JUN   2021

TELLING THE
TECHNICAL SERVICES
STORY

TELLING THE TECHNICAL SERVICES STORY

COMMUNICATING VALUE

EDITED BY

KIMBERLEY A. EDWARDS

and

TRICIA MACKENZIE

IN COLLABORATION WITH CORE PUBLISHING

ALA
Editions

CHICAGO   2021

KIMBERLEY A. EDWARDS is the head of database integrity and analysis at George Mason University Libraries. She received her MLIS from the University of Kentucky, and prior to her current role she worked in the circulation and technical services departments of several college and government libraries. She has presented on collection management and analysis tools and techniques at a range of national and international conferences.

TRICIA MACKENZIE is the head of metadata services at George Mason University Libraries. She received her MLS with a specialization in digital libraries from Indiana University and has an MA in history from Southern Illinois University–Edwardsville. Prior to her current role, she was the metadata librarian at George Mason University Libraries. She has presented at regional, national, and international conferences on topics relating to cataloging and metadata creation and quality control, authority control, and data management.

ISBN: 978-0-8389-4946-7 (paper)

Library of Congress Cataloging-in-Publication Data
Names: Edwards, Kimberley A., editor. | Mackenzie, Tricia (Tricia Wall), editor.
Title: Telling the technical services story : communicating value / edited by Kimberley A.
    Edwards and Tricia Mackenzie in collaboration with Core Publishing.
Description: Chicago : ALA Editions, 2021. | Includes bibliographical references and index.
    | Summary: "This contributed work provides useful tips for telling a compelling story
    about the value of technical services work. With this collection, you'll learn about specific
    initiatives to improve communication within departments, across the library, and campus
    wide"—Provided by publisher.
Identifiers: LCCN 2020058696 | ISBN 9780838949467 (paperback)
Subjects: LCSH: Technical services (Libraries)—United States. | Communication in library
    science—Technological innovations—United States—Case studies.
Classification: LCC Z688.6.U6 T45 2021 | DDC 025/.020973—dc23
LC record available at https://lccn.loc.gov/2020058696

Cover image © kentoh/Adobe Stock. Text design in the Chaparral, Gotham, and Bell Gothic typefaces.

♾ This paper meets the requirements of ANSI/NISO Z39.48-1992 (Permanence of Paper).
Printed in the United States of America

25 24 23 22 21   5 4 3 2 1

Contents

Introduction

The work of technical services librarians and staff has long since moved beyond an exclusive focus on the daily acquisition, cataloging, and processing of materials. In this era of increased cross-departmental collaboration, evolving technology, shrinking budgets, and the misconception by some that researchers only need access to a Google search box, the staff in technical services departments must be able to communicate the role their work plays in supporting the mission of both their library and their larger institution. This book illustrates effective strategies that technical services departments have used to facilitate such communication.

The book's case studies are divided into three parts focusing on the intended audience, moving from internal communication to interdepartmental communication, and ending with communication external to the library. The chapters in this book were written by staff in research institutions across the United States, and though this may limit the book's scope in some ways, we feel that these studies can nevertheless provide a road map for an array of libraries.

The book's first part, "Communication within the Department," illustrates ways to improve communications within a technical services department. Autumn Faulkner and Emily Sanford start off by describing their department's complete overhaul of its documentation, thereby both improving the department's work product and fostering equity. In the next chapter, Patrick Flanigan shows the ways in which Basecamp can be used to support healthy communication throughout a department. Following that, Gwen Gregory explains the myriad benefits that can come from regular technical services retreats. In the final chapter of this part, Melissa Moll and Shelby Strommer describe how they implemented multidirectional communication strategies to coordinate a large-scale collections project.

The chapters in part II, "Communication across Library Departments," depict the ways in which collaboration has been fostered with library colleagues outside of technical services. This part begins with a chapter by Kaylan Ellis, Jennifer Donley, and Christopher Deems, who created a community of practice between the technical services and systems departments in their libraries. In the next chapter, Xiying Mi, Bonita Pollock, and Brian Falato show how they established a series of cataloging classes for the public services department, thereby enhancing the cataloging knowledge of public-facing staff to better facilitate their work while simultaneously demonstrating the value of cataloging. In their chapter, Erin Block and Kimberly Lawler demonstrate how they used Trello to streamline the communication related to e-resource purchasing and activation across departments. Meghan Burke took a different approach to e-resource management at her library and established an e-resource ticketing system using Google tools to improve error notification and resolution. Jennifer Mezick and Elyssa M. Gould conclude part II with a description of how they improved their collection development processes by strengthening communication between technical services and subject librarians.

In the book's third and final part, "Communication outside the Library," the authors describe their experiences reaching beyond the library's walls to better promote and further the work of their institutions. Anna Seiffert begins by explaining how her library improved the way it communicates information about its budget to its parent institution's administration and faculty. In the next chapter, Hilary Hargis and Jenny Novacescu provide an overview of marketing concepts and show how technical services departments can aid directly in the marketing work of a library. In their chapter, Heather Jeffcoat, Marlee Givens, Sofia Slutskaya, and Karen E. Viars show how their library addressed the growing shift to an electronic resource-focused collection and how that move was communicated to the campus community. Maggie Dull's department approached campus outreach in a different way, launching a service to provide metadata support for various stakeholder projects outside the library. In the last chapter, Jamie Hazlitt and Glenn Johnson-Grau describe a multifaceted weeding project that incorporated extensive and successful outreach and collaboration with faculty.

Facilitating better communication within our libraries is something we all strive to embrace. We hope that the following chapters provide useful information for all types of libraries and show the many ways that technical services departments can and do successfully tell their stories every day.

PART I

COMMUNICATION WITHIN THE DEPARTMENT

AUTUMN FAULKNER AND
EMILY SANFORD

1

Usable Documentation for Technical Services

How to Win Friends and Confluence People

When considering good communication in the workplace, documentation is perhaps not the first thought that springs to mind—often it is an afterthought and develops ad hoc when the occasion dictates, and is jotted down quickly and watched over by accidental custodians. The importance of documentation, however, can be seen in how it sprouts up even when there is no particular plan for curating it. It pops up higgledy-piggledy in personal caches—on sticky notes, on printouts, in Google Docs, in saved e-mails, or in computer files. It exists in (sometimes) organized forms in unit wikis, intranets, and three-ring binders. Indeed, documentation is a natural by-product of the complex and precise work of technical services.

It is not a controversial statement to say that good documentation is useful. (In this context, *documentation* is understood as written instructions or information to guide workplace processes, and good documentation may be taken to mean documentation that is cohesive, formalized, and regularly maintained.) And yet this crucial form of communication often gets short shrift. There are many valid reasons why documentation slips to the bottom of the to-do list. It can be complicated and messy. Like a car or a toddler, it requires frequent maintenance and monitoring. It is not flashy and requires time and energy that can already be in short supply in a busy workplace. However, we contend that intentional strategies around documentation support efficiency, workplace equity, and institutional memory.

THE BENEFITS OF DOCUMENTATION

The project discussed in this chapter was born out of a perceived need for a strategy to better care for our Technical Services Division's documentation at Michigan State University (MSU) Libraries. We wanted to alleviate pain points for those creating content and those consuming it by providing an organized and extensible framework and an easy-to-use interface. We applied research, project planning, and various user experience (UX) methods to accomplish our goal. In writing about our processes, we hope to provide something useful and applicable from our project that libraries can adapt for their own use.

When conducting a mental review of your unit's documentation, you should decide what level of effort is worthwhile and consider the two primary outcomes of *good* documentation: (1) quality and (2) equity.

Why We Wanted to Do It

Documentation Supports High-Quality Work

There is a direct line from good documentation to quality work. Traditional technical services (TS) work is detailed and highly structured by its very nature. The work must support multiple workflows that acquire, describe, process, track, and maintain a diverse set of materials through their library life cycle. In the last few decades, libraries have expanded their missions and incorporated more nontraditional items into their collections to support the research and information needs of their communities. TS rules and systems built to encapsulate the standard book have adapted to ingest nontraditional items, like online streaming media, cake pans, and soldering kits (to name a few). Now more than ever, our workflows cross traditional TS team lines. These workflows are complicated and often involve multiple individuals, if not multiple teams.

In this environment, shared documentation is vital to high-quality, accurate work. If reliable and easily referenced, it can reduce cognitive load, mistakes, redundancies, and questions. It can also ensure that library materials are treated consistently and follow more efficient paths to availability. Predictable data equals good discovery—as much for acquisitions staff creating fund code lists as for the front-end library user searching the catalog. Finally, documentation functions as an archive. TS work does not exist in a vacuum. The database represents an accumulation of past decisions and projects. Data created today must live and thrive in that existing ecosystem. Having documentation helps mitigate the loss of institutional memory that follows retirements and system migrations. It further provides the bedrock on which we may build future library technical services environments.

Documentation Fosters Workplace Equity

Just like other forms of workplace communication, documentation is crucial to staff empowerment. Through the distribution of shared knowledge and expertise, documentation ensures equal access to critical information, mitigates incidental or intentional gatekeeping, creates transparency in local decision-making and cross-divisional communication, and promotes the responsible stewardship of staff time and energy.

Transparency, accessibility, shared expertise, stewardship—any library strategic plan will include some of these as goals, and it is easy to connect them to workplace well-being. Good documentation means that newly trained Staff Member A knows to bring certain types of materials to a certain shelf for processing instead of bringing it to Staff Member B by mistake. While, of course, this should be no big deal in a collegial environment, we should not discount the everyday power dynamics of workplace interactions. What if Staff Member B is not comfortable correcting another person's mistakes and feels pressured instead to take on unassigned work? Inadequate documentation can potentially place staff in positions of insecurity, anxiety, or indecision.

Good documentation, by contrast, builds confidence and trust. Staff members exercise their own competencies and agency by searching for and following procedures; they spend less time navigating "who," "what," and "how" questions and have more capacity for questions of effectiveness. When an entire workflow is mapped out and visible, all those involved have access to the big picture and can be equal participants in workflow design.

A Note about Care

We have discussed quality and equity as two important outcomes of good documentation. To view both of these from a more philosophical perspective, think of good documentation as a way of showing care—care for our end-users and care for our staff. Consider the four elements of the feminist care ethic as outlined by Joan Tronto and Bernice Fischer[1] and paraphrased for this context:

Attentiveness: awareness of and scanning for need
Responsibility: willingness to address need
Competence: skillful and appropriate methods of addressing that need
Responsiveness: consideration of users' positions and their perceptions of
    provided care

Effective documentation addresses each of these elements. We are attentive to the needs of our users, whose ability to access library resources quickly and intuitively depends on smooth workflows in TS. We are attentive to the needs of our staff by acknowledging the cognitive load of TS work and recognizing that it is unreasonable to expect them to commit thousands of details to memory. We accept the responsibility of providing reliable and accessible information to end-users and staff, and we commit to doing this competently and iteratively, in response to changing systems, materials, and use cases.

The last two elements are crucial. Any equity and empowerment that documentation achieves, and any return on investment of time and effort, are predicated on staff finding that documentation to be truly usable.

WHY WE NEEDED TO DO IT

The MSU Libraries' Technical Services Division comprises seven subunits: Acquisitions, Catalog Maintenance, Cataloging & Metadata Services, Copy Cataloging, Metadata Management (authorities work), Catalog Services (system management of the integrated library system, or ILS), and Electronic Resources. The division has a complement of approximately forty full-time employees who work together to acquire, catalog, process, and maintain library resources. With so many teams and staff members, not to mention student workers, we rely heavily on communication to coordinate our many workflows and processes. Our TS documentation has historically served as a central place for procedures, policies, and statistics-gathering. The division's documentation had been through several iterations over the decades as technology evolved, bouncing from binders to website to wiki to Drupal. The documentation had been edited or amended by various editors as needed and as time allowed. This unintentionally gave rise to a disjointed organization of topics, duplication, and conflicting or outdated information. The whole thing had ballooned to 300+ pages, which were punctuated with the names of former systems and staff members. All these factors meant that staff spent considerable time slogging through bloated and sometimes unreliable information. Content creators had a basic template to work with, but were essentially starting from scratch each time they needed to write a new procedure. Any changes to the menu options or templates required Web Services' assistance and permission.

Before we launched our project, the libraries' public-facing Drupal website was the repository for TS documentation. Its placement there was intentional to align with the university's land-grant philosophy of openly sharing information with the wider community for their use and benefit (a philosophy we replicated in our current site by making it publicly accessible). But the location on the libraries' main website also triggered logistical issues. The search function searched the whole website, making it difficult to narrow a search to strictly TS documentation web pages. Searching "microfilm" in this interface would return relevant LibGuides for patrons on using microfilm, alongside TS internal documentation detailing local procedures for assigning call numbers to microfilm. This was as frustrating for TS staff as it was potentially confusing for users. Any changes to the documentation site's web pages, no matter how small, required Web Services' assistance to go live—typically at least a 24-hour turnaround. While our Web Services colleagues were responsive and helpful, these added steps were ultimately unsustainable for us considering the numerous edits our many pages warranted, and it felt like an underutilization of their skills and time.

ANALYSIS AND DEVELOPMENT OF THE PROJECT PLAN

Project Plan and Goals

We had long discussed a project to evaluate the division's documentation. The project fell into our niche areas of interest. As catalogers, we rely on, recognize, and value good, organized documentation. Faulkner, as manager of the Copy Cataloging Team, often writes procedures and onboards new staff who rely heavily on documentation. Sanford, who spends part of her time within the libraries' User Experience Unit (UX), has long had an interest in the intersection between UX and technical services. In late 2017 our schedules aligned, and we got a green light to proceed with the project from our administrators. We understood that this would be a time-intensive undertaking with many moving parts, as well as a project we were pursuing in addition to our regular work. To that end, we developed a project plan to guide us and keep us on track. Our goals for the project were informed by our understanding of the documentation's pain points, which we have outlined in the above paragraphs. Our delineated project goals included:

- Improved information architecture for the overall site
- Increased findability and readability of procedures for users
- A simplified process to create/write/edit content (interface, guidelines, templates, built-in infrastructure, and accessibility)
- Future-proofing (accounting for future growth and developing a mechanism for routine reviews of content)
- Identifying gaps in the documentation of current workflows

To meet these goals, we developed a project checklist, shown in figure 1.1, with a multiphase approach.

Project Checklist

Phase	Status	Comments
Concept	Done	Identify goals and plan an outline for project - get support of AD and assistant AD
Survey	Done	Analyze documentation pages of BTAA & similarly-sized peer research libraries.
Investigate	Done	Identify needs for TS documentation. Analyze content management systems to organize documentation - Drupal & Confluence. Present results.
Research	Done	Research and understand best practices around information architecture and document design.
Planning	Done	Complete affinity diagram, identify out-of-date pages, plan infrastructure & permissions.
Execution	In Process	Subscribe to CMS, set-up space (templates & permissions), move content, train staff, launch, refocus Drupal page.
Review	On-track	Identify gaps & one-person workflows, set-up review mechanism, analyze effectiveness.

FIGURE 1.1
A presentation slide from a report to colleagues on our project's road map as it neared completion

Initial Analysis and Assessment

Using Google Forms, Sanford built a survey to gauge the staff's confidence in and usage of the existing documentation site. We had a good response rate of approximately 45 percent. Both closed- and open-ended questions were utilized to gather the data. The results confirmed our own observations—the site was unsearchable, hard to navigate, and out of date. The survey did not reveal any new insights, but provided confirmation that we were moving in the right direction. If you are working with a medium to large staff (anonymity is important; too small a staff and anonymity is hard to maintain), a survey might be a good first step to identify problem areas and hidden blind spots. Google Forms is free and relatively easy to use. All surveys are not created equal, and investing time into research on good survey development is a key first step.[2] It is also helpful to have a colleague complete a run-through of the survey to provide feedback and catch any assumptions or mistakes. Reading up on informed consent in survey deployment is also a must.

Having ascertained what our users thought, we turned to external examples of technical services documentation for ideas. Why reinvent the wheel? Comparative analysis, another user experience tool, is a process that identifies tools and strategies that already exist and could be adapted for use. Sanford completed a comparative analysis of the TS documentation sites of like-sized university libraries, especially our peers in the Big Ten Academic Alliance. That analysis found, among other things, a new tool we had not previously encountered: Confluence, a part of Atlassian's suite of products. Several university libraries and technical service departments were using it for their intranet and/or documentation sites.

Accessible Design and Architecture

With identified user needs and comparative analysis in hand, we began investigating best practices around accessible design and information architecture. An entire chapter could be written about our findings, so we encourage you to consult our project archive (https://tinyurl.com/MSULTSarchive) if you wish to explore further, but here are the key takeaways:

The page and site design should aim to reduce cognitive load.

- Written technical procedures involve a significant demand on the reader's "internal storage."[3]
- The style and formatting of presented text have a direct effect on reader comprehension.
- Too many choices or too much information at once increases cognitive load and hinders decision-making. Navigation choices should be lean at the top.[4]

The page and site design should ensure accessibility.

- An online procedures site is better than paper documents or files stored on individual machines.
- Standardized structural elements should be used both site-wide and in individual pages to assist screen-reading software.
- We should comply with the Web Content Accessibility Guidelines 2.0 (WCAG) (www.w3.org/TR/WCAG20/) recommendations and perform screen-reader testing.

To accomplish both of these mandates, we drew upon the Gestalt theory of design, the principles of plain language,[5] and the principles of information architecture. Gestalt theory orients itself to the tendency of the human brain to sort and synthesize pieces of information into an easily comprehensible whole. To best accommodate this instinctive behavior, the presentation of information should adhere to the principles illustrated in figure 1.2. The plain language approach emphasizes logic, context, conciseness, and clean design as aids to comprehension. The principles of information architecture encourage a clear demarcation of different types of content, meaningful choices, layered content, hierarchical presentation, and intuitive categorization and classification.

Using these principles and our known user needs, Faulkner generated a list of optimal features for our new documentation site:

- General
  - » Discoverable on the Web
  - » Intuitive editing interface
  - » Immediate publishing

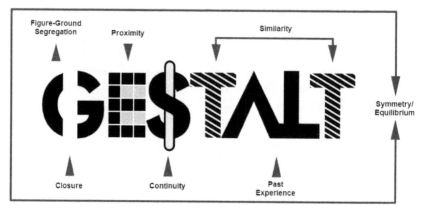

FIGURE 1.2

This graphic illustrates each principle of the Gestalt theory of design. *Gestalt* is German for "a unified whole," and these principles help to create quick recognition of that whole. When applied to text, as shown here, the principles work together to reduce cognitive load for the reader.

Figure-Ground Segregation Image courtesy of Turner & Schomberg (2016), licensed under CC BY 4.0; retrieved from http://www.inthelibrarywiththeleadpipe.org/2016/accessibility.

- Architecture and organization
  - » Tagging and searching
  - » Sidebar navigation with page trees and nesting
- Style and design
  - » Overall clean design with ample white space and contrast
  - » Page templates
  - » Quick creation of visual elements like lists, tables, lines, blocks, and so on
  - » Ability to attach images and files

IMPLEMENTATION

Why We Chose Confluence

When it came to the choice of a new platform to host the documentation site, we considered all the options known to us and identified in our comparative analysis. It came down to three contenders for a new platform: (1) a wiki, (2) an internal Drupal site developed for us by Web Services, and (3) Confluence. Using our needs list, we assessed each content management system.

Confluence is a "team collaboration software" that has document storage functionality and wiki-like features. When compared with our list of desired features, it clearly offered the most bang for our buck. With a low cost and with little customization work needed on our end, it provided almost all the usability we were hoping to attain.

Our initial investigation revealed that Confluence offers different tiers of users (or log-ins) and we could make our pages viewable by anyone—an important tenet to maintain to support our land-grant mission. We could also choose to host the site locally or use their cloud-based version. Confluence offers a seven-day free trial that we took advantage of (www.atlassian.com/try/cloud/signup?bundle=confluence&edition=premium). The trial gave us access to a sandbox environment in which to tinker with the administrative options, customizability, and overall site usability. We developed a prototype during the trial, which we were then able to share with our TS management team to demonstrate our vision for the site.

Content Creation

The price plan we chose includes ten log-ins for administration and content creation. (In the time since we chose our paid plan, Confluence has debuted a free plan with ten log-ins, although it has fewer customizations available and limits administration options.) Permissions in the plan we chose are layered and easily toggled, making it possible to enable or disable users easily, and to restrict access to some content or functions as needed. The editing interface is intuitive and includes drop-in design elements like rule lines, tables, panels, blocks, and more. More importantly, pages can be published or updated immediately. Versioning and page editing histories remove much of the burdensome work of regular maintenance and updating. Finally, Confluence makes it simple to attach images with alt text and many other types of files. Integrations are available for Office documents, Google Suite documents, and more.

Style and Design

Our research repeatedly emphasized the need for clean design, white space, and the proper use of page elements for screen readers. We found the overall style settings of the Confluence space to be in harmony with these principles. The page template tool promotes the consistent use of local design choices, which reduces the cognitive load for content creators. The latter do not need to remember all the principles of accessibility and usability—for the most part, these are baked into the template, and writers can focus purely on content.

Additionally, by using the macros mentioned above in combination with templates, pages can be set up to have distinct and uniform "blocks" for different types of content, allowing the reader's eye to quickly jump to the same spot every time to find certain information.

Organization and Architecture

Confluence's out-of-the-box site navigation tallies with all the best practices we compiled in our research. A hierarchical left-hand sidebar menu is the primary means of presentation, but a powerful search function and a tagging feature provide two alternate methods for quick access. The page tree in the sidebar menu can be nested to many levels, and the order and grouping of pages can be easily changed with drag-and-drop.

Another bonus is automatic link management. Editors can insert child pages without manual linking, don't have to create their own URLs for their pages, and can insert links to other pages using automatic lookup. As page titles change or pages are moved around in the page tree, URLs dynamically update wherever they occur throughout the space. In a page deletion dialogue, editors are notified where that page link is referenced so maintenance can be performed accordingly.

Product Support

The Confluence user community offers robust discussion forums and feature voting, and we found Atlassian's customer support to be highly responsive even before we purchased their product (we submitted a ticket during our free seven-day trial period and they responded).

Drawbacks

The counts against Confluence included some limitations around home page display and hierarchy position that required a local workaround, the inability to create aliases for URLs using natural language, and the default inclusion of a large user icon and "last updated" block at the top of each page that we consider to be disruptive to an otherwise clean flow of information.

We took our analysis of all three options to the TS management team. In the end, Confluence ended up meeting most of our needs with the most out-of-the-box features, and it allowed us to design a site that we could manage without having to do a lot of coding or tinkering with what was there.

Affinity Diagramming: A UX Approach

With our platform choice made, we turned our focus to content. Web Services generated an inventory for us of the existing web pages of documentation (all 306 of them). Working from a spreadsheet, and in coordination with TS managers and other content owners, we deleted old content and merged similar procedures. When we could quickly update content, we did so as we encountered it. Anything that would require more time or consultation to update, we marked for future attention.

We next needed to create new navigation and structure for the site. The old site had been organized by teams (i.e., units) within technical services. Certainly, this makes sense from a content owner and traditional TS structure point of view. But, as already discussed, the lines have become increasingly blurred between TS teams. Arranging by unit also requires the user to know what team is responsible—or in some cases *used* to be responsible—for the procedure to locate it. It can also break up a workflow into several procedures when it crosses teams, which leads to duplicate information and confusion. Our research and discussions, therefore, convinced us that arranging procedures by function instead would improve findability and, to some extent, future-proof procedures as teams evolve and merge.

"Affinity diagramming" is a form of content-mapping and is another user experience or contextual inquiry tool. It is the process of breaking ideas or data into chunks and grouping them together relationally to explore natural links and organization. Approaching our large set of data, we opted to complete an affinity diagram to develop top-level navigation and to categorize individual procedures and policies underneath. Affinity diagramming is a time-intensive process, and it took us several working days to complete from beginning to end. The steps in the process are described below.

Step 1

We recorded each web page's name on separate sticky notes, color-coordinating for its type of documentation; for example, procedure vs. policy. While the color-coordinating did not always figure into our organization of the page, it did help us understand how many types of documentation we had (and perhaps was a cataloging occupational hazard by-product). We used a black marker and wrote in large font for better visibility.

Step 2

We set up using a large, blank wall on which to organize and arrange the sticky notes (figure 1.3). We grouped similar sticky notes together, discussing aloud as we went along and always reaching mutual agreement. We used another color of notes (bright pink) to assign temporary category names under which we were then sorting the notes to help us keep track of our categories (figure 1.4). We arranged and rearranged the notes as we went along, slowly developing a complete diagram and organizing a new structure for the site.

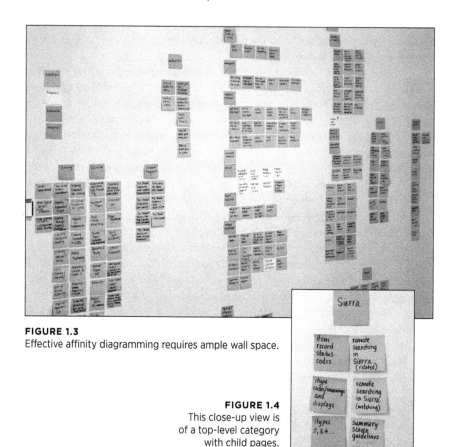

FIGURE 1.3
Effective affinity diagramming requires ample wall space.

FIGURE 1.4
This close-up view is
of a top-level category
with child pages.

Step 3

We finalized the category names, which in turn became our top-level navigation. We worked to keep the category names simple and explanatory; for example, "physical processing." Finally, we recorded our diagram in a spreadsheet (figure 1.5) and took pictures of our wall affinity diagram as a backup.

We took the future into consideration as much as possible throughout the process. The top-level navigation was purposely made to be general rather than specific, so it could easily accommodate future content (one of the failings of the old site was its rigid structure). Knowing that a system migration was in our immediate future, we grouped the system-centric (Innovative's Sierra) procedures together so we could easily find and archive (or jettison) them after the system migration. We shared our new organizational scheme with the TS management team to gather input and feedback from them. With our finalized structure in hand, we were well set up for the site design and migration phase.

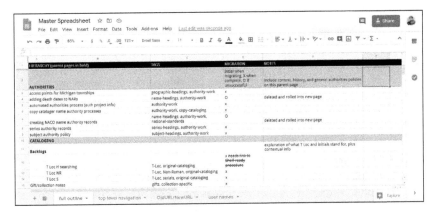

FIGURE 1.5
Excerpt of master spreadsheet with top-level navigation and nested children

Setting up the Space

Again, our research guided our site design choices. Confluence permits multiple spaces within one instance, and we decided that one unified space was the best choice for our documentation. Next, we decided to limit page nesting to three levels, which prevents users from getting lost in a hierarchy or having too many choices.

For consistent design and accessibility, Faulkner designed four templates in Confluence: two for top-level and intermediate parent pages in the navigation hierarchy, and two for short- and long-form procedures.

Following the principles of identifying different types of content and maintaining similarity in presentation, each page template includes a brief section at the top for the summary and context, a linked table of contents, a side panel for any relevant policies, and a panel for content ownership and date updated. These are delineated from the procedures themselves using strong visual cues (see figure 1.6).

To reduce cognitive load when scanning lengthy, detailed instructions, the long-form template includes headings and rule lines to demarcate sections/steps, and a linked table of contents and "Back to top" links for quick in-page navigation. The short-form template is only used when the entire text of the procedures can fit on the screen with no scrolling, thus eliminating the need for a table of contents.

Both templates use headings and white space to support contrast, figure-ground separation, and good screen reader progressions. Confluence templates allow for written instructions not visible in the final, published document, which we used to include brief guidelines for content creators drawn from WCAG 2.0, Gestalt theory, and plain language principles. All of these guidelines (listed below) aim to reduce cognitive "noise" and assist users in quick identification and comprehension:

- In the summary block, give one or two sentences about what the procedure covers and identify its intended audience, so users understand where they are and what to expect from the content.
- In general, use bulleted and numbered lists instead of paragraphs of text; each step of a procedure should have its own separate line and/or section.
- Use macros like tables, note panels, and other design elements to make information concise, identifiable, and linear.
- Add the content creator's name, e-mail, and date created/updated.
- Add tags from the provided tag library.

Finally, Sanford created a style guide for content editors that contains detailed information about best practices for page creation, and our colleague Tim Kiser, who joined us at this stage of the project, developed a library

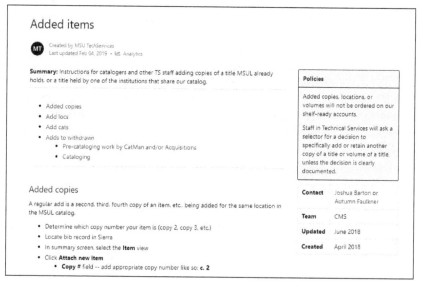

FIGURE 1.6
This is a page from the MSU Libraries' documentation site that uses the long-form procedures template mentioned in text. Note the discrete zones for different types of information. Also note the disparity between the automatically supplied "last updated" date directly below the title and the date supplied manually by the content creators. We chose to supply our own "last updated" dates because they are more meaningful; the automatically supplied date might represent an insignificant change, like a typo correction.

of controlled tags to ensure that those terms did not become diluted or duplicative.

To view all of this in action and further improvements we've made, visit the MSU Libraries' Technical Services documentation site at https://tinyurl .com/MSULTS.

Migration and Testing

After creating top-level parent pages, the three of us began copy/pasting content from Drupal into new Confluence pages, using the aforementioned spreadsheet to track our progress. (If you're undertaking a similar project, this is a great time to closely review the content and make sweeping edits as needed, or flag the content for future follow-up.) For each page copied over, we chose the appropriate template, tidied up the formatting (though we found that headings and styles ported over quite conveniently in many cases), wrote brief summaries, added policies and tags, and assigned content owners.

Before launching the site, a colleague with accessibility-testing experience ran diagnostics for us. The Confluence space performed well in screen-reading tests, though not without some hiccups. While we would have preferred a perfect performance, it was clear that Confluence's navigation and design features would still improve our documentation's accessibility across the board.

IMPACT

Our documentation site went live on May 15, 2018, after a brief training for staff who had editor roles. The training took perhaps one hour, after which participants were able to hit the ground running. We received positive feedback from TS staff at large as well, as from non-TS colleagues in the library. We were asked by various interested library units to share about our process, after which our library's Conservation Lab team decided to implement a Confluence space of their own.

Knowing that it was important to measure site usage going forward, Sanford set up a Google Analytics dashboard for the new space. (Confluence has since integrated analytics into their cloud-based platform.) From implementation through May 28, 2020, the site has seen 85 unique visitors. These visitors accounted for 2,645 sessions, which works out to approximately 32 sessions per user. The site's web pages have been viewed 13,430 times. This works out to nearly 560 pages viewed per month, or approximately 26 times per workday. We do not have analytics for the Drupal site before the migration, nor would there be a one-to-one comparison, considering that we winnowed out many pages of content.

What the numbers do show is that the site is consulted repeatedly by a small number of regular users, from which we can infer (and support with anecdotal data) that Confluence saves time for staff and managers—one of our long-term goals.

The COVID-19 pandemic of 2020–21 has revealed further benefits of a robust and user-friendly documentation space. When the crisis struck, the MSU Libraries had less than a week to prepare for the move from in-building to remote work. For TS staff, this meant the rapid generation of project work, associated procedures, and general guidance to support work-from-home processes. We were able to design, populate, and share out a new Confluence space with its own custom procedures template in a day, and other staff were contributing to and consulting this site with no issues the following day.

Having an existing platform with low barriers and a familiar setup was crucial for those staffers who are either creating or accessing COVID-19 procedures. No one had to adjust to new interfaces or systems in an already stressful and demanding situation, and we linked to the new telecommuting space from our existing documentation space so it was immediately accessible.

We add this additional point in favor of investing in good documentation: by doing so, you save yourself heartache and give your staff some much-needed consistency when and if things shift to crisis mode. The crisis need not necessarily be a global pandemic, either. Perhaps it's a reorganization, a system migration, a flood in the library, or a sudden change in budgets or leadership. In all such cases, good documentation means more informed decisions, less chaos, and a solid shared basis for moving forward.

CONCLUSION

Our project is ongoing. Its future directions include continued assessment, iterative design, and the documentation of hidden workflows and knowledge gaps. Our ultimate goal is to make the site a living, evolving document to avoid having to repeat the project in ten years. In this chapter, we have provided a detailed account of our project, research, and tools. We hope it provides a useful road map for individuals interested in undertaking a similar endeavor. Our project archive, available at https://tinyurl.com/MSULTSarchive, has additional resources and project artifacts for reference and use.

Each organization would benefit from making a conscious decision about how to invest time and effort in its documentation, based on staff needs, existing resources, and any prevailing institutional priorities. Making no decision at all often means letting ad hoc documentation sprout up like weeds and remain patchy and untended. In that scenario, precious staff time is often wasted from the start. By contrast, any intentional approach will ensure that you're working more effectively, even if your strategy is to identify constraints and adopt a minimal approach. Ultimately, small investments in documentation can pay big dividends in improved workplace communication.

REFERENCES

Brown, D. "Eight Principles of Information Architecture." *Bulletin of the Association for Information Science and Technology* 36, no. 6 (2010): 30–34. doi:10.1002/bult.2010.1720360609.

Dam, Rikke Friss, and Teo Yu Siang. 2020. "Affinity Diagrams – Learn How to Cluster and Bundle Ideas and Facts." 2020. Interactive Design Foundation. www.interaction-design.org/literature/article/affinity-diagrams-learn-how-to-cluster-and-bundle-ideas-and-facts.

Farrell, Susan. "28 Tips for Creating Great Qualitative Surveys." September 25, 2016. Nielsen Norman Group. www.nngroup.com/articles/qualitative-surveys.

Guthrie, J. T., S. Bennett, and S. Weber. "Processing Procedural Documents: A Cognitive Model for Following Written Directions." *Educational Psychology Review* 3, no. 3 (1991): 249–65.

McCrudden, M., G. Schraw, K. Hartley, and A. K. Kenneth. "The Influence of Presentation, Organization, and Example Context on Text Learning." *Journal of Experimental Education* 72, no. 4 (2004): 289–306. doi:10.3200/JEXE.72.4.289-306.

Patrick, M., and C. Fitz. "Using Gestalt Theory to Teach Document Design and Graphics." *Technical Communication Quarterly* 2, no. 4 (1993): 389–410. doi:10.1080/10572259309364549.

Pernice, Kara. "Affinity Diagramming for Collaboratively Sorting UX Findings and Design Ideas." February 18, 2018. Nielsen Norman Group. www.nngroup.com/articles/affinity-diagram.

Sander-Staudt, M. "Care Ethics." *Internet Encyclopedia of Philosophy.* www.iep.utm.edu/care-eth/#SSH1cv.

Tronto, J. *Moral Boundaries: A Political Argument for an Ethic of Care.* New York: Routledge, 1994.

Turner, J., and J. Schomberg. "Inclusivity, Gestalt Principles, and Plain Language in Document Design." *In the Library with the Lead Pipe*, June 29, 2016. www.inthelibrarywiththeleadpipe.org/2016/accessibility.

———. "Inclusivity Through Documentation: Using Gestalt Principles and Plain Language to Create Effective Documents" [presentation slides]. 2017. Cornerstone: Minnesota State University – Mankato. https://cornerstone.lib.mnsu.edu/cgi/viewcontent.cgi?article=1142&context=lib_services_fac_pubs.

NOTES

1. J. Tronto, *Moral Boundaries: A Political Argument for an Ethic of Care* (New York: Routledge, 1994).
2. Susan Farrell, "28 Tips for Creating Great Qualitative Surveys," September 25, 2016, Nielsen Norman Group, www.nngroup.com/articles/qualitative-surveys.

3. J. T. Guthrie, S. Bennett, and S. Weber, "Processing Procedural Documents: A Cognitive Model for Following Written Directions," *Educational Psychology Review* 3, no. 3 (1991): 249–65.

4. D. Brown, "Eight Principles of Information Architecture," *Bulletin of the Association for Information Science and Technology* 36, no. 6 (2010): 30–34. doi:10.1002/bult.2010.1720360609.

5. J. Turner and J. Schomberg, "Inclusivity, Gestalt Principles, and Plain Language in Document Design," *In the Library with the Lead Pipe*, June 29, 2016, www.inthelibrarywiththeleadpipe.org/2016/accessibility.

PATRICK FLANIGAN

2

Using Basecamp Project Management Software to Improve Communication and Efficiency

Improved communication and collaboration are things that libraries strive for even under normal circumstances. During the COVID-19 pandemic, however, many library professionals began to work remotely from their institutions and became physically isolated from their coworkers and colleagues. Being removed from the office environment made normal everyday tasks difficult and the need for strong and efficient channels of communication even more vital than usual. Project management methods and tools, which libraries have long utilized, are now more relevant than ever.

In fall 2018, the San Diego State University (SDSU) Library's Information and Digital Technologies Department launched a pilot study of Basecamp, the online project management software. Departments and units were encouraged to test out the software and provide feedback. The SDSU Library had used Basecamp sparingly in 2017 during the migration to Ex-Libris's Alma, a library services platform (LSP). Then, in January 2018, the SDSU Library's Monograph Unit (hereafter referred to as the Unit) hired additional staff members to address a backlog of materials donated to Special Collections that were in need of cataloging. The timing of the hiring of new staff and the recent migration to a new LSP created the perfect opportunity to explore the possibilities of what Basecamp might offer.

Basecamp promotes itself as "more than just a project management tool." It enables collaborators who work on teams or projects to be more efficient by providing them with a structured means for communication and organization. Basecamp was launched as a web-based project management tool in 2004, and has undergone several iterations since then. The version used by the Unit was Basecamp 3, released in 2014.

Messaging, calendars, archiving, and document management are tools that many libraries are using, and much of this functionality can be found in other software or applications, such as Trello, Asana, and Slack. Basecamp improves the efficiency of project- or team-based activities by combining these communication channels and resources into one place, thereby reducing the amount of meetings and time needed for members and stakeholders to be brought up to speed.

The Monograph Unit is one part of the Content Organization and Management Department (COM), known previously as the Technical Services Department, and is responsible for the cataloging and processing of monographic items in a variety of formats, with a strong emphasis on Special Collections print materials donated to the library. Working on these materials requires communication and capturing decisions with many stakeholders. Depending on the donation, a monograph's provenance and how it is described in a bibliographic record will vary. This chapter will detail how Basecamp initially helped the Unit at SDSU Library address special collection projects, the ongoing needs of the COM Department (including working remotely during the COVID-19 pandemic), and the challenges and weaknesses that we found.

BEFORE BASECAMP

Though the technology used by libraries and other organizations has changed, the need for communication in a technical services department has always existed. Whether it is a retrospective cataloging project, a migration to a new integrated library system (ILS) or LSP, or ongoing team efforts, success is often determined by communication. Singh reported that "in reviewing the narratives of highly successful project teams, it is clearly evident that effective communication is the most important contributor to project success."[1] This should come as no surprise to library professionals who have been involved in work efforts that were unsuccessful or more challenging than they needed to be due to communication issues. Basecamp succinctly states this on their site: "Poor communication creates more work."[2]

The one mainstay of communication in libraries has been meetings. If ideas need to be shared or decisions made, meetings were the solution. The minutes of a meeting would capture who was in the meeting, the agendas, what information was shared, and how decisions were made. The detail and accuracy of those minutes depend on the effort made by the "minutes taker." Depending on the decade, the minutes existed as a memo or as an e-mail that was circulated. Recipients of the minutes would be individually responsible for organizing and archiving them. Organizations would archive these documents in a physical file drawer or on a shared drive on the company network. If the minutes were ever to be referenced following a meeting, it required that someone knew the minutes existed and the exact way to discover the documentation.

Prior to utilizing Basecamp, the Unit used a network shared drive to house Microsoft Word documents of policies, processes, and minutes. The Technical Services portion of the shared drive was divided into subfolders for each unit in the department; that is, Monographs, Serials, Government Publications, and Acquisitions. A document addressing multiple units in Technical Services would often be stored in the unit folder of the creator of the document. However, this approach generally made it difficult to find and access documents. It wasn't until the migration to Alma and the hiring of new staff that this inefficiency was addressed.

In preparation for that migration, steps were taken to resolve inaccuracies and inconsistencies in the library's current catalog. One thing that became apparent when looking at our bibliographic records was the evolution of cataloging practices over the years. Finding the policies, processes, or decisions that explained past cataloging workflows often required assistance from a staff member who had worked at the time the decision was made and knew that a document existed. This meant that finding out how and why practices evolved required reaching out to colleagues with institutional memory and performing additional detective work.

Searching File Explorer in the network drive could lead to a document that detailed how donor gift notes were to be formatted, but the discovery was dependent on documents having a descriptive file name. The absence of standardized file-naming conventions provided more challenges. More detective work would be required because it meant that an individual would have to guess how another person had approached file-naming and management.

A second problem often emerged when a file was not modified after it was created and subsequent changes to the content were only communicated via e-mail. Someone arriving at the organization after those e-mails were sent would miss out on that information and would spend a lot of time attempting to acquire it.

This problem also occurred with regard to stakeholders. The Unit often struggled in identifying stakeholders when it came to projects such as the Alma migration or creating new practices for cataloging new types of materials. Despite the best efforts made to include all who were performing the work or would be affected by it, often a stakeholder would be missed or added later, and they too would spend time and effort getting up to speed.

At the SDSU Library e-mail was, and still is, a main channel of communication. E-mail clients are accessible from desktops or mobile devices and make it easy to search for older communications. An individual can also utilize folders for archiving messages. The problem with e-mail is that it requires the sender of the e-mail to include all individuals who need to receive the communication at the beginning and to have a subject heading that is descriptive of the information being communicated. If an individual was not included at the beginning of the communication, it requires effort to loop them back in. The thread nature of e-mails also makes it harder to follow the flow of communication, especially when it involves a long exchange.

USING BASECAMP

Basic Project Management

As stated above, the Unit began exploring Basecamp as a means of improving intradepartmental communication after the SDSU Library launched a pilot study of the tool in 2018. The first and primary way the Unit began using Basecamp was as a project management tool. The initial project the Unit piloted was searching for missing books, and this mostly involved assigning "To-do's," Basecamp's task-assigning feature (figure 2.1). The To-do feature was successful in dividing up the work and tracking the progress being made. As the To-do's are completed, the project manager or person assigning the task is notified and then can manage any remaining work as necessary.

Because of the success of that initial project, Basecamp has become the go-to tool to help divide up and track the work on all large projects with multiple contributors. In the past two years the Unit has used Basecamp for projects such as withdrawing thousands of reels of microfilm that were damaged by a plumbing leak, withdrawing physical government publication items made redundant by electronic copies, and the cataloging of hundreds of streaming video titles when the vendor-supplied bibliographic records for them were deemed insufficient.

With staff in the Unit working remotely due to the COVID-19 pandemic, opportunities to work on catalog cleanup projects as well as other new projects have occurred. In the summer of 2020 a project to correct a migration error of the enumeration fields within item records was identified. It was a given that Basecamp would be the tool used in managing the project, as it would require dividing up and assigning large amounts of work. While the project seemed intimidating, it is reassuring to know that this tool exists to help manage the workflow.

Assigning tasks in Basecamp for these projects has benefited both the project manager and the team members because it is easy to keep track of

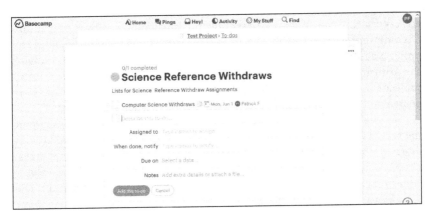

FIGURE 2.1
A blank To-do

work that may need to be done urgently, or to notify people that a project can be worked on at a slower pace. For example, due to increased user demand, it might be necessary to set an earlier deadline for the addition of a large number of individual e-book titles to the catalog, whereas an ongoing project of removing confirmed missing items can have a deadline set further out.

Cataloging Projects

As mentioned earlier, the Unit hired two temporary catalogers in 2018 to work on a large backlog of collections that were donated to Special Collections. While all of the uncataloged materials were somewhat similar, the approaches to cataloging them had distinct differences and requirements. Each collection had specific criteria, specific stakeholders in the departments of Special Collections and Technical Services, and most importantly, each collection required established channels of communication. The donated collections were perfect candidates to utilize a project management approach, an idea supported by Daugherty and Hines in their monograph *Project Management in the Workplace*: "With the advent of systemic project management, stakeholders are identified at the outset and the project team establishes clear communication channels for both input and output of information."[3]

As the Basecamp pilot progressed, the two temporary catalogers, who were already working on cataloging the donated books, expressed frustration with long e-mail threads, cluttered department drives, and busy schedules, which made Basecamp very appealing. Following the completion of the first cataloging project, both the catalogers and the cataloging lead agreed to use Basecamp for upcoming projects.

The positive effects of using Basecamp were felt almost immediately. Documents that were being housed on the Unit's Google Drive could be easily accessed within the project on Basecamp, but most important was the capture of communication. Stakeholders in Special Collections were included in the project, so if questions arose regarding what to do with a duplicate copy or the printing of labels for the book flags, they could be answered easily for all project contributors to see. Using the Message Board feature, questions were posted and answered quickly and in a thread-like fashion.

As the Unit worked on more cataloging projects for Special Collections, the activity in the Message Board feature increased as those involved became more comfortable with the tool. In a project for cataloging pulp serial magazines, a serials cataloger was added to the project and was helpful in resolving issues quickly as they arose. The serials cataloger worked part-time in a separate physical area of the library, but Basecamp made it easy to collaborate because messages and questions would get answered without getting lost in an e-mail in-box. Despite being a late addition to the project, the serials cataloger had no problems adjusting to using Basecamp.

The success with the Special Collections projects led to our using Basecamp for more cataloging projects. It has been used for large donations of gift books, music collections, music scores, e-books, and streaming videos. Because each cataloging project will have its own criteria and standards, using Basecamp to house all the communication and resources for the project in one place has improved efficiency.

Communication and Collaboration

When working on projects, the Unit has shifted to using Basecamp as its main source of communication. As new projects are created and tasks are assigned to an individual, the last line in the instructions is "communicate all issues and questions through Basecamp." The success of using a project management approach is determined by the buy-in of stakeholders, and improving communication among stakeholders is one of the best ways to enlist their support for the approach. McCready and Clark illustrate the importance of communication, stating: "unanswered questions from stakeholders will breed confusion, cause them to create hypothetical answers, and inspire disparate expectations . . . a lack of communication is one of the most cited reasons for project failure."[4]

What has worked very well for the Unit is that even if a stakeholder isn't logging into Basecamp daily, as long as they are attached to the project, they will receive notifications on activity within the project, such as questions that need answering. The stakeholder is able to click a link in the body of the notification that is delivered via e-mail or desktop notification and thus go directly to the discussion in Basecamp.

Basecamp has many features for enabling communication, which means that depending on the type of communication needed, an easy option is usually available. The most prominent method used by the Unit is the Message Board feature. With each project having its own Message Board, questions or issues that are posted on it are seen by the stakeholders and contributors in a topic heading with a chat-style format, where a response follows the most recent message. With the Message Board feature embedded into the project, the discussions stay on topic, whereas with other current tools that have chat features such as Zoom or Slack, work discussions often stray off topic.

Basecamp notifies members on a project of new Message Board posts that list the topic in the notification. When working on cataloging projects, the Unit often uses the Message Board to post questions clarifying the issue of capturing provenance. The questions are easily seen by the stakeholders in Special Collections, and their responses are shared with all involved. This feature makes it easy to collaborate and contribute to the discussions in decision-making. In the event that a decision or discussion regarding a project happened outside of Basecamp, the Unit makes the effort to post the information in the Message Board so that all involved are up-to-date and the information is captured within the project.

Another benefit of having the communications and decisions within a project captured in Basecamp is that it makes it easy to reference them when working on another project that may have a similar issue, which is often the case for the Unit. This feature helps us save time finding a consensus among stakeholders without the extra work of scheduling a meeting. With Unit staff working at home during the COVID-19 pandemic and dealing with the challenges of working in an at-home environment, the Message Board allows project contributors to collaborate at times that are convenient for them. Hempel summarized this perfectly when reviewing Basecamp for *Wired* in 2015, noting that "your mind works better when you can put something down and revisit it later," and "efficient communication is when the right people are able to have the right conversation at the right time."[5] Work during the COVID-19 pandemic requires flexibility and efficiency, and Basecamp helps with both. "Communication shouldn't require schedule synchronization. Calendars have nothing to do with communication. Writing, rather than speaking or meeting, is independent of schedule and far more direct."[6]

Basecamp also allows for discussions to happen within sections of a project. Features such as To-do's or Documents offer a "Discussion" window where messages can be posted back and forth. This has benefited the Unit if the instructions in a To-do needed clarification, or if an anomaly appeared for an individual while performing the task, as contributors could communicate at that level. Knowing when to have something communicated at the project level with Message Boards or at the task level with Discussions is very intuitive.

Basecamp's top navigation assists in keeping communications easy to manage. The "Hey!" feature in the top navigation works as an aggregator of

FIGURE 2.2
Hey! notifications

all communications, reminders, and Projects and Teams activities (figure 2.2). The Hey! feature contains everything an individual needs to know with regard to what is going on in their Basecamp work. Most importantly, it displays all communications and notifications for an individual that are within Basecamp. The Unit often works on multiple projects simultaneously, and managing communications within those projects is very easy with this feature.

If a quick, direct communication between two individuals is needed, the Ping feature allows for this to occur at the Basecamp level. The Unit didn't use this feature initially, but it is now used more often, as working from home and within Basecamp has increased. The Ping communication exchanges are also captured in the Hey! feature.

Having discovered the value of having a defined channel of communication and an organized structure that captures information, the Unit decided to look for opportunities to apply a project management approach to its ongoing or daily work and collaboration. Basecamp offers two distinct sections with the same functionality, "Projects" and "Teams," and after using the tool for Projects, the Unit decided to use the Teams feature.

The Unit has found Teams most helpful with regard to educational resources and professional development. When employees of the Unit participated in the Name Authority Cooperative Program's (NACO's) Funnel training, a Team was created in Basecamp that "is all things NACO-related." Because authority work will be a constant need and keeping up-to-date is crucial, the team was formed to include individuals who were receiving training, as well as those already performing NACO authority work. Basecamp's tools allowed those new to authority work to communicate and collaborate more effectively with members who have authority work expertise.

During the COVID-19 pandemic, the head of COM created an opportunity for many library employees to enroll in an online RDA Lab class. Online meetings for those in the class were scheduled by the head of COM to help collaborate on class assignments and discuss RDA. When the discussion came to what communication channel to use, all members of the Unit pushed to use Basecamp over other tools such as Zoom's chat feature or Google Hangouts. The class members who were not in the Unit were shown how Basecamp is used for the NACO Funnel team and agreed to use Basecamp for RDA Lab class communications and the tracking of documents.

Contributors

When preparing for this chapter and speaking with contributors within the Unit to determine what they liked most about using Basecamp, the common theme was how easy it is to find what they need when working on projects. Basecamp makes searching through e-mail easier as well. When a person sends a message or posts a question in Basecamp, an e-mail notification is sent with a subject heading indicating the project and area being referenced. For example, a discussion within a To-do about withdrawing Government Publication items would read: "Re: (Gov Pubs Ongoing Projects) Contributor 2nd Tab of Gov Pub Withdraws."

Having all of the resources needed for a project stored in Basecamp has also been very helpful. Contributors have found that storing documents within the Docs & Files section lends itself to intuitive file management through the creation of folders, with space for a description of the document as well as an area for discussion. This allows contributors to save time because that structure reduces confusion. The Unit found that using Docs & Files to link directly to Google documents was the best method for our workflow, as opposed to creating documents directly within Basecamp. While it may seem redundant to create a document in Google and then paste the link of the Google document into a Basecamp document, having a path embedded in the project saves time, and the use of Google documents allows for fluid editing and simultaneous viewing of the document. In the event that a significant update or edit is made to the document, a simple mention in the discussion attached to the document will alert all members working on the project.

Project Managers or Leads

As a project manager or lead, it is easy to sing the praises of Basecamp because it allows the manager of a project to easily keep in touch with contributors, see their progress, and most importantly, manage workloads. Embedding resources and documents within a project ensures that contributors are working with a current resource.

As stated earlier, the ability to add members to a project or team and let them see the history of communications and documents is very valuable. If a project grows and needs more contributors, being able to simply add a person to a project and have them able to get up to speed quickly with access not only to all the documents relevant to the project, but to all of the discussion that has occurred, saves time for both the project manager and the newly added team member.

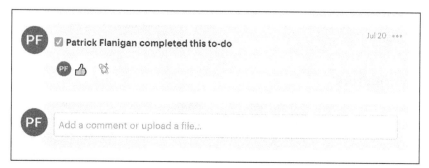

FIGURE 2.3
Boost emoji on a completed To-do

A small but very positive feature in Basecamp is the "Boost" feature (figure 2.3). When a To-do is completed, a notification is sent to the project manager and anyone else on the alerts list. Within the notification of the completed To-do there is a prompt to "boost" the individual with some text or an emoji such as a happy face, thumbs up, or some other sign of appreciation. The Unit has started using the Boost feature and has found it to have a positive effect. In a study of the role of communication in project management, Singh found that acknowledging achievements and communicating appreciation was a value among successful teams. "The highly successful project teams developed greater admiration and respect for each other through candid recognition of the contributions of their members. In fact, they made sure, in their team contract, that the contributions of project members would be acknowledged and communicated in a transparent manner."[7] Having the Boost feature baked into the scheduling tasks and communications makes it easy to acknowledge the completion of a task with positive signs of appreciation. For the Unit, Boosts have fostered collaboration, besides helping in the success of a project and improving the morale of a team.

The activity on a project or team effort will always be archived within Basecamp, and this is a huge positive for project leads and managers. The Unit appreciates this feature because it is an easy way to refer back when asked about the progress on a project at a current moment, or to determine when a decision was made.

In addition, when it is time for yearly evaluations, managers and contributors in the Unit can go to Basecamp and look at the Activity feature (figure 2.4) in the top navigation to see a history of their own activity, or those whose work they've managed. With Unit employees now working at home as well as from the library, Basecamp is keeping an archive of all their efforts both within and sometimes outside of their job description. At a time when many struggle to remember the work they did the previous week, having a history of all their efforts and accomplishments is beneficial and rewarding.

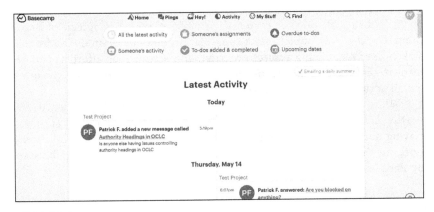

FIGURE 2.4
Activity feed in Basecamp

CHALLENGES TO USING BASECAMP

Overall, the adoption of Basecamp has been successful for the Unit at the SDSU Library. The use of Basecamp has resulted in fewer e-mail chains and fewer meetings, especially because stakeholders can view progress and discussions at any time. The numerous avenues for communication, the use of Boosts, and the archival features of Basecamp have helped improve morale in the department and have led to greater cohesion and cross-training. Unfortunately, there have also been challenges to using Basecamp that have prevented it from being embraced and integrated fully into the COM Department and the SDSU Library as a whole.

Because using Basecamp started as a pilot and the use of it was voluntary, there is limited buy-in across the entire library. The library has not taken the steps to adopt it as an organizational tool required on all projects or by all departments, partly due to the SDSU migrating to SharePoint for document management and archiving. The Unit had a need for Basecamp with the addition of new staff and projects, but not all departments have as many projects as a unit in a technical services department.

The technology gap among staff members has also proved to be a challenge. While some staffers are very fluent and comfortable using online tools through things like social media or learning management systems, many others are not. Basecamp's features are available in other established tools, and it is also not the only project management tool available. This has led to many employees preferring to stick with the communication methods and tools they are comfortable with.

This use of other communication and organization tools created a challenge for project managers and team members. It became very important to be vigilant in capturing communications or decisions made outside of Basecamp. For the Unit, sometimes a conversation in a hall or an e-mail from a stakeholder regarding a project occurred, and a conscious effort had to be made to capture the information and put it in Basecamp, either by copying an e-mail or by summarizing a conversation.

While Basecamp does its best to integrate with Google, in the case of hosting documents in Basecamp it can feel redundant and inefficient at times. Having documents in Google Drive provides security and enables collaboration, but the extra step to then incorporate them into Basecamp can be seen by some as a bit of a hassle.

CONCLUSION

Communication is often cited as a crucial factor in successful projects and the lack of communication as the cause of failed efforts. Basecamp can benefit libraries by being a defined channel for communication among project teams and departments. It tracks all project progress and communications and allows this information to be delivered quickly and easily to contributors who join the project later.

Overall, Basecamp has greatly improved the Unit's communication, collaboration, and morale by serving as a hub for discussions about projects and policies. Hempel states: "the upshot is that Basecamp works well, even if only a couple of the people working on a project choose to work in Basecamp."[8] This was exactly the case for the Unit, even if it would work better still if more people in the organization embraced the use of Basecamp. It saves valuable time by helping those using it get up to speed quickly and not have to hunt for communications and information. The need to work efficiently and communicate with online tools will be essential, given the uncertain times ahead. For a library or technical services department that is challenged with juggling multiple projects and regular work efforts simultaneously, Basecamp is a solution that can make communication and organization more efficient without much effort.

BIBLIOGRAPHY

Basecamp. "The Basecamp Guide to Internal Communication," last modified May 21, 2020. https://basecamp.com/guides/how-we-communicate.

Gumares, Anastasia, Laurie McGowan, Miranda VanNevel, and Zheng Wang. "The Value of Full-Time Project Management Positions: PMO Nuts and Bolts at Hesburgh Libraries." In *Project Management in the Library Workplace*, ed. Alice

Daugherty and Samantha Schmehl Hines, 199–228. Advances in Library Administration and Organization. Bingley, UK: Emerald, 2018.

Hempel, Jessi. "Basecamp 3 Will Change the Way You Think about Work—Again." *Wired,* November 4, 2015. www.wired.com/2015/11/basecamp-3-will-change -the-way-you-think-about-workagain/

McCready, Kate, and Kirsten Clark. "Academic Library Implementation of Project Management Standards." In *Project Management in the Library Workplace*, ed. Alice Daugherty and Samantha Schmehl Hines, 133–50. Advances in Library Administration and Organization. Bingley, UK: Emerald, 2018.

Singh, Rajesh. "The Role of Communication in Project Management." *Information Outlook* 20, no. 5 (September 2016): 4–6. http://libproxy.sdsu.edu/login?url =https://search-proquest-com.libproxy.sdsu.edu/docview/1836966517? accountid=13758.

NOTES

1. Rajesh Singh, "The Role of Communication in Project Management," *Information Outlook* 20, no. 5 (September 2016): 4–6. https://search-proquest-com.lib proxy.sdsu.edu/docview/1836966517?accountid=13758.

2. Basecamp, "The Basecamp Guide to Internal Communication," last modified May 21, 2020, https://basecamp.com/guides/how-we-communicate.

3. Anastasia Gumares et al., "The Value of Full-Time Project Management Positions: PMO Nuts and Bolts at Hesburgh Libraries," in *Project Management in the Library Workplace*, ed. Alice Daugherty and Samantha Schmehl Hines (Bingley, UK: Emerald, 2018), 199–228.

4. Kate McCready and Kirsten Clark, "Academic Library Implementation of Project Management Standards," in *Project Management in the Library Workplace*, ed. Alice Daugherty and Samantha Schmehl Hines (Bingley, UK: Emerald, 2018), 133–50.

5. Jessi Hempel, "Basecamp 3 Will Change the Way You Think about Work— Again," *Wired,* November 4, 2015, www.wired.com/2015/11/basecamp -3-will-change-the-way-you-think-about-workagain.

6. Basecamp, "Basecamp Guide to Internal Communication."

7. Singh, "The Role of Communication in Project Management," 5.

8. Hempel, "Basecamp 3 Will Change the Way You Think about Work—Again."

GWEN MEYER GREGORY

3
Retreating to Advance Together

Communicating through Internal
and External Retreats

I t can be challenging to step away from our daily work in technical services. There are always invoices to be paid, licenses to be reviewed, and books to be cataloged. However, when we take a deep breath and "escape" together as a group, we can build new bonds and come up with fresh ideas. Leaving the day-to-day behind, spending time together in a different environment, and participating in thought-provoking activities can lead to many positive results.

BACKGROUND

The University of Illinois at Chicago (UIC) is a large urban research university with a student population of 33,500 (22,000 undergraduate, 11, 500 graduate and professional). The campus has a substantial research enterprise as well as the largest medical school in the United States. The UIC community also includes 2,800 faculty members and 6,000 staff. The UIC Library is comprised of five sites across the state: two libraries in Chicago, as well as ones in Rockford, Peoria, and Urbana. Within the library, the acquisitions, cataloging, electronic resources, and collection maintenance for all of the UIC Library sites are managed centrally by the Resource Acquisition and Management (RAM)

Department, which was created in 2010 as a result of a merger of the Cataloging and Acquisitions departments. The department currently includes 5 faculty librarians, 15 paraprofessionals, and 12–15 student employees, though these numbers have varied slightly over the time frame described in this chapter.

I began work as head of the RAM Department in May 2012. The previous head of this new department had departed soon after it was created, and no interim head had been appointed. As a result, some parts of the merger and subsequent reorganization had not been fully implemented, and staff members felt that their ideas and perspectives were not well represented to the library administration. Several staff members also retired around the time I joined the department, which added to the feeling of instability.

As I got to know the department, I saw many excellent people focused on their individual work, but lacking understanding of each other's responsibilities or what we accomplished in total and how the pieces fit together. The creation of a new mission statement and strategic plan for the entire library, however, gave us an opportunity to clearly align the department's work to the library's overall mission. Drawing from my experience at other libraries, I suggested that we hold a departmental retreat. This idea was met with both enthusiasm and confusion; some staff members were not familiar with the retreat concept, and others were jaded about meetings in general.

We created a team of several volunteers to work on our first retreat. As the department head, I led the planning, obtained funding from library administrators, and coordinated participation from those outside the department. Between 2014 and 2019, the RAM Department at the UIC Library held five retreats (see figure 3.1). Planning these enabled a number of departmental staff members to develop and practice their leadership skills.

Date	Length	Topic(s)
August 2014	Full day	Mission statement
March 2015	Half day	Internal and external communication
October 2015	Full day	Technology, department initiatives, and goals
January 2017	Half day	Collaboration (invited participants from other departments)
February 2019	Three-quarters day	Reorganization, department initiatives, and goals

FIGURE 3.1
Chronology of RAM Department retreats

LIBRARY RETREATS

Retreats are generally defined as events where a work group leaves their usual working space to gather elsewhere for a defined length of time and engage in planned activities while avoiding outside interruptions. Retreats are longer than normal meetings and focus on longer-term issues and concerns. The reasons to hold a retreat are varied but include fostering change, creating a collective vision, exploring staffers' fundamental concerns, and making tough decisions. The support and encouragement of departmental and library leadership is key for an effective retreat. Managers should be prepared to implement the changes suggested at a retreat, thus demonstrating that the process is taken seriously.

Bolman and Gallos's four frames model provides insights into some of the potential benefits of retreats.[1] In fact, these frames (structural, political, human resource, and symbolic) are applicable to many workplace situations found in academia and in organizations generally. Each frame may be appropriate in different situations; an effective leader can use them all as needed.

> *Structural frame*: Focuses on process and rationality, and therefore comes naturally to many workers in technical services. The retreat can be a powerful analytical tool, providing space and perspective to understand departmental structures and workflows.
>
> *Political frame*: Important in building relationships within and throughout the organization. A retreat is an occasion to build coalitions and negotiate as well as to plan strategies.
>
> *Human resource frame*: Focuses on communication and developing people. Relationship-building, including developing confidence and trust in each other and in leaders, can be a part of the retreat.
>
> *Symbolic frame*: Uses ceremony and ritual to tell our story and create a shared vision. The retreat is a space to develop our culture as well as our vision of ourselves.

All of these frames depend on communication; without connecting to each other, the organization, and the world, we are unable to work together effectively and efficiently.

Within the library field, retreats have long been used for team-building and improving communication.[2] This is true for technical services units as well. For example, one large university library's technical services department held a retreat focused on restructuring its workflows.[3] An outside facilitator helped design a card-sort activity which resulted in new departmental organizational models. The activity divided employees into four random groups that then used sticky notes to analyze the department's work tasks. This activity succeeded in engaging everyone in the process and ensuring that their ideas were heard and collected. Other technical services units have held retreats focused on building teams, improving communications, enhancing social bonds, and creating momentum for change. Interviews with librarians who planned and conducted those retreats showed positive comments and results. In addition, those interviewed emphasized the need for proper planning and facilitation, as well as gathering feedback from participants. All the librarians said they would encourage future retreats or similar group events.

PLANNING

When planning a retreat there are several factors to consider. The retreat should be related to the day-to-day work but not focus exclusively on the details. A variety of participants should be part of the group tasked with planning the retreat, and a facilitator from outside the group is recommended, both to display neutrality and to promote participation by the group's leaders. The facilitator may be from another library department, from another part of the organization, or hired from outside the organization.[4]

The RAM Department's first retreat in 2014 was experimental in that most staff members had never participated in such an event. An intrepid group of volunteers, led by me and including one other faculty member and four paraprofessionals, agreed to work on the planning. As it was our first retreat, much discussion was required to determine our goals and how we wanted the event to proceed. We met every week or two for the four months before the retreat took place. Individual planning team members took on responsibility for coordinating separate activities related to the retreat. For example, one person took the lead on managing the food, and two others worked together on games and team-building. As the department head, I scheduled meetings and obtained funding from the library administration to pay for food, supplies, and the room rental. In later retreats I also asked for volunteers to work the events.

The planning process for each of our retreats was similar and usually started with decisions regarding its date and location. We found that planning may take several months, so it was good to begin discussions around these points early. Our main costs were generally food and the space rental, so those were important considerations throughout the planning process.

> *Date and time:* Keep in mind any scheduling restrictions such as holidays, school vacations, and the individual schedules or shifts of participants. The date will help you to determine a location that is available at the time you need it, as well as help with planning other logistics such as food.

Prior notification: To avoid any confusion with colleagues in other library departments, we notified them of a retreat's dates and times. Some staff members also left a message stating that they would reply to requests the day after the retreat.

Location: We have found that a location away from the usual work space is preferable. This helped people to mentally separate from their daily tasks, as well as providing freedom from interruptions. In our first retreat, we visited several locations before determining that using a room at the student center was convenient and within our price range. In subsequent retreats we also used other locations in the library building. Additional possibilities may include hotels or retreat centers. It is crucial in all these discussions to keep the transportation needs of participants in mind, as travel off site might require a bus or other option.

Once the date, time, and location were set, we tackled other tasks in the planning process, such as food and activities. With a team working on the event, specific tasks can be assigned to individuals who can report back to the team on their progress. Individual staff members enjoyed working on these activities because they provided some variety from their daily jobs.

Themes are one more option to consider. We found that themes provided opportunities for decorating and other creative outlets. For example, our retreat after our departmental reorganization was themed "Under Construction." We used yellow warning tape, construction worker vests, and themed napkins and plates to create an engaging atmosphere for the day. The themes of our other retreats have included "Back to the Future" and "Tropical Vacation."

Finally, as mentioned earlier, a facilitator is crucial for a successful retreat. As part of the planning process, I asked the planning team who they would like to have facilitate, and they preferred an internal person. Because of this we have generally had the department head act as the facilitator for our retreats. However, some sources recommend an outside facilitator, in part because this allows all department members to participate fully.[5] This is something we have discussed, and we will consider how it can be accomplished for future retreats.

After holding several retreats in close succession, we have concluded that a full department retreat is probably best every two years or so, depending on the major activities and events impacting us. For example, we are currently migrating to a new library management system, and a retreat focusing on the impacts of that project and assessing what we need to do next will be planned for after the implementation. This retreat may include outside participants who also use the system.

Activities

While planning the first retreat, we developed an agenda that would serve as a model for future events, with a mix of work-related small and large group discussion, team-building activities, goal-setting for the department, and social time. We incorporated as much interaction into the retreat as possible, encouraging communication in a number of ways. The participants took part in several icebreakers to help them learn more about each other. They were also divided into small discussion groups, which then reported back to the entire group at a later point. These agendas were essential because they let participants know what to expect and when. (See figure 3.2 for a sample agenda.)

Each retreat was planned with a blend of practical and entertaining activities, all with an emphasis on communicating with colleagues. Common elements across all retreats included icebreakers, team-building activities, food, visits from library administrators, and the development of an end product such as a mission statement or departmental goals.

Though seemingly less crucial, the fun activities are definitely an important part of the experience. They allow colleagues to get to know each other in a new way, which promotes better communication. While you may think that everyone already knows each other, there are many icebreakers available online that will reveal new things. You should aim for activities that include

Time	Activity
9:00–9:15	Introduction/welcome
9:15–9:30	Icebreaker
9:30–10:00	Small group discussion: collaboration
10:00–10:30	Small groups report out
10:30–10:45	Break
10:45–11:00	Small group discussion: project ideas
11:00–11:45	Small groups report out
11:45–12:30	Lunch/relaxation
12:30–1:15	Wrap-up/future steps
1:15–1:30	Teambuilding activity
1:30–1:45	Farewell/special guest

FIGURE 3.2
Sample retreat agenda

FIGURE 3.3
The author with UIC mascot Sparky

everyone and which can be completed in the amount of time allotted. Opportunities to stand up and move around will wake people up and stimulate creativity. Team-building games may fit better toward the end of the retreat, providing a chance to blow off steam after in-depth discussions. Teams can be assigned by having people number off to provide random groupings. Personality quizzes and tests are also engaging activities for a retreat because they can provide colleagues with insight into how to work with each other more effectively. In one of our retreats, we each completed the True Colors personality test.[6] After a short presentation on the test's results and what they meant, we split into groups by color. Each group discussed their communication style and how they would like others to communicate with them. The groups then shared these ideas, helping colleagues to develop better strategies for working together.

Discussion and goal-setting are challenging work and everyone will appreciate a break, so it is also important to set aside social time as part of the retreat. Participants enjoy having a chance during lunch to socialize. One of the most enjoyable parts of our 2017 retreat was the visit of our campus mascot, Sparky D. Dragon, as the farewell guest (figure 3.3). Everyone enjoyed posing for photos with Sparky, and the campus spirit office was happy to provide the visit at no charge.

Outside Staff

Though this was more challenging to organize, including staff from other departments who had not previously joined our retreats helped us expand our communication within the library. The success of planning a cross-departmental retreat required buy-in from the heads of the other departments, followed by willing participation from selected staff members in those departments. Together, our team built an agenda that we hoped would be interesting and understandable to all involved, and we made special efforts to welcome all participants. We used this cross-departmental retreat as an opportunity to build relationships and strengthen communications with our library colleagues. Some of the participants external to our department were long-term library staff who were nevertheless surprised to learn details about our department's operations. They were impressed by the full engagement of technical services staff in the retreat process, as well as our commitment to creating and executing our goals. Technical services staff appreciated the opportunities to explain their work to external colleagues and to work together on developing new processes and services that benefited both internal and external users.

Assessment

The final step for each retreat was to conduct an online assessment of the event. It is best to have the survey ready to go before the retreat in order to request feedback while the experience is still fresh in participants' minds. The results from these assessments have provided us with data to help in planning future events. The response rates for the surveys were generally good, ranging around 40–60 percent.

An online survey, using a tool like Survey Monkey or Qualtrics, makes collecting, analyzing, and sharing the results easy. (See figure 3.4 for a sample and figure 3.5 for selected results.) In these evaluations, respondents were generally asked to rate each aspect of the retreat on a scale from very good to very poor in order to get their feedback on all the activities. Many parts of the surveys requested qualitative answers using comments boxes. We asked for comments on any specific activities and what participants liked most and least about the retreat. Finally, we requested suggestions for future retreats or activities, as well as final comments.

The respondents rated most activities positively, but it was easy to see which activities were the most and the least popular. Lunch was usually rated highly, while some specific icebreakers did not work out as planned. The respondents often had helpful and detailed suggestions that we took to heart. In future retreats, for example, we shortened the length of the retreat, invited staff members from other departments, and planned the team-building activities more carefully.

In our retreats we continue to provide snacks, drinks, and lunch and to incorporate fun activities like icebreakers. Each time we start to plan a retreat, we review the previous evaluation results and incorporate what we have learned into the new event. Having the department head lead the planning and assessment has provided continuity, as it would be easy to lose track of previous survey results and documentation such as agendas and notes.

Please rate the following activities at the retreat:					
Activity	Very Good	Good	Fair	Poor	Very Poor
Icebreaker	O	O	O	O	O
Tech topic session in Idea Commons	O	O	O	O	O
Strategic initiatives discussion with Mary Case	O	O	O	O	O
Costume content/ other free time activities	O	O	O	O	O
Small group discussion and reporting	O	O	O	O	O
Full group discussion	O	O	O	O	O
Teambuilding activity	O	O	O	O	O
Wrap-up and future planning	O	O	O	O	O
Preretreat communications (agenda, flyers, etc.)	O	O	O	O	O
Lunch	O	O	O	O	O
Snacks and other refreshments	O	O	O	O	O
Location/room	O	O	O	O	O
Breaks	O	O	O	O	O

Do you have comments on any specific activities?

What did you like most about the retreat?

What did you like least about the retreat?

What ideas or suggestions do you have for future department retreats or activities?

Please add any other comments about the retreat.

FIGURE 3.4
Sample evaluation of a retreat

Date	2014	March 2015	October 2015	2017	2019
Number of respondents	11	12	8	18 (12 RAM, 6 other depart- ments)	7
Percent responding	61	67	44	60	39
Most popular	Mission statement discus- sion and creation	Lunch	Food, internal commu- nications discussion	Small group dis- cussion, location	Ice- breaker
Least popular	Location/ room	Tech topics	Games	Handouts	NA

Sample Comments:

"The discussion surrounding the mission statement was very engaging and everyone had an opportunity to participate. It really helped to us to better define what the RAM Department is."—2014

"From the notes, I think I see everyone on agreement on communication being an issue everyone is willing to work on."—2015

"I liked learning more about my coworkers."—2015

"Coming together and getting a better understanding of how one does their job and how it affects another person or unit. Communication is always good."—2017

"I liked that one of the activities really reflected how our department is: everyone was giving their advice and helping in completing the obstacle course."—2019

FIGURE 3.5
Sample evaluation of a retreat

OUR EVENTS

Developing a mission statement for the department was an important goal for our first retreat in 2014. Working with the associate dean, we reviewed the library's mission statement and strategic plan, and during the retreat we broke up into groups to brainstorm ideas about our own department's mis- sion. After lunch and downtime, we came together to discuss the ideas gener- ated and narrow them down in a facilitated discussion. The result was a concise statement of just twenty words: "RAM acquires, organizes, and maintains information resources, providing access for users by working in collaboration with internal and global partners." This mission statement has proved to be a terrific focus for us in the ensuing years. We include it in our annual report, have it printed on bookmarks that are given to new staff and visitors, and display it on a banner at the entrance to our physical office area.

Our second retreat, which we called a retreat refresher, was a half-day event in March 2015. This retreat focused on communication, both within the department and with outside clients. We watched Seth Godin's TED talk "This Is Broken,"[7] an entertaining discussion of the ways that marketing, signs, and other methods we use to communicate can fail. We used Godin's examples to spur discussion of ways that our current communication was ineffective. For example, had we created complex signs or forms to interact with our customers rather than fundamentally changing our processes so that they work better? We again used the technique of small group discussion followed by large group reporting, with the sessions focusing on internal and external communication. The result was a number of new ideas to improve our communication, including ways to better indicate location changes, creating e-resource tutorials and guides, and providing more guidance for library liaisons and others on e-books and how to access them.

In October 2015, at our third retreat, we focused on developing specific goals and initiatives based on our department's mission and the library's strategic plan. As an introduction to the topic, the library dean spoke with us about current campus and library initiatives. We then conducted small and large group discussions of important roles the department could play in meeting the library's goals. The result was a number of initiatives for the department, which included better cross-departmental communication, learning more about the library's special collections, and providing more guidance about e-books and how they work. Teams were formed to work on several of these goals. The day also included other elements, such as an introduction to several technology resources useful for department staff: the library wiki, macros for cataloging, and cloud storage via Google Drive and Box. The retreat lasted for a full day, with lunch provided.

Our fourth retreat took place in January 2017. At this event, staff members from several other departments were invited to participate in many of the sessions. Colleagues from the circulation, systems, reference, special collections, and digital programs areas were invited. This was a natural outgrowth of our emphasis on external communications. We hoped that by having external players involved in our discussion, we could learn from them and craft new ways to enhance our relationships. We consciously focused discussion on how the RAM Department could meet the needs of outside colleagues and their departments, and it was very helpful to get comments directly from our internal stakeholders. As a result, the new item-processing instructions and forms were revised and a library-wide metadata task force was formed. The participants also formed social relationships, which provided new paths for interdepartmental interactions. This retreat lasted for a full day with lunch provided, although the external participants were not required to attend for the entire time. We asked that they be there in the morning, and then invited them to stay for lunch. The post-lunch activities were optional for them.

Our most recent retreat was in February 2019. This event occupied most of a day and included lunch. A major departmental restructuring had taken place in the latter half of 2018, and as a result this retreat was focused on discussions of and refinements to the new structure. We began by reviewing the library's latest strategic plan, followed by conversations regarding the current state of our department's internal and external communications. We ended by developing goals for the next year and formed teams to work toward those ends. The goals included the creation of a team to work on improving relations with subject liaisons and other staff, improving communications with the business office, and having each unit within the department hold regular unit meetings. Since the retreat, we have discussed progress on these goals at our monthly department meetings. The teams working on two of the original goals ended up converging and merging into a single team focusing on outreach. One year after the retreat, we had accomplished all the goal activities and were ready to start planning for a new retreat.

CONCLUSION

Communication has been an ongoing theme in our retreats. We have designed activities specifically to help us get to know each other and our individual communication styles better. The time away from our usual tasks was well-spent, allowing us to examine our work in new ways and to develop longer-term plans, many of which were related to communication within the department as well as externally. Colleagues learned about each other by participating in exercises and developing goals together. We took time to think deeply about our internal customers in other library departments, looking at recurring challenges and developing goals to improve our services. These included establishing new outreach specifically for liaison librarians, as well as a cross-departmental task force to develop clearer procedures for the handling of rush items.

Research suggests that nourishing positive relationships at work is a powerful way to improve workplace satisfaction, and we have learned that we benefit from this personally and as a group.[8] Increasing and improving communication builds relationships as we learn about each other. This takes place through games and social time, as well as through team-building and workflow analysis. Our experience has shown that even staff members who are reluctant to participate at first can warm up to the retreat environment and benefit from joining in. Our department plans to continue holding retreats in the future and we are looking forward to our next event, following our migration to a new library management system.

REFERENCES

Bergin, Meghan Banach, and Sally Krash. "Creative Solutions to Technical Services Staffing Challenges in an Academic Library." In *Library Technical Services: Adapting to a Changing Environment*, 237–52. Lafayette, IN: Purdue University Press, 2020.

Bolman, Lee G., and Joan V. Gallos. *Reframing Academic Leadership*. San Francisco: Jossey-Bass, 2011.

Campbell, Sheila, and Merianne Liteman. *Retreats That Work*. San Francisco: Jossey-Bass, 2003.

Cross, Rob. "To Be Happier at Work, Invest More in Your Relationships." *Harvard Business Review Online*, July 2019. https://hbr.org/2019/07/to-be-happier-at-work-invest-more-in-your-relationships.

Fischer, Christine. "Re: TS Retreats," e-mail to the author, February 24, 2020.

Godin, Seth. "This Is Broken," TED: Ideas Worth Spreading. www.ted.com/talks/seth_godin_this_is_broken_1.

Granskog, Kay. "RE: Have You Held Retreats for Your Technical Services Department?" E-mail to the author, February 18, 2020.

Langley, Anne, and Andrea Baruzzi. "So You Want to Have a Library Retreat? Planning, Facilitating, and Outcomes." *College & Research Library News* 75, no. 5 (2014): 250–53.

Roper, Jennifer O'Brien. "RE: Have You Held Retreats for Your Technical Services Department?" E-mail to the author, February 28, 2020.

Simmons, Lisa. "How to Host a Fun and Productive Staff Retreat." Desk Demon. http://us.deskdemon.com/pages/us/meeting/fun-productive-staff-retreat.

True Colors Intl. "What Is True Colors?" https://truecolorsintl.com/what-is-true-colors/.

NOTES

1. Lee G. Bolman and Joan V. Gallos, *Reframing Academic Leadership* (San Francisco: Jossey-Bass, 2011).
2. Anne Langley and Andrea Baruzzi, "So You Want to Have a Library Retreat? Planning, Facilitating, and Outcomes," *College & Research Library News* 75, no. 5 (2014): 250–53.
3. Meghan Banach Bergin and Sally Krash, "Creative Solutions to Technical Services Staffing Challenges in an Academic Library," in *Library Technical*

Services: Adapting to a Changing Environment (Lafayette, IN: Purdue University Press, 2020), 237–52.

4. Sheila Campbell and Merianne Liteman, *Retreats That Work* (San Francisco: Jossey-Bass, 2003).

5. Campbell and Liteman, *Retreats That Work*.

6. True Colors Intl., "What Is True Colors?"

7. Godin, "This Is Broken."

8. Cross, "To Be Happier at Work."

MELISSA MOLL AND
SHELBY STROMMER

4

Up, Down, and Sideways

Multidirectional Communication within a
Multifaceted Technical Services Project

The University of Iowa (UI) Libraries is the largest library system in the state of Iowa, with more than five million volumes housed in seven libraries across campus, plus an off-site storage facility. During the 2016–17 academic year, large collection moves provided a real-time case study of communication within technical services at the UI Libraries. With a mix of permanent staff, temporary hires, and student employees, the Preservation and Conservation Department and the Cataloging-Metadata Department collaboratively spearheaded major facets of the collections relocation project. Especially when the project scope grew and the timeline shrank, efficient communication strategies became as important as knowing how to shrink-wrap a bound volume or edit a holdings record.

Over three decades, a large area in the basement of the main library became a storage repository for less-circulated items and materials from closed branch libraries. The volumes were shelved in their order of transfer to the basement, with notes added to holdings records alerting staff to general shelf locations. By 2016, the space held approximately 425,000 volumes in a range of physical conditions, and the accumulated impact of both deliberate decisions and unanticipated events triggered a domino effect of interrelated collections projects centered on this main library basement storage area.

One unanticipated event came in the summer of 2008, when historic flooding in eastern Iowa caused $750 million in damage to the University of Iowa campus. While in the end the main library's basement suffered only minor flooding, hundreds of volunteers responded to a call and formed book brigades that moved nearly 100,000 volumes and manuscript boxes from lower shelves in the basement to the upper floors of the library.[1] The campus's music and art buildings adjoined the Iowa River and suffered extensive destruction, impacting the branch libraries that they housed.[2] The art library reopened in 2011, while the main library hosted the music library for eight years until the launch of a new music building for the fall 2016 semester.[3]

The flood of 2008 became a crisis that prompted a collections shift. A temporary off-site warehouse facilitated the collections moves, especially the displacement of main library materials when the music library moved in. During the flood recovery, many campus efforts—including the off-site warehouse—depended in part on approval and funding from the U.S. Federal Emergency Management Agency. When the new music building and music library opened in summer 2016, the UI Libraries also opened a new, permanent high-density storage annex about a mile away from the previous warehouse. The new annex holds a maximum 4.8 million items and features 22-foot high shelving and a special cold storage room for media.[4]

In mid-2016, changing campus priorities and needs prompted a reevaluation of the space within the main library's basement. As the university-level deliberations and decisions evolved over the following months, library staff began planning to vacate a portion of the basement that was used for materials storage. Their work in late 2016 and early 2017 was paced and deliberate, especially as it coincided with a major system migration within the UI Libraries and the openings of the new off-site annex and the music library. Midway through the spring 2017 semester, however, the university timeline for the main library space suddenly shifted. Within the UI Libraries, work to clear the basement storage shelves rapidly scaled up. Thirty-eight staff members across the Cataloging-Metadata and Preservation and Conservation departments participated in the collections project in some capacity, creating an interdepartmental team of full-time employees, student workers, and temporary hires. This technical services team connected to other departments and teams that oversaw many additional aspects of the UI Libraries' collective response.

From summer 2016 through summer 2017, the scope of the collections project within technical services grew to meet rapidly developing needs and priorities. In the main library basement, project staff assessed over 425,000 volumes for condition issues, separating those approved for immediate relocation to the off-site annex from others requiring preservation treatment and stabilization prior to transfer. The staff also cleaned, verified, and shrink-wrapped a large portion of the 33,000 volumes that were held back.

Beyond materials in basement storage, the project rehoused, labeled, and bar-coded 16-mm films in preparation for cold storage; assessed and withdrew thousands of duplicate items from the circulating collection; transferred the library's preservation print leaf masters; and implemented cataloging procedures for retaining, transferring, and withdrawing items as part of shared print agreements. The project timeline coincided with a vacancy in the Cataloging-Metadata Department head position. For the collections project, this meant that many department head-level decisions were made instead at the project level—and thus effective communication became even more important to tie together everyone from the project team members to related teams, to permanent and interim supervisors, to the library administration.

PRIMARY QUESTIONS FOR BUILDING MULTIDIRECTIONAL COMMUNICATION

Amid complex parameters and high expectations for deliverables, the collections project became a laboratory for experimenting with communication methods within technical services. As the two project leads—one of us from the preservation side and one from cataloging—we led the day-to-day project management within the two departments. One project risk was certain: without reliable, extensible, and sustainable communication channels, we would increase confusion and diminish productivity. Communication had to flow up, down, across, and around to reach everyone involved. Two primary questions guided us in determining where to build communication pathways: "Who does this affect?" and "Who do we not realize that this will affect?"

Library staff fell into both categories: those known, and those unforeseen to be impacted by the project. Continuous communication through multiple platforms enabled our project team members to complete a revolving series of interconnected projects and asynchronous tasks within work spaces that spanned three floors of the main library building. Where one team member or workflow ended, the next began. Beyond our immediate project team, we cast a wider communications net to connect with known stakeholders and to prevent inadvertent information gaps that could impact the work of our colleagues within technical services and related project teams.

The Hippocratic oath of "First, do no harm" applies to technical services work and to technical services communication as well. Answering the question "Who (or what) does this affect?" seems an obvious first step in preventing harm to materials, data, and working relationships with colleagues. The second question—"Who (or what) do we *not* realize that this will affect?"—aims to surface those harms that may not be readily apparent at first glance; that is, those risks from blind spots in knowledge or communication that could detrimentally impact project outcomes. For us, intentionally answering these two questions helped to pinpoint and establish communication pathways that flowed up, down, and sideways.

COMMUNICATING PROJECT DETAILS

As with many technical services tasks, clearly communicating the details of the collections project—answers to the who, what, when, where, why, and how questions—coordinated people, materials, and spaces while streamlining processes and avoiding redundancies. None of our communication methods were groundbreaking, but together they established and disseminated transparent workflows. Low-tech solutions organized physical spaces and physical items, a virtual hub gathered the project team's resources, in-person connections served as launching points for later work, and statistics-gathering tools provided real-time project assessments. Spending time envisioning and establishing details early in the project saved time later and facilitated quicker adaptations when needs and parameters changed.

A project centered on physical collections required physical communication methods that tracked materials routing and processing. With multiple work spaces and staging areas across three floors of the library, physical signage became an essential communication tool. Signs reminded team members of key steps and procedures, marked progress at the end of one shift and identified the place to begin for the next, and tracked which items on which book carts, shelves, and staging areas were at which point of which process. Paper flags marked volumes that required special preservation treatment or a second look at the bibliographic record. A bulletin board near project team workstations provided a central location for posting work schedules and progress reports. These low-tech signs, flags, and boards communicated high-value information to team members as they shifted from task to task and to team leads as we identified backlogs and redirected efforts accordingly.

A cloud-based shared folder served as a centralized hub for the project team's virtual communications. Because student employees cannot access our staff intranet or shared server, we turned to online document-sharing tools like Microsoft OneDrive, Google Drive, and Box that were available to all team members. The virtual hub gathered how-to documentation detailing step-by-step procedures, flow charts illustrating materials routing and key decision points, operational spreadsheets to track progress, and links to web-based statistics forms and helpful online resources. As a one-stop shop for all project documents, the virtual communication hub linked team members to up-to-the-minute, point-of-need information regardless of where or when they worked.

Along with low-tech physical signage and a higher-tech virtual hub, in-person communication proved essential to transmitting project details. In addition to informal check-ins with project staff throughout the workday, more formal training sessions incorporated multiple learning styles through demonstrations, hands-on practice, and reference documents with both written instructions and illustrations. To gather the entire team together, we borrowed and modified a tactic from "agile project management" and held scrum meetings at the beginning of each week. Agile project management is a cyclical management technique based on a set of principles originally designed for software development. It aims to reduce a project's time frame by "motivating the team, welcoming constant change, using face-to-face communication, keeping the process simple, and creating an environment for excellence."[5] The iterative focus of agile project management and regular scrum meetings proved a good fit for the frequently shifting demands of the collections move process. During our Monday morning scrums, team members stood in a circle near the project bulletin board to share updates, raise and address questions and concerns, and establish priorities for the week ahead. The fifteen-minute meetings allowed enough time to communicate essential details while remaining brief enough to avoid unnecessary distractions and "rabbit holes." They provided stability, predictability, and opportunity for regular feedback. With team members working at different times and at different locations in the building, the scrums gathered everyone together and built a sense of camaraderie and team identity. They also empowered team members by affording them the opportunity to ask questions and voice concerns, fostering a sense of ownership in the project.

Each project workflow built in statistics-gathering points, with the input method depending on the need at hand. Paper and pencil placed at strategic points was a quick and easy way for project staff to log statistics as they worked, a method particularly useful for hands-on tasks away from a computer workstation but requiring manual data-gathering and calculation. Shared spreadsheets housed in the virtual hub offered ready online access and built-in number-crunching features to automate statistical calculations. Web forms, such as those offered by Microsoft and Google, provided simpler user interfaces for team members to report statistics and data easily into a spreadsheet. While the collections project utilized all three of these statistics-gathering methods, the data collected remained consistent. For each task, team members recorded the date, their name, the time spent on the given task, and how many items had been completed. The resulting statistics tracked progress to date and also provided data to map out likely future progress, resource needs, and timelines.

COMMUNICATING A POSITIVE TEAM ENVIRONMENT

Many tasks in the collections project were decidedly unglamorous, repetitive, and tedious. Team members often worked in cramped and dusty conditions, pushing heavy carts up and down ramps. Communicating a positive team environment helped to alleviate the monotony of some project components and to remedy issues more easily as they arose. We endeavored to foster this culture of teamwork, collaboration, and learning through both our actions and our words.

As team leads, we often worked alongside and together with other team members—a form of communication via action and "sweat equity" that wordlessly transmitted expectations for everyone. Many of the items in the main library basement suffered from varying degrees of red rot, a type of deterioration in which the leather becomes desiccated and flakes off in a rust-colored powder that is prone to stain the hands and clothes of anyone handling the books. The team lead on the cataloging side established several "red rot days," during which she and several team members wore clothes that could be ruined and then worked through the afflicted volumes. On the preservation side, the team lead spent hours each week working directly with the project team pushing heavy carts across the basement and moving books caked in decades of dust and covered in red rot. By not being afraid to get our hands dirty, quite literally, we demonstrated to our project team the importance of this behind-the-scenes labor and established a "we're all in this together" mindset.

Cultivating an open atmosphere—where questions were encouraged and learning was expected—balanced the needs of veteran student staff members' cross-training to perform a wider range of duties, additional student and temporary employees newly hired for the project, and parameters that often felt more like shifting sand than hard bedrock. We expected team members to learn new tasks and procedures on the fly and adapt quickly to changes, and our role as team leads was to support and facilitate their work. We ended scrum meetings and training sessions by asking "What questions do we have?" rather than "Does anyone have any questions?" This simple wording shift let team members know that we both expected and welcomed their questions, and helped build an environment where they did not feel intimidated or shy about asking questions of their supervisors or raising issues in front of the group. We were learning together.

Low- and no-cost offerings conveyed our sincere appreciation for the team's efforts, especially when they willingly took on added responsibilities above and beyond their initial job descriptions. To celebrate project milestones, coffee and homemade treats proved especially popular among our student employees. Other simple gestures like a genuine thank-you for a job well done or handwritten cards for graduating students showed our team members that we cared about them as employees and as people. At the end of one major phase of the collections project, an associate university librarian personally attended a scrum meeting to thank the team members for all their hard work. Hearing this appreciation from a member of the library administration emphasized the importance of their efforts and allowed the team to see the impact of their work within the larger library context.

Beyond their practical value in protecting clothes while handling dusty items from the basement, lab coats and aprons from the library's conservation lab became surprisingly useful tools to encourage and motivate student employees. Early on, the students expressed their enjoyment of "dressing up" in the lab coats, and the novelty of wearing them became an incentive that made tasks like cleaning a mountain of dirty volumes seem a little more fun. The coats also communicated a symbolic value, becoming a uniform that created a sense of team identity. With the lab coats, the project team and therefore the project work felt more official, increasing the students' respect and motivation for the tasks at hand.

Because many project team members were student employees, we aspired to create an environment in which they could gain marketable skills and hone their strengths in preparation for post-academic careers. Several of our staff were concurrently pursuing library science degrees, and the collections project provided hands-on training and experience working with fragile collections materials and metadata in an academic library setting. Students in non-library career paths developed transferable skills such as teamwork, problem-solving, and leadership. We communicated this culture of learning and development both indirectly, by providing team members with opportunities to learn new tasks and take on additional responsibilities, and directly, by asking them to reflect on how their experiences, skills, and accomplishments could benefit them in future positions. To help with the latter, we took inspiration from the Iowa GROW (Guided Reflection on Work) program, developed by the University of Iowa's Division of Student Life. Iowa GROW uses a series of short, guided conversations to help students draw connections between their classes, on-the-job learning, and their future professions.[6]

COMMUNICATING PROGRESS

Both within and outside of the project team, communicating our progress became a way to tell the story of the team's efforts within technical services and highlight the positive impact made toward library-wide goals. Much of the project work involved repetitive tasks performed on large numbers of items. When cleaning, shrink-wrapping, verifying, or withdrawing seemingly endless streams of individual volumes, a sense of accomplishment could remain

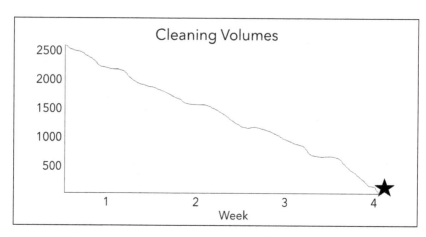

FIGURE 4.1
Example of a burn-down chart

elusive. To visually represent these monotonous yet cumulative efforts, we borrowed another technique from agile project management. During the weekly scrums, we gathered near a bulletin board filled with "burn-down" charts (figure 4.1) that communicated visible reflections of our progress. The vertical axis represented numbers of items, with the horizontal axis denoting time. Each burn-down chart became a midpoint goal and a milestone for the project team to celebrate upon completion.

To reach a broader audience and address potential communication gaps, we sent weekly e-mail blasts to both team members and tangential colleagues and administrators. These brief Friday e-mails provided regular progress reports, relaying high-level updates, statistics, and priorities to everyone involved with or affected by the project. Each weekly e-mail followed the same format: first, status updates including statistics for that week and for the project to date; second, a look ahead to priority tasks or scrum topics for the week to come; third, progress summaries of ongoing subprojects; and finally, reminders like altered work schedules or the location of extra cleaning equipment and protective gear. For project team members, the Friday e-mails were both written acknowledgments of their efforts and mini-agendas for Monday morning scrums. For decision-makers within our technical services departments and administration, the e-mails functioned as executive summaries, while for colleagues in related departments they provided alerts of incoming materials fully processed by our team.

Toward the end of the project, we created an infographic summarizing the substantial impact of the team's work over the course of the year (figure 4.2). Doubling as a final report, the infographic communicated the project's achievements far more effectively than a text-heavy document. For library supervisors and administrators, the infographic translated often hidden technical services work into a relatable, dramatic narrative that told the story behind the facts and figures. It confirmed the project's return on investment of time, labor, and materials. For the project team, the infographic linked their item-by-item efforts within technical services to the bigger picture of the library's overall mission. By the time we produced the infographic, several of the student workers on the team had graduated and moved on to new jobs or degree programs. One final e-mail update to distribute the infographic provided an avenue to officially thank them for their individual and collective efforts toward the progress we made together.

To produce the infographic, we used one of several available free or low-cost infographic software options, along with images and clip art in the public domain. Our final draft of the document balanced statistics with story. Numbers held a prominent place, highlighting project achievements such as the over 400,000 items visually assessed and the 2,000 16-mm films rehoused. A "hidden treasures" section relayed the drama of notable volumes found in the library basement and transferred to special collections, safekeeping a Greek

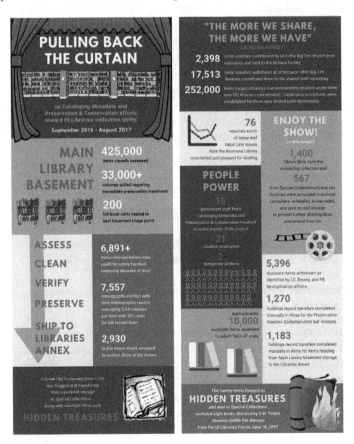

FIGURE 4.2
Examples of a technical services infographic

Old Testament from 1730, and eight books showing visible damage from a library fire at the University of Iowa in 1897. Another section visually portrayed a workflow to assess, clean, verify, preserve, and ship materials to our off-site library annex.

By highlighting the contributions of our technical services departments, we pulled their behind-the-scenes work out into the spotlight and promoted a more realistic assessment of the time, staff, and funding required to achieve stated goals. Tools like burn-down charts, regular e-mail updates, and infographics communicated our progress on current or completed technical services projects, and also laid the groundwork to propose and plan future initiatives.

KEY INSIGHTS

Over the course of the project year, intentional communication built a framework that enabled our technical services departments to successfully collaborate on a multifaceted project, meet seemingly impossible deadlines, motivate our staff, and convey our progress to stakeholders. None of our communication strategies and tools were particularly novel. Many of them required little to no financial outlay, like a burn-down chart on a half-sheet of paper or a batch of scones to celebrate the burn-down chart's completion. Some needed relatively little effort to develop and maintain, while others demanded substantial investments of time and energy but usually paid off by anticipating bottlenecks in staffing, equipment, or materials. Our key takeaways included:

- Identifying where to build communication pathways by asking the questions "Who does this affect?" and "Who do we not realize this will affect?"
- Utilizing statistics to document our progress and estimate future resource needs
- Creating a culture of teamwork, collaboration, high expectations, and learning through intentional actions and words
- Especially for repetitive tasks, finding ways to illustrate, convey, and celebrate the progress made

Another crucial lesson: choosing communication methods that worked for us, our project team, and our supervisors. That seems obvious, but the method had to match the need, otherwise it became a waste of time, energy, and resources. During initial planning stages, the process of creating and debating flow charts helped us to envision workflows and potential roadblocks. These flow charts were immensely useful to the two of us as team leads, but their complexity did not fit the needs of either the supervisors to whom we reported or the team members who joined in the work. For those two groups, simplicity and ease of use were primary factors in communication. When making the case to ramp up the work, numbers proved persuasive. Statistics kept during an initial test phase sold administrators on the need to hire temporary staff and increase student employees' hours to provide the people power to meet desired deadlines.

Communication mishaps became reset points and growth lessons. At times we failed to cast a wide enough net when answering the question "Who do we not realize that this will affect?" Our periodic high-level project summaries to all technical services colleagues may have eased those situations. Secondly, clear statements to prospective employees about the grimy nature of some project tasks greatly benefited their later buy-in. We were less intentional in communicating this to existing staff who transferred over, to the detriment of the project output and the staff members' satisfaction with the job. Finally, an interdepartmental project may sometimes conflict with the established hierarchical structure of many technical services departments. Stating who has the authority to make project decisions and to communicate those decisions out clarifies everyone's expectations and responsibilities.

During the rush of the project year, taking time to communicate to our "future selves" and our future technical services colleagues received short shrift. When a main project deadline suddenly moved up, we prioritized speed and sacrificed full bibliographic control for items from the main library basement that required preservation treatment prior to moving them to off-site storage. This decision to rapidly assess, pull, and stockpile thousands of volumes met stakeholder deadlines but essentially rendered these items inaccessible. The project team completed work on a portion of this backlog, and progress on the rest continues as time and staffing allow. In the years since the collections project, new priorities and personnel mean that other colleagues now have responsibility for overseeing continuing work on the basement stockpile. A more detailed written assessment of the remaining items could have provided a helpful form of succession planning—a guidebook for our future colleagues.

After the project's conclusion, communication ties between the Preservation and Cataloging departments continued to strengthen and formalize. Our interdepartmental project team built in cross-training, and the resulting broadened understanding of each other's roles aided the development of regular day-to-day workflows. The ties were also formalized when the project lead from the Preservation and Conservation Department became the official liaison to the Cataloging-Metadata Department. This responsibility was added to her job description, and cataloging colleagues now had an official point of contact for preservation questions and consultation.

CONCLUSION

When establishing multi-directional communication within technical services, you should envision or assess where the impediments to forward action lie. Sometimes a well-placed sign or a quickly scannable book flag meets the communication at the point of need. Sometimes a positive environment enriches both the work and our collective work life. Sometimes taking a moment to recognize a goal met builds energy toward meeting the next goalpost. Conduits that are reliable, extensible, and sustainable travel up, down, and sideways to build communication networks that move technical services work and the mission of a library forward.

REFERENCES

Buser, Robin A., Miriam Pollack, and Bruce E. Massis. *Project Management for Libraries: A Practical Approach.* Jefferson, NC: McFarland, 2014.

Buturugă, Oana Cristina, Vasile Mirel Gogoi, and Ioana Alexandra Prodan. "Agile Project Management Tools." *Economy Informatics* 16, no. 1 (2016): 19–26.

Connerly, Charles, Lucie Laurian, and James Throgmorton. "Planning for Floods at the University of Iowa: A Challenge for Resilience and Sustainability." *Journal of Planning History* 16, no. 1 (2017): 50–73. doi:10.1177/1538513216646131.

Goldberg, Beverly. "Iowa Libraries Bear Brunt of Midwest Floods." *American Libraries* 39, no. 7 (2008): 22–23.

Hirst, Donna. "Editorial Board Thoughts." *Information Technology and Libraries* 27, no. 4 (2008): 5–8.

Niemi-Grundström, Minna. "Developing, Evaluating and Managing Library with Agile Methods." *Library Management* 35, no. 6 (2014): 481–85.

Sims, Chris, and Hillary Louise Johnson. *Scrum: A Breathtakingly Brief and Agile Introduction.* Dymaxicon, 2012.

Soderdahl, Paul A. "The Iowa Flood of 2008: Putting the Disaster Response Plan to the Test." Paper presented at the 78th International Federation of Library Associations and Institutions General Conference and Assembly, Helsinki, Finland, August 2012. www.ifla.org/past-wlic/2012/216-soderdahl-en.pdf.

———. "The University of Iowa and the Flood of 2008: A Case Study." In *Technology Disaster Response and Recovery Planning: A LITA Guide,* ed. Mary Mallery, 73–81. Chicago: American Library Association, 2015.

Stoddard, Morgan M., Bill Gillis, and Peter Cohn. "Agile Project Management in Libraries: Creating Collaborative, Resilient, Responsive Organizations." *Journal of Library Administration* 59, no. 5 (2019): 492–511. doi:10.1080/01930826.2019.1616971.

University of Iowa. "Iowa GROW." https://vp.studentlife.uiowa.edu/priorities/grow.

University of Iowa Libraries. "Annex: UI Libraries Opens New Cost-Efficient Facility." *Bindings* (Winter 2017): 8–9. https://ir.uiowa.edu/lib_bindings/29.

NOTES

1. Donna Hirst, "Editorial Board Thoughts," *Information Technology and Libraries* 27, no. 4 (2008): 5–8.

2. Paul A. Soderdahl, "The Iowa Flood of 2008: Putting the Disaster Response Plan to the Test" (presentation, 78th International Federation of Library Associations and Institutions General Conference and Assembly, Helsinki, Finland, August 2012), www.ifla.org/past-wlic/2012/216-soderdahl-en.pdf.

3. Paul A. Soderdahl, "The University of Iowa and the Flood of 2008: A Case Study," in *Technology Disaster Response and Recovery Planning: A LITA Guide*, ed. Mary Mallery (Chicago: American Library Association, 2015), 80.

4. University of Iowa Libraries, "Annex: UI Libraries Opens New Cost-Efficient Facility," *Bindings* (Winter 2017): 8–9, https://ir.uiowa.edu/lib_bindings/29.

5. Robin A. Buser, Miriam Pollack, and Bruce E. Massis, *Project Management for Libraries: A Practical Approach* (Jefferson, NC: McFarland, 2014), 108.

6. University of Iowa, "Iowa GROW," https://vp.studentlife.uiowa.edu/priorities/grow.

PART II

COMMUNICATION ACROSS LIBRARY DEPARTMENTS

KAYLAN ELLIS, JENNIFER DONLEY,
AND CHRISTOPHER DEEMS

5
Small but Mighty

Cultivating a Community of Practice to
Document the Past and Prepare for the Future

This chapter chronicles the collaborative efforts to improve internal communication and documentation related to technical services operations in the two campus libraries at Ohio Northern University (ONU). For over three decades, the working relationships between the technical services departments in the undergraduate library and the law library had been limited. A nearly complete turnover of library personnel and the subsequent hiring of many early career professionals, including the authors, set the stage for the community of practice (COP) that would be developed by the current team of librarians at ONU.

The newly minted librarians who joined the technical services-related departments in the undergraduate Heterick Memorial Library and the Taggart Law Library were drawn to one another by a common need to understand their roles and the demands of their respective libraries, to tackle long-standing problems in novel ways, and to document their efforts in order to mitigate future knowledge drains. As the only librarians in ONU's historically independent departments of cataloging, systems, and law library technical services, they desperately needed connections with other librarians who understood the issues inherent to technical services.

By subverting the established norms regarding librarian collaboration, the authors eliminated silos, strengthened relationships between the two libraries, and inadvertently developed a small yet powerful COP, culminating in enhanced operations and project outcomes, and the creation of a repository for institutional memory. The following case study can serve as a model for interdepartmental cooperation at other institutions, particularly those with smaller libraries whose technical librarians may operate alone or in silos.

LITERATURE REVIEW

A review of the literature identifies a wealth of material related to communication, collaboration, and documentation in academic library technical services, as well as many articles discussing the role of COPs in libraries. What appears to be lacking, however, are articles at the intersection of these four topic areas that relate specifically to technical services departments in academic libraries.

Several articles call for shifts in workplace culture and the adoption of procedures throughout the department that address how information is conveyed, or processes are documented, in order to improve communication in technical services departments. Research has examined the resistance to collaborative work environments and technology,[1] alongside the increasing need for such environments in order to develop stronger libraries and departments.[2] Siewert and Louderback cover several documentation hurdles, such as the absence of procedural documentation for positions that have been held by the same individuals for many years.[3] They also highlight how a lack of succession planning leads to a loss of institutional memory when these individuals retire or leave their current positions.[4] Related to the aforementioned resistance to collaboration is the trend in academia to reward individualism and protect information instead of sharing information collectively, which often bleeds into academic library practices.[5] Some studies, however, report that larger libraries often make internal documentation available online to other institutions, a trend toward open access that will hopefully spread to smaller libraries.[6]

Libraries are learning communities whose practice is strengthened by effective communication and collaboration, and there are many discipline-specific articles that discuss communities of practice within libraries. An exhaustive search of the literature cannot be claimed by the authors, but one of the topics we did not encounter was the role of COPs (and not just teams) within library technical services departments and how advantageous they can be for smaller libraries. Researchers such as Bartlett and Acadia[7] discuss the importance of COPs in larger libraries, but assert that it "might be relatively easier to build a sense of community in a small library."[8] While this sense of community might be easier to cultivate in a smaller library, departments can still be compartmentalized, which makes sharing knowledge, building partnerships, and succession planning more difficult.[9] Smaller libraries, where a single individual might comprise an entire department, are deeply impacted by workforce turnover because there are fewer individuals at any given time to fill institutional memory knowledge gaps.[10]

As will be supported throughout this case study, the hiring of technical services librarians who are willing to readily engage and collaborate with coworkers, and who enjoy working as a team toward unified goals, presents technical services departments in smaller academic libraries with the perfect opportunity to cultivate their own COPs. Even when not hiring, working with existing teammates to cultivate an open and cross-trained environment within the current workplace culture can potentially achieve the same desired COP outcome.

BACKGROUND

Ohio Northern University is located in Ada, Ohio, a rural village of 5,500 people situated about 70 miles south of Toledo. The private, United Methodist Church-affiliated institution comprises five liberal arts and professional colleges, with 2,800 undergraduates and more than 150 law students as of 2019. The undergraduate Heterick Memorial Library (HML) employs five librarians, one archivist, and four staff members. The HML librarians all participate in the library's departmental liaison program, collection development and reference activities, and information literacy instruction. The Taggart Law Library (TLL) serves the law school as well as the broader ONU community, with three librarians and three staff members supporting the program of legal education through circulation and reference services, workshops, and by hosting various law school events. Librarians from both the undergraduate and law libraries hold tenure-track faculty status and participate in institutional governance alongside teaching faculty, with library representatives involved in committees, councils, and task forces at all levels across the university.

Like many of the libraries profiled in the recent literature, both ONU libraries experienced several notable retirements, departures, and other staffing changes within a short period of time, resulting in a massive loss of institutional memory. The entire slate of library professionals at HML turned over within the span of ten years, and the cataloging librarian and systems librarian positions were refilled twice. The law library simultaneously experienced a similar turnover of librarians, including the technical services librarian's transition into a part-time role for three years before entering full retirement. The HML systems librarian and cataloging librarian had served for twenty-five and thirty-one years, respectively, and the TLL technical services librarian had held her position for over forty-one years.

Though relations among librarians within each library and between the two libraries were cordial, collaboration was limited, and a proprietary atmosphere and intentional independence clouded most projects. Librarians were hesitant to reach out to one another, instead pressing on alone or setting aside projects when faced with significant challenges rather than asking for help. Although these librarians may have seen themselves as part of a cohesive group or department, the lack of cross-training[11] and the dearth of shared procedural documentation[12]—an unfortunate but unsurprising situation common to academic libraries—indicated that there was room for improvement.

To be clear, it is not our intention to besmirch our predecessors. Their behaviors reflected the broader workplace culture and were not indicative of interpersonal rivalries or personality flaws. These talented individuals operated within a culture in which seeking assistance or partnerships seemingly implied that an individual was not willing or able to address an issue on their own. With no external spark or top-down directive that encouraged collaboration, there was little incentive to challenge the status quo.

Because succession planning had not been formally addressed by the library, few detailed procedures existed after the period of personnel turnover. What historical documentation endured was mostly vendor manuals and contracts. The departures of two librarians were timed so that they could spend up to three months working with their respective successors in order to pass on the entirety of the job orally—in retrospect, an inefficient and costly approach that could have been avoided with proper documentation and succession planning.

Two of the three authors had direct interim predecessors who left ONU before earning tenure. While these individuals did attempt to create procedural documentation before they left, it proved limited in scope because succession planning was not a formalized practice and they had inherited little documentation themselves. It was not until Donley and Ellis were hired that the documentation and succession-planning procedures in the technical services departments began to change. After starting their jobs with a dearth of documentation and guidance, the urge to set themselves and their future successors up for success made creating a repository of institutional knowledge a priority.

For all three authors, ONU marked the beginning of our professional careers as faculty librarians. Jennifer Donley was the earliest hire, assuming the role of HML's cataloging librarian in 2009. Kaylan Ellis became TLL's technical services librarian in 2016, followed in 2018 by Christopher Deems as the HML-based systems librarian. Because we were recent library school graduates at the time of hire, the campus libraries benefited from a regular influx of fresh perspectives and the introduction of new standards, trends, and ideas.

Our positions represent full-fledged departments in larger university libraries, but at ONU they reflect a department of one librarian who may have, at most, one assistant. TLL must maintain its independence in accordance with the American Bar Association's requirements for law school accreditation, but the two libraries are still very intertwined. Deems serves as the systems librarian for both libraries, which share a catalog, discovery layer, and various other electronic resources. We are also each other's best sounding boards, as the only three librarians on campus who can converse fluently in cataloging and systems-related jargon.

The proliferation of collaborative technology over the last decade has significantly impacted the way librarians are able to interact with each other and with patrons. Learning itself is becoming increasingly collaborative, and group projects are now the norm even in online library science courses. Advances in technology and shifts in workplace culture, such as the embrace of social media, were already occurring elsewhere on campus when we arrived, and these changes laid the groundwork for the COP that we have subsequently and successfully built together.

CASE STUDY

After years of working together closely, meeting regularly, and collaborating on projects, we realized that the academic buzzword "community of practice" was applicable to the collaborative working relationships we had developed. In their foundational text *Cultivating Communities of Practice: A Guide for Managing Knowledge*, authors Wenger, McDermott, and Snyder[13] define COPs as "groups of people who share a concern, a set of problems, or a passion about a topic, and who deepen their knowledge and expertise in this area by interacting on an ongoing basis."[14] The text identifies seven principles necessary for the cultivation of a COP—a road map we had unknowingly followed, and one that other groups could adopt to develop a similarly successful team structure:

1. Design for evolution.
2. Open a dialogue between inside and outside perspectives.
3. Invite different levels of participation.
4. Develop both public and private community spaces.
5. Focus on value.
6. Combine familiarity and excitement.
7. Create a rhythm for the community.[15]

Our utilization of each of these principles will be discussed in the subsections below.

Design for Evolution

We were brought together by a mutual need to educate ourselves and preserve the institutional knowledge we were acquiring as solo departmental librarians in separate technical services units at the same institution. Our pursuit of these shared goals facilitated the development of strong bonds as we realized we were not isolated individuals, but rather part of a cohesive team poised to tackle issues together. This partnership has demonstrated that the whole is greater than the sum of its parts, enabling far better outcomes than any one individual could have produced on their own. Wenger, McDermott, and Snyder found that "communities typically build on preexisting personal networks,"[16] and our libraries did have a long-standing tradition in which the HML and TLL librarians met weekly for lunch, though these occurred less frequently as our predecessors retired. This led Donley and Ellis to recognize the need for intentionally scheduled time to talk so that long periods of time did not pass between our sharing experiences and ideas face-to-face. These intentional meetings were not approached with any preconceived notion of what we wanted or expected to come out of them—we simply set aside time to talk. The meetings evolved into a weekly Google Calendar appointment, and we began to record minutes in a shared folder on Google Drive and to create progress notes for outlined projects on Google Keep.

Open a Dialogue between Inside and Outside Perspectives

Both inside and outside perspectives are crucial for successful community design. Without outside perspectives, members can overlook how their decisions impact other areas and can miss opportunities to collaborate with individuals beyond the usual suspects. Regularly incorporating outside perspectives from other librarians into our discussions allowed all the ONU librarians to develop more robust and nuanced understandings of the undergraduate and law library operations. On multiple occasions we invited additional librarians to attend our weekly meetings and contribute to specific discussions, or to join the conversation after stopping by to ask an unrelated question. Inviting nonmembers to participate removes the need to follow up and allows all parties to be present while new information, details, and concerns are discussed.

Invite Different Levels of Participation

Participation among the three authors has always varied, partly due to our positions and our arrivals at the institution. Donley and Ellis were initially drawn together as sole catalogers at separate ONU libraries that shared an integrated library system (ILS). In 2018 our systems librarian, who had been at the institution for five years following her predecessor's retirement after twenty-five years, took a job elsewhere, and the need for collaborative succession planning arose. The systems librarian position, while based out of HML, serves both libraries. Although a search for a replacement was approved and

Deems would begin working later that year, Donley and Ellis covered many of the systems responsibilities for several months.

During those months of sharing systems duties, we discovered how related many aspects of the position were to our own cataloging and electronic resources responsibilities. We identified new ways to collaborate, streamline, and document those interrelated processes for all three positions and created a list of potential future collaborations. When Deems arrived, we invited him to several meetings in order to share the history and context of procedures and projects relevant to his position, as well as the limited documentation we had been able to compile. We realized that he could also benefit from regularly scheduled interactions, and we would benefit from his input into our discussions. In order not to overwhelm him with weekly meetings, and to leave time for exploring cataloging concepts in-depth, we scheduled Deems into every other meeting. Outside of meetings, the three of us regularly included each other on e-mail threads dealing with technical support tickets, ILS oddities, and tech-related ideas. This practice kept everyone informed, created an e-mail archive for each of us, and allowed us to speak up when we had something to contribute.

Develop Both Public and Private Community Spaces

A mix of public and private spaces and interactions strengthened our community structure and our knowledge base simultaneously. As the group evolved, we found that in addition to meeting in person, it was helpful to create virtual spaces to support our frequent discussions and collaborations. We began attending technical services conferences and webinars together, which provided additional opportunities to discuss new information we had absorbed, and we continued our practices of regular meetings and periodically having lunch with the other librarians. According to Wenger, McDermott, and Snyder, "these informal, 'back channel' discussions actually help orchestrate the public space and are key to successful meetings. They ensure that the spontaneous topics raised at the meetings are valuable to the whole and that the people attending will have something useful to add."[17] We took a renewed interest in expanding an existing but sparse LibGuides-based intranet, and we uploaded recently codified local procedures for institution-specific ILS codes, as well as historical information regarding past projects. Wherever a platform permitted collaboration and seemed uniquely advantageous, such as Google Keep, Trello, or Slack, we created an account. We shared information about formal and informal resources for hive-mind inquiry such as that on electronic discussion lists, forums, and the Facebook group "Troublesome Catalogers and Magical Metadata Fairies." Random e-mails and phone calls occurred between meetings, often to celebrate victories such as resolved service tickets or discounted pricing on a webinar.

Focus on Value

Focusing on value helped our small community of practice to succeed even in its earliest and most informal stages. While we were most aware of our developing sense of camaraderie, Wenger, McDermott, and Snyder affirm that "the full value of a community is often not apparent when it is first formed."[18] We quickly recognized that our discussions, which incorporated consultation and feedback, were generating feasible project outlines for daunting backlogs as well as exciting new ideas. As we became aware of our group's growing value, we also became more formalized with our documentation and intentional in our plans, confirming Wenger, McDermott, and Snyder's assertion that "as the community grows, developing a systematic body of knowledge that can be easily accessed becomes more important."[19] We found this to be particularly true regarding minutes, which at first seemed excessive because we had just planned time to talk, but by the next meeting the details of the previous conversation had dulled and we were grateful for those notes. We also became formulaic in our approach to project lists on Google Keep. Each project included a description, potential hurdles, and relevant updates, and was ranked based on its status, such as Priority, Current, Waiting, Future, and Ongoing. Inactive items (Abandoned or Completed) were relocated to a separate list, allowing us to track progress without cluttering up our active list. This system helped us plan ahead based on the need for and benefits of a project, its anticipated costs, and the time required.

Combine Familiarity and Excitement

Our meetings have always begun informally; without watching the clock, we catch up on current events and personal happenings, and as our chat winds down we transition to work-specific topics. Occasionally we plan to grab lunch with the other librarians after the meeting, bringing all of the librarians together and allowing us to revisit some of our recent discussions for additional feedback. In a work environment where we often spend hours alone in our offices, focused intently on projects and rarely breaking for conversation with coworkers, this is a welcome reprieve that both energizes us and helps strengthen our larger community's bond.

The crucial element that allows us to incorporate familiarity and excitement into our meetings by informally catching up, and then smoothly transitioning to more formal work-related subjects, is shared passion. We are each driven by the same two urges: first, to better understand the functionality of the technology in use from cataloging and systems perspectives in order to optimize technical services operations; and second, to leave more robust frameworks for our future successors than those that we inherited. We would not have applied for our positions if we did not care about delivering results to patrons, but our practice has been elevated to a truly enjoyable endeavor as we experience the thrill of collaboratively identifying problems, breaking them down, and building foolproof solutions.

Create a Rhythm for the Community

When we began working together, the ONU librarian community had an irregular rhythm for interactions. Apart from university gatherings that brought us all together, the HML and TLL librarians typically only gathered together for group lunches. While those lunches were enjoyable, discipline-specific discussions about cataloging and systems felt exclusionary at a table alongside reference and instruction librarians. Those coveted conversations needed their own schedule, and thus a seed was planted for regular technical services-related meetings.

Developing a COP did not hinder our creativity and individuality. Regular "state of the union" conversations in which we shared our current projects and concerns helped us tackle issues, anticipate future challenges, and refine procedures. Even casual conversations resulted in learning, planning, and growth, as regular opportunities to talk shop introduced new concepts, built trust, and benefited the entire library community.

REFLECTION

We unintentionally created a community of practice for our small group that aligns with the definition of a COP, but when we realized what we had achieved, we were able to turn to the literature and learn how to strengthen and sustain our little community. Our intentional efforts had been focused on improving our current situations, and those efforts resulted in a complete review of internal documentation, a series of shared responsibilities and resources, and the development of a mutually beneficial inter-library partnership. We have cross-trained, served as representatives for each other at consortial meetings, and consulted with one another on projects impacting individual departments or the broader library system. The COP structure we have embraced enables us to nimbly tackle technological challenges and the evolving needs of students and faculty, while preserving the insights gleaned for future ONU librarians to use.

As previously referenced, Bartlett and Acadia suggest that COPs are of greater value to larger libraries because it is easier for small libraries to develop a sense of community.[20] While our COP is small in stature, it demonstrates the value of COPs regardless of an institution's size. A compact campus does not negate the need for intentional communication and collaboration between units. Members are rewarded with a deeper understanding of the tools of the trade and by the experience itself. Communicating with other professionals who share similar concerns and levels of intellectual curiosity, and learning together and developing new strategies and approaches, do not have to be relegated to a university event or an annual library conference. Instead, those same stimulating conversations can be embedded within a library's culture, constantly reinvigorating participants and keeping the passion for the work at the forefront. Though technical services librarians bring different experiences and personalities to their positions, we are united by a common purpose: to support information literacy and access to knowledge. The passionate pursuit of that purpose can help break down barriers and overcome silos and stereotypes. Even if the group lacks formal avenues for collaboration, technical services librarians are well-versed in creating crosswalks to facilitate communication, and the resulting connections will be worth the investment.

Over the course of evaluating and revising our operations, several practices that we have adopted and shortfalls that we have avoided stand out as the keys to our COP's success, and we offer them as considerations for a group seeking to replicate our results:

- Start small and allow the community's structure to develop organically at first. Intentionally carve out time to keep the conversations going, and then try to schedule standing weekly or monthly meetings.
- Agendas can stifle the flow of conversation; some of our most advantageous conversations and project ideas resulted from unstructured conversations or from revisiting the notes from previous meetings.
- Take minutes whenever meetings occur and transcribe them quickly to preserve the meaning of scribbles and side notes, and to highlight action items or resolutions.
- Work together to create official, detailed procedures for ongoing processes and special projects, even if only one person is responsible. Document the motivation behind changes to procedures, the impetus for a project, and the factors influencing its design.
- Librarians must be open to learning from new hires; early career librarians bring cutting-edge knowledge, and new hires bring fresh perspectives. Seniority is invaluable with respect to the institutional memory gathered over the years, but clinging to "the way we've always done things" will inhibit growth and innovation.
- Ensure that documented discussions and workflows are preserved online in an organized, searchable repository. Take advantage of free technology, such as Google Drive, and use tags, folders, and file-naming conventions to facilitate repository navigation. Test out various organizational, project management, and file storage platforms and don't be afraid

to implement and overlap more than one, creating links or crosswalks as needed.

- Internal documentation should be viewed as a collection of living documents. Processes change, new users find gaps in procedural steps, and revisions to policies and workflows will be needed. Documenting policy development with detailed road maps will limit confusion and avoid repeated mistakes.

- Succession planning should not be relegated to the end of a career or two weeks before a departure, but should instead begin on the first day of hire. By documenting the questions, tips, and insights gleaned from the very beginning, all positions can contribute to the foundational framework for a powerful knowledge base.

- Be willing to trust in one another. Every professional has areas of expertise and comfort, as well as unique approaches to problem-solving and communication. Focus on the common passions, goals, and problems driving the community, and recognize each other's strengths. Prioritize transparency and clarity in all communication, and revisit goals often to track progress, reorient, and reinvigorate the team as needed.

- Ultimately, the best resources we have are our colleagues, so cultivating strong working relationships is crucial. Solid partnerships and sound procedural frameworks enable teams to tackle even the most disruptive issues as a cohesive unit.

CONCLUSION

Our community of practice succeeded because we communicated frequently, embraced collaboration, and made deliberate efforts to document *everything*. We assert that the act of creating a COP, intentionally or unintentionally, facilitates a more efficient, cooperative, and productive working environment even in smaller libraries with an existing sense of community. This approach to interdepartmental communication will likely appeal to other technical librarians with methodical personality types like ours, as it provides structure and purpose for moving projects forward while addressing the eternal struggle of balancing limited time with competing priorities.

This chapter was written during the initial months of the COVID-19 crisis. After transforming the opaque and siloed departments we inherited into transparent and unified technical services operations, we managed to navigate the impacts that a global pandemic had on our libraries by staying connected remotely. We gather now via Google Meet, but our ability to benefit from and grow our community of practice endures. Though the landscape has shifted and the future is uncertain, the need for community resilience and a collaborative culture is more urgent than ever before. As your institution establishes a new normal during and after the crisis, consider using this time of change as an opportunity to lay the groundwork for your library or technical services department's own community of practice.

REFERENCES

Andreadis, Debra K., Christopher D. Barth, Lynn Scott Cochrane, and Karen E. Greever. "Cooperative Work Redesign in Library Technical Services at Denison University and Kenyon College." In *Library Workflow Redesign: Six Case Studies*, ed. Marilyn Mitchell, 39–49. Washington, DC: Council on Library and Information Resources, 2007.

Bazirjian, Rosann, and Rebecca Mugridge, eds. *Teams in Library Technical Services*. Lanham, MD: Scarecrow, 2006.

Mitchell, Marilyn. "Library Workflow Redesign: Concepts and Results." In *Library Workflow Redesign: Six Case Studies*, ed. Marilyn Mitchell, 1–7. Washington, DC: Council on Library and Information Resources, 2007.

Morris, Anthony. *Emerging Issues in Academic Library Cataloging and Technical Services*. 2019 edition. New York: Primary Research Group, 2019.

Paramonova, I. E. "Information Interactions: The Criteria of the Choice of Communication Channels in a Scientific and Technical Library." *Scientific and Technical Information Processing* 46, no. 3 (2019): 181–86. https://doi.org/10.3103/S0147688219030067.

Parrott, Justin. "Communication and Collaboration in Library Technical Services: A Case Study of New York University in Abu Dhabi." *New Review of Academic Librarianship* 22, no. 2–3 (2016): 294–303. https://doi.org/10.1080/13614533.2016.1181663.

Wood, Elizabeth J., Rush Miller, and Amy Knapp. *Beyond Survival: Managing Academic Libraries in Transition*. Westport, CT: Libraries Unlimited, 2007.

NOTES

1. John Lubans Jr., "Letting Go: A Reflection on Teams That Were," in Teams in Library Technical Services, ed. Rosann Bazirjian and Rebecca Mugridge (Lanham, MD: Scarecrow, 2006), 155–70.

2. Anne Chase and Tony Krug, "New Techniques in Library Technical Services at the Appalachian College Association," in *Library Workflow Redesign: Six Case Studies*, ed. Marilyn Mitchell (Washington, DC: Council on Library and Information Resources, 2007), 8–20.

3. Karl G. Siewert and Pamela Louderback, "The 'Bus Proof' Library: Technical Succession Planning, Knowledge Transfer, and Institutional Memory," *Journal of Library Administration* 59, no. 4 (2019): 455–74, https://doi.org/10.1080/01930826.2019.1593716.

4. Nancy J. Weiner, "Securing Knowledge before Employee Departure: Do Wikis Work?" in *Libraries That Learn: Keys to Managing Organizational Knowledge*, ed. Jennifer A. Bartlett and Spencer Acadia (Chicago: American Library Association, 2019), 137–44.

5. Spencer Acadia and Jennifer A. Bartlett, "Challenges and Issues in Managing Organizational Knowledge," in *Libraries That Learn: Keys to Managing Organizational Knowledge*, ed. Jennifer A. Bartlett and Spencer Acadia (Chicago: American Library Association, 2019), 23–48.

6. Anna R. Craft, "Online Documentation Portals in Library Technical Services: Shedding Light on Local Practices and Procedures," *Serials Review* 45, no. 3 (2019): 171–75, https://doi.org/10.1080/00987913.2019.1645531.

7. Jennifer A. Bartlett and Spencer Acadia, "Conceptual and Technological Tools for Knowledge Management," in *Libraries That Learn: Keys to Managing Organizational Knowledge*, ed. Jennifer A. Bartlett and Spencer Acadia (Chicago: American Library Association, 2019), 49–66.

8. Bartlett and Acadia, "Conceptual and Technological Tools for Knowledge Management," 52.

9. Acadia and Bartlett, "Challenges and Issues in Managing Organizational Knowledge."

10. Weiner, "Securing Knowledge before Employee Departure."

11. Weiner, "Securing Knowledge before Employee Departure."

12. Siewert and Louderback, "The 'Bus Proof' Library."

13. Etienne Wenger, Richard A. McDermott, and William Snyder, *Cultivating Communities of Practice: A Guide to Managing Knowledge* (Boston: Harvard Business Review Press, 2002).

14. Wenger et al., *Cultivating Communities of Practice*, 4.

15. Wenger et al., *Cultivating Communities of Practice*, 51.

16. Wenger et al., *Cultivating Communities of Practice*, 51

17. Wenger et al., *Cultivating Communities of Practice*, 59.

18. Wenger et al., *Cultivating Communities of Practice*, 59.

19. Wenger et al., *Cultivating Communities of Practice*, 59.

20. Bartlett and Acadia, "Conceptual and Technological Tools for Knowledge Management."

XIYING MI, BONITA POLLOCK,
AND BRIAN FALATO

6

Interdepartmental Communication through Informational Classes

Creating a Community of Cataloging and Metadata Stakeholders in an Academic Library

The activities of technical services workers are often a mystery to those in other areas of the library. As the cataloging maven and former ALA president Michael Gorman wrote, a common perception of this group is that it "is concerned with esoteric 'technical' matters and, populated by reclusive adepts, has concerns which are mysterious and methods which are suspect." The misunderstanding is furthered by library science journals. According to Gorman, "the widening gap between journals devoted to automation/technical services matters and those devoted to public services matters" means that "each of these types of journal is barely comprehensible to those on the other 'side.'"[1]

A lack of communication and understanding can turn cataloging and the rest of technical services into a silo that has little contact with others. This can hurt organizational effectiveness and, ultimately, impact the quality of services the library offers to the public.

The perception that cataloging in particular is some kind of "dark art" that can't be understood by non-practitioners can have serious consequences, from a diminution of cataloging's importance to views by some administrators that cataloging personnel can be cut because automation, batch-loading, and outsourcing can handle the job well enough.

A first step to better communication is explaining to the rest of the library what cataloging does and how it benefits patrons. The University of South Florida (USF) Tampa Library put this idea into practice by offering a series of informational classes to employees in the library. The goal was to explain the various fields in a catalog record and show how this metadata could be used to improve search accuracy and the retrieval of library resources.

At the USF Tampa Library, the technical services department is called Collections and Discovery. It encompasses the units Acquisitions and Collection Development, Electronic Resources, Cataloging and Metadata (including metadata for digital collections), Catalog Maintenance, and Preservation. The communication between these units is strong because they work closely together to provide library resources for the university populace. As a department, all staff members meet biweekly to discuss issues and problems in order to keep the communication channels open to all members. On top of that, the unit heads meet weekly to make sure that emergent and time-sensitive matters get communicated. At the individual unit level, Acquisitions and Cataloging communicate frequently during the processing of new materials. Cataloging and Electronic Resources commonly work together with Acquisitions to purchase and provide access to e-resources in the catalog and the discovery layer. The Catalog Maintenance and Preservation units are also in constant communication with Cataloging and Metadata to maintain the library catalog and physical collection. The department holds frequent cross-unit meetings to discuss projects which involve personnel from various units.

Electronic formats for books, journals, and videos are preferred, so the batch-loading of records takes up a large part of cataloging activities. This includes both collections that have been purchased and those available through demand-driven acquisitions and evidence-based acquisitions programs. Tangible items are still purchased when specifically requested or there is no electronic version available, so the "traditional" cataloging process of handling one item at a time is still done. The department is also responsible for providing metadata for collections that have been digitized in-house. This requires the Cataloging and Metadata Unit to communicate with staff from the Special Collections Department and Digital Collections to provide quality metadata for library resources.

The Cataloging and Metadata Unit is also involved in special initiatives. A legislative mandate to reduce the cost of textbooks at state universities has led to the Textbook Affordability Project (TAP), in which e-books are offered as an alternative to printed texts. Cataloging and Metadata personnel developed an "Ebooks for the Classroom" (EB+) database that shows e-books available as an inducement for professors to adopt the e-book versions in their classes. The planning and creation of the EB+ database requires cooperation and communication across various departments, including Metadata and Cataloging, TAP staff, software programmers, Electronic Resources, and Acquisitions. An EB+ team composed of representatives from these areas meets biweekly to discuss the project and see to its maintenance and development.

Members of the department are also involved in linked data projects that will showcase the library's digital collections. The linked data team has representatives from Digital Collections, Cataloging and Metadata, Electronic Resources, Digital Scholarship, and IT staff. This team meets weekly to discuss the ongoing linked-data projects and serves as a governing body to develop policy and procedures for converting the library's digital collections into linked open data. Communication between the members of this team provides a balanced perspective on how to best utilize library resources to improve the access and discoverability of collections through linked data technology.

The Collections and Discovery units are all located on the top floor of the Tampa Library building and have very little interaction with patrons, Access Services, or public services personnel. Communications within the department and with Digital Collections and TAP is excellent because all are located in the same area and collaborate frequently on various projects. Communication outside the department with librarians who are working with students and faculty, and with Access Services, which runs the circulation desk, is more limited. As Walton et al. pointed out in their historical study, communication obstacles can arise from a lack of knowledge of others' work and from physical distance.[2] This lack of communication between departments is a common problem and has been an area that the library as a whole is seeking to address.

THE RATIONALE FOR CLASSES

Through its work, the Cataloging and Metadata Unit (hereafter the Unit) provides the foundation for public services, Digital Collections, and TAP. However, it usually does not have direct contact with library users. Most direct patron contact is handled by the Access Services team at the circulation desk or by the public services librarians, who provide help to students and faculty such as library instruction and research assistance. Facing these communication barriers, the Unit hoped to break this pattern and take a proactive approach in presenting the importance of cataloging and metadata to other departments, especially those working in public services areas. Communication between the Cataloging and Metadata Unit and these other areas was therefore crucial. Hilkka Orava discussed this communication need in an IFLA conference presentation: "The better the interactive network that we manage to create with our clients who are the best experts of their own information needs and fields of interest, the better our service satisfies the users. The service improves, and promotion comes as a bonus: active clients tell others who are interested about what has been acquired, and all involved feel that this is their library."[3]

As part of the process to better inform other areas about the work of the Cataloging and Metadata Unit, the idea of basic metadata classes was formed. Providing face-to-face informational classes to small groups gave us an opportunity for verbal, written, and visual communication with colleagues. An in-person format was also excellent for participant interaction, providing a forum in which to ask questions and receive instant feedback. E-mail and other formats don't provide the variety of communication styles and immediate feedback needed to effectively communicate complex issues in cataloging and metadata. The goal of the classes was to provide a venue for the Unit to connect with its colleagues in other departments of the library. Through the classes, it was hoped that information could be exchanged, needs heard, and a common understanding established.

The objectives of the classes were to inform colleagues how cataloging impacts the different functions of the library catalog, how metadata and cataloging support the discovery and access of library resources, and what the ongoing metadata and cataloging projects are, as well as how they will impact others in the library. It was hoped that this would clear up misconceptions and provide a greater understanding of the role and importance of cataloging and metadata.

PLANNING AND DESIGN PROCESS

A metadata class proposal was presented to the library administration. It stressed the communication blind spots between departments that the classes could address. The head deans approved the proposal and agreed that it was an excellent venue to communicate between departments in the library. From there, the Cataloging and Metadata Unit designated a task force consisting of the three librarians in the Unit, who are the authors of this chapter. The task force met to discuss the goals and objectives of the project and to determine a course of action for planning and implementing the informational classes. The goal was to improve communication between the departments by sharing knowledge on topics of common interest. One of the reasons the task force felt this was important was to help improve the search functionality of the catalog by showing library staff and faculty how metadata affects the search results in the catalog and discovery layers. Another reason the task force wanted to communicate with others was because the library had recently hired quite a few new employees, and the task force wanted to provide information to them about cataloging and how the Unit functions.

At the planning stage for the classes, there were three questions the task force needed to answer. The first question was who would be the target audience for these classes. Determining who would probably be attending helped the task force plan the content of the lessons and gave an indication of how best to communicate that information. The task force had a reasonable idea of who might attend the classes based on their knowledge of staff work assignments and areas of interest, yet it was hoped to get as many attendees as possible. To help determine the audience, the task force designed a library-wide survey to gauge interest in the classes. The task force also spoke personally with library staff and faculty members who were most likely to be interested in the classes, and thus obtained feedback on attendance firsthand. The classes were then designed to meet the needs of known participants, while still attracting as wide an audience as possible.

The second question the task force tried to answer was what to communicate in the classes. What would be the most applicable and interesting information that other colleagues wanted to hear about the Unit and its services and functions? There are many operations going on within the Cataloging and Metadata Unit, yet some would not concern colleagues in other areas. The task force needed to pick those that would be most useful and meaningful. The task force was also interested in sharing with colleagues the importance of cataloging and how it affects the workflow of others working in the library. To accomplish this goal, a library-wide survey was created that included questions about topics of interest to people attending the classes. The task force had a predetermined list of possible topics and asked the participants to select the topics they were interested in learning more about. A suggestion box was included for topics not mentioned on the list.

The third question was how to best use the Unit's personnel to address the topics in the most effective way. The three librarians in the Cataloging and Metadata Unit have their own individual expertise. At the planning stage, these librarians devised topics based on their areas of work. One would cover general cataloging rules and operations. Another would cover electronic resource cataloging procedures, the design of the USF library catalog, and its searching functions. The third librarian would cover digital library metadata management and the projects happening in that area.

To answer the three questions we posed, the aforementioned survey was designed to encourage others to share their thoughts. The task force designed the survey to gauge the interest of participants, what departments were interested, and what topics were of the most interest. The whole library was invited to participate in the survey. See figure 6.1 for a list of the survey questions. A detailed description of the survey and its results follows.

In the survey, the task force asked if metadata classes would be of interest to the library. Participants interested in taking part were asked to identify themselves and their area of work, so that the task force could get demographic information and be able to design the class content to fit participants'

Metadata Cataloging Informational Classes Survey Questions

1. Would you be interested in attending metadata classes on various topics? If so, please enter your name so we may send you further information.

2. Which metadata/cataloging topics are you interested in learning more about? (Choose all that apply.)

   ☐ Learning what metadata is
   ☐ Reading a MARC record
   ☐ Understanding fundamental metadata fields
   ☐ Understanding different catalog record formats (books, ebooks, streaming media, images, etc.)
   ☐ Constructing a metadata record
   ☐ How to format your metadata for a project
   ☐ How to update and enhance current metadata to increase searching and discoverability
   ☐ How metadata impacts the OPAC display and search options
   ☐ Linked Data: What is it and how can it benefit libraries

3. If you are a supervisor, would you be willing to send your staff or student workers to any of these sessions?

4. What other metadata session topics would be beneficial to you?

5. What is your job classification (Faculty, Staff, Student Worker, Admin, etc.)?

6. What department of the library do you work in (Access Services, Collections and Discovery, Research and Instructions, Digital Scholarship Services, Digital Heritage and Humanities Collections, Digital Collections, Special Collections, etc.)?

FIGURE 6.1
Survey questions

needs. Nine cataloging/metadata topics were listed in the survey. These topics ranged from basic cataloging/metadata knowledge to new buzzwords in the field such as "linked data."

The Qualtrix survey provided an effective way to reach all library staff simultaneously through the library e-mail list. Overall, 22 of the 88 library employees responded to the survey. Over half of these responses came from people in areas located on the same floor as the Cataloging and Metadata Unit, and this reinforced the theory that physical proximity affects communication efforts.

In the survey results, seventeen people expressed an interest in attending metadata classes and the other five respondents were maybes. This indicated to the task force that only those interested in the classes actually responded to the survey. Most of the library supervisors responded to the survey and said they would be willing to send their staff to the metadata classes if they were interested in attending. From the survey results, it was determined that the main audience for the classes would be from Digital Collections, Collections and Discovery, and the Library Student Success and liaison librarians. These were all people who used the catalog system and had some knowledge of how the catalog worked. See figure 6.2 for the survey results by department or unit.

Reviewing the results of the survey, the number one topic involved linked data, in which 99 percent of the participants expressed an interest. The next topic in terms of interest concerned how to update and enhance current metadata to improve searching and discovery. Over 90 percent of the respondents expressed an interest in this topic, reinforcing the task force's belief that other departments are interested in how metadata can improve their workflow and job tasks. Other topics that received more than 80 percent of the votes

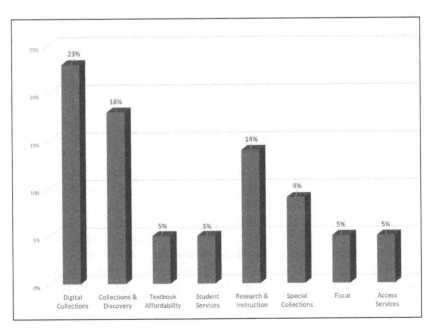

FIGURE 6.2
Expressions of interest in the survey by department

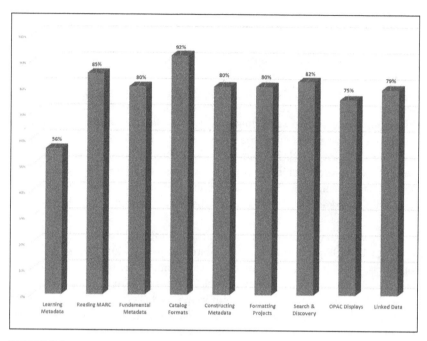

FIGURE 6.3
Survey results on class topics

included understanding the fields in catalog records, constructing a metadata record, understanding fundamental metadata fields, and how to format metadata for a project. For a complete graph of the survey results on class topics, see figure 6.3.

COMMUNICATION PLAN

After conducting the survey, the task force determined that only one-fourth of the library's staff had responded to the survey. To increase the attendance of the metadata classes, the task force devised a communication plan to spread the word. This involved getting buy-in from the administrators to support the classes so that the supervisors in the library could endorse the plan and allow interested staff members to attend the classes. The communication plan consisted of three parts: the task force (1) created a series of e-mails to advertise the classes, (2) communicated directly with coworkers to promote the classes and invite attendees, and (3) solicited feedback from participants to improve the classes and plan future events.

The first part of the communication plan involved a series of e-mails designed to advertise the metadata classes and encourage library staff to register for the classes. These e-mails went out about six weeks before the classes started to give people plenty of time to plan. Reminder e-mails were then sent out every two weeks until the classes started. Once the classes started, an e-mail went out on the Friday before each class to remind participants and to highlight the topic of the week. This was done to spark interest and invite attendees who had not previously registered to attend. After each class, another e-mail was sent out with a short survey thanking the person for attending, sharing the slides from the session, and asking for feedback on what the participant found useful about the class.

Another part of the plan involved communicating directly with coworkers. This took the form of issuing face-to-face invitations to faculty and staff who the task force determined might have an interest in metadata. The classes were also mentioned in departmental and library-wide meetings. Word-of-mouth promotion was thus built up through these efforts.

The last part of the communication plan involved direct feedback from the class participants. At the end of each class session, time was left for questions from the audience, and the presenters asked what the attendees liked or disliked about the class. Topics for future metadata classes were also solicited from the audience, and participants were encouraged to invite others to future classes.

With this communication plan, the task force hoped that the entire library would be made aware of the metadata classes and topics being offered, and that faculty and staff would understand how these classes might be beneficial to their work. The hope was also that this would open the door to increased communication and collaboration between departments.

CLASS IMPLEMENTATION

The task force analyzed the survey results and decided on six topics that would cover most of the areas in which people were interested: (1) what is metadata, (2) how to figure out titles, creators, publishers, dates, and subjects, (3) the relationship between Mango (the USF library catalog) and MARC, (4) the cataloging of non-book materials, (5) metadata projects in the library, and (6) USF libraries' foray into linked data. There would be six class sessions in all. For each session, slides were developed to give the participants both written and visual information to help understand the topic. The presentations were designed to include as much audience participation as possible by asking questions, playing metadata trivia games for candy, and having group discussions.

Our first session was intended as a brief introduction to cataloging and metadata. This would be especially helpful for those staff members who did not have much previous experience in libraries or had not been exposed to the concepts. The task force also wanted to use this session to test the waters, so that the audience's general understanding of concepts could be determined. This would help the task force to develop the depth and scope of the following classes.

Session two introduced the basic elements of cataloging and metadata. This helped participants understand how the various pieces in a catalog record fit together and what information is critical and irreplaceable for a record. The session also allowed participants to share their perspective on what is most useful to them when searching the catalog as part of their job responsibilities.

The third session covered the relationship between MARC and the local library catalog (Mango). This session showed how cataloging/metadata impacts the search functions in the catalog, and how these functions could be used effectively. The session allowed the participants to give feedback on how they use Mango and how metadata could be improved to better facilitate end-users.

Session four focused on cataloging non-book materials. This covered the cataloging information provided for the various formats and how the formats could be used to limit and improve search results. Various types of formats were discussed, including audiovisual media, maps, musical scores, and e-books. A discussion of the various e-book programs used at USF was outlined, including how demand-driven acquisitions and evidence-based acquisitions programs function. How these various formats display in the catalog and how to best search for different formats was also discussed.

This was followed by a session where we introduced various projects taking place in the Cataloging and Metadata Unit, in collaboration with the Digital Collections Unit. Information on the many digital collections that have been developed had not been communicated to colleagues in other departments in an effective way. This class shared information on the projects that had been worked on in the past three years, and informed participants about the digital collections currently available in the library.

The final session talked about the linked data project initiated in the library. Linked data has been a big topic in the cataloging/metadata field in recent years, and the USF Tampa Library has a linked data team that has been exploring this area for the last two years. This session gave a great opportunity for the task force to communicate its work. The session included new trends in metadata and explored how the Cataloging and Metadata Unit could collaborate with colleagues to make library resources more findable and accessible.

The classes were scheduled for six consecutive weeks on the same day and time for continuity. The hope was that this would increase attendance by making it easier for participants to remember the time and date. The day and time were determined based on the results of a Doodle poll. Given the busy schedules of library employees, it was critical to get consensus on a day and time that would allow the most participants to attend.

The presenters used PowerPoint to help deliver the class content and designed interactive activities to engage the audience. PowerPoint was a way to visually present the information through pictures, screenshots, and bullet points of the content. It also allowed the presenters to type up the class content outline in the notes, which helped them stay on track in the presentation. These notes were sent out in the PowerPoint slides after the class, so attendees could study them further.

Quizzes were another critical component to strengthen class communication. They helped engage the audience in the presentation, and also helped the presenter to check how well the content was being received. In the classes, presenters embedded questions in the presentation. Those in the audience who correctly answered the questions would get a piece of candy. Sometimes the presenter would just start a conversation with a question, to effectively draw information out from the audience and exchange ideas.

During the weeks that classes were scheduled, weekly e-mails were sent out to the whole library to remind everyone about the class time and the week's topic. The weekly e-mail newsletter sent to all library employees also contained the class information and an invitation to join.

The presenters kept a sign-in sheet to track the audience at each session. The attendance varied from 20 to 24 people, which is approximately 25 percent of all the employees in the library. The attendees received a survey after the class asking about their opinions of the class.

ASSESSMENT AFTER THE CLASSES

The Qualtrix survey tool was also used to collect after-class feedback and the attendees' satisfaction rate. The survey asked if the classes had been helpful overall, and inquired about the usefulness of each individual class. Additionally, it asked about any changes participants would like to see, and if there were any topics for future classes they would like presented. See figure 6.4 for the follow-up class survey questions.

The survey participants unanimously said that the classes had a positive impact on their daily jobs. The satisfaction rate for individual sessions varied from 67 to 89 percent. While only a few participants responded to the survey for each class (the average response was nine), the task force garnered some excellent feedback from participants during the class sessions themselves. Many participants expressed how helpful they found the classes and said that the information provided was very useful for filling in gaps in their knowledge. Several new employees told the task force that the classes had helped them better understand the catalog and how to search it effectively. Many people expressed an interest in learning more about the metadata projects at the library.

Metadata Information Classes Follow-Up Survey Questions

1. Were the classes helpful to your daily job? Rate the usefulness of the class on a scale of 1–4, where 1 is least useful and 4 is most useful.

2. Did session one "what is metadata" meet your expectations? Rate the usefulness of the class on a scale of 1–4, where 1 is least useful and 4 is most useful.

3. Did session two "how to figure out titles, creators, publishers, dates, and subjects" meet your expectations? Rate the usefulness of the class on a scale of 1–4, where 1 is least useful and 4 is most useful.

4. Did session three "the relationship between Mango and Marc" meet your expectations? Rate the usefulness of the class on a scale of 1–4, where 1 is least useful and 4 is most useful.

5. Did session four "from soup to nuts (or serials to realia)" meet your expectations? Rate the usefulness of the class on a scale of 1–4, where 1 is least useful and 4 is most useful.

6. Did session five "metadata projects in the library" meet your expectations? Rate the usefulness of the class on a scale of 1–4, where 1 is least useful and 4 is most useful.

7. Did session six "USF Libraries' foray into the Semantic Web" meet your expectations? Rate the usefulness of the class on a scale of 1–4, where 1 is least useful and 4 is most useful.

8. List the most useful things you have learned from the classes.

9. If you can make changes, what would you change about the classes?

10. If there are future metadata classes, what other topics do you want to hear about or what topics in this series do you want to hear more about?

FIGURE 6.4
Follow-up class survey questions

The follow-up survey showed that most of the class topics were well received. The most popular class was the metadata introduction class, which was attended by many of the newer employees at the library. Next was the third class which was on the online public access catalog (OPAC), and then the classes on digital collections and linked data. See figure 6.5 for the survey results on individual classes.

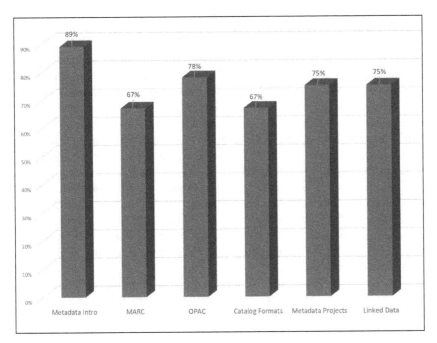

FIGURE 6.5
Follow-up survey results on the usefulness of the classes

The survey also asked about any changes participants desired or topics for future classes. One suggestion was holding classes on types of metadata other than descriptive, such as technical, administrative, and provenance. Another suggestion was to include simple handouts of the main points to help the participants remember important metadata concepts. Many attendees expressed, in both the survey and in verbal feedback, an interest in having more metadata classes that would highlight the library's digital collection projects. Others were interested in a more hands-on approach, which would give them the opportunity to make metadata records. The task force plans to take all these suggestions into consideration for future classes.

The task force was recognized by the library administration for its work. The dean of the USF Tampa Libraries acknowledged the Metadata and Cataloging Unit for its efforts in helping to improve communication throughout the library. The assistant dean in charge of Collections and Discovery sent the task force a letter of commendation, stating: "The value of metadata in the profession has long been underestimated, so bringing this to light in an engaging and comprehensible way is a great achievement. The feedback I have heard indicates that library staff were highly impressed with your professional presentation of the subject matter. We all look forward to future class series from the three of you unraveling the mysteries of metadata."[4]

FUTURE GOALS

Some colleagues who missed sessions asked if the task force could put on similar sessions in the future. And the library administration asked that more sessions be given to increase the communication around the whole library.

Accordingly, the task force is planning for a second round of classes. Ideas in consideration for the second round include presenting more in-depth discussions on metadata creation and its application, and showcasing the library's digital collections and the metadata work involved. The task force plans to incorporate many of the suggestions given by attendees, including providing handouts and having more hands-on classes. Future class topics would also provide updates on the library's current digital collections and linked data projects. This would provide valuable information to the library personnel who use these collections. One department in the library mentioned the possibility of a future collaboration with the linked data team, which could become another class topic.

The planning team would like to record future sessions, providing access to those who could not be present. This would also expand the audience outside the library by posting the recordings on the library's website and on social media. The task force plans to investigate ways to improve survey participation and other forms of communication to encourage a greater attendance. Communication in the classroom could be enhanced by using more engaged learning techniques, such as hands-on sessions and fostering more group discussions in the classes.

CONCLUSION

The series of classes has shown that communication between the Cataloging and Metadata Unit and other areas of the library is critical. Cataloging/metadata librarians need to be proactive to create communication opportunities with colleagues from other departments. By providing information about what the Unit does and the value of cataloging, the "false dualism" (in Margaret Bing's words) between technical and public services can be erased. As Bing says, "there is no person in the library who is not doing public service."[5] The Cataloging and Metadata Unit wants to build on this spirit and sense of cooperation for future endeavors.

REFERENCES

Bing, Margaret. "The False Dualism: Technical Services vs. Public Services." *Journal of Library Administration* 29, no. 2 (1999): 24.

Davis, Carol Ann. E-mail to the authors, October 28, 2019.

Gorman, Michael. "The Ecumenical Library." In *Reference Services and Technical Services: Interactions in Library Practice*, ed. Gordon Stevenson and Sally Stevenson, 56. New York: Haworth, 1984.

Orava, Hilkka. "Marketing Is an Attitude of Mind." In *Adapting Marketing to Libraries in a Changing and World-Wide Environment: Papers Presented at the 63rd IFLA Conference, Copenhagen, September 1997*, 88. Munich: Saur, 2000.

Walton, Richard E., John M. Dutton, and Thomas P. Cafferty. "Organizational Context and Interdepartmental Conflict." *Administrative Science Quarterly* 14 (1969): 523.

NOTES

1. Michael Gorman, "The Ecumenical Library," in *Reference Services and Technical Services: Interactions in Library Practice*, ed. Gordon Stevenson and Sally Stevenson (New York: Haworth Press, 1984), 56.

2. Hilkka Orava, "Marketing is an Attitude of Mind," in *Adapting Marketing to Libraries in a Changing and World-Wide Environment: Papers Presented at the 63rd IFLA Conference*, Copenhagen, September 1997 (Munich: Saur, 2000), 88.

3. Richard E. Walton, John M. Dutton, and Thomas P. Cafferty, "Organizational Context and Interdepartmental Conflict," *Administrative Science Quarterly* 14 (1969): 523.

4. Carol Ann Davis, email to the authors, Oct. 28, 2019.

5. Margaret Bing, "The False Dualism: Technical Services vs. Public Services," *Journal of Library Administration* 29, no. 2 (1999): 24.

ERIN BLOCK AND
KIMBERLY LAWLER

7

Improving Interdepartmental Communication and Workflows

A Survey of Workflow Tools and the
Implementation of Trello at the University
of Colorado Boulder Libraries

Managing the life cycle of electronic resources is a complicated process that remains a pain point for many libraries. It often involves the cross-departmental distribution of information, which can result in information being lost, underutilized, or not shared with the correct units and employees. This situation can then result in the library being more reactive than proactive. At the University of Colorado Boulder Libraries (CU Boulder), units from multiple departments worked together to review and implement a workflow that improves upon the way information about electronic resources is communicated. In order to proceed with this task, members from the Collection Development, Acquisitions, and Access & Discovery units researched and trialed different online workflow tools to find the best option for improving our communications about new, renewal, and trial electronic resources. In the end, our team identified the workflow management tool Trello as the best option to achieve better communication and more efficient processes for managing new electronic resources.

BACKGROUND AND ORGANIZATIONAL STRUCTURE

The University of Colorado Boulder is the flagship university in a multi-campus system in the state of Colorado. A public research university, the University of Colorado Boulder has five libraries on campus. Given the size of the University of Colorado Boulder Libraries (hereafter the Libraries), the process of acquiring and making electronic resources discoverable is a complex one. With multiple departments, units, and people involved, ensuring that information is shared across all departments and that employees are receiving the appropriate information can be challenging. Moreover, good interdepartmental communication is also essential in order to improve accessibility for the Libraries' users.

The units responsible for this work are the Access & Discovery unit within the Metadata Services Department and the Acquisitions and Collection Development units within the Scholarly Resource Development Department (see figure 7.1). In the past, they have been separate departments within the same

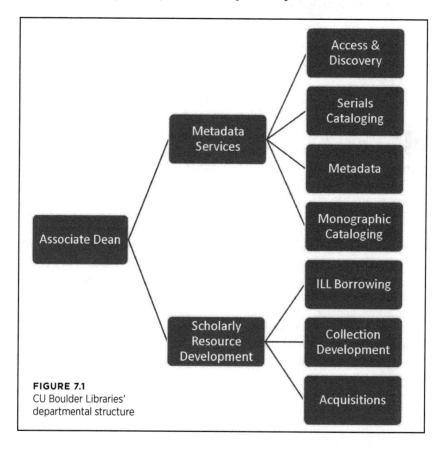

FIGURE 7.1
CU Boulder Libraries'
departmental structure

division and under the same associate dean. However, the libraries are currently undergoing a reorganization and this may change, making the establishment of a central place for storing and sharing information between them even more crucial.

Within the CU Boulder Libraries, Collection Development usually initiates the cycle of obtaining electronic resources. Requests most often stem from the Libraries' subject specialists and liaisons, who request new e-journals, e-books, databases, and many other types of electronic resources. Collection Development supplies funding information and then contacts the Acquisitions unit to request additional necessary information.

Once the Acquisitions unit is informed of a request, their role is to contact the vendor or publisher of the electronic resource under consideration to determine whether we will be able to subscribe to or purchase the material. The vital information for this type of exchange includes pricing, licensing terms or terms and conditions, perpetual access rights, and concurrent user limits. After gathering the requested information, it can then be passed along to the Collection Development unit. If approved, the Acquisitions unit then negotiates any signed agreement or terms and conditions if necessary, and receives and routes the invoices for payment. All access information can then be sent to the Access & Discovery unit.

From there, Access & Discovery makes the electronic resources discoverable by working with the vendor, tracking the materials in our knowledge base, or working with other metadata services colleagues to get the electronic resource cataloged and accessible in our catalog and our discovery layer. This unit is also responsible for troubleshooting issues and resolving any access problems that may arise. Trials for many different types of electronic resources are also set up and handled by the Access & Discovery unit.

At the end of the workflow, Access & Discovery informs Collection Development when materials are available for use. Following that, Collection Development informs the Libraries and its users. Depending on the resource, this is done by notifying librarian subject specialists, faculty members who requested the resource, the library's SharePoint site, and even social media.

To communicate this pertinent information, the units historically used e-mail as the key tool. E-mails were used to share information between departments regarding electronic resource requests, pricing, access, trials, purchases, and more. In addition, subject specialists would send e-mails detailing new databases they were interested in trialing, forwarding the information to employees working in any or all of the aforementioned units. The subject specialists would communicate back and forth to request trial information, pricing, access rights types, and much more, leading to a decision on whether we were allowed to make the purchase or not, and then deciding which funds could be allocated for payment. Under this workflow, all the details relevant to the request and subsequent purchase of a resource were contained in multiple e-mails across various units. All in all, there were a multitude of hands on the keyboard, sending e-mails to make sure electronic resources were accessible and available to the Libraries' users, but all without a formalized workflow to keep track of everything. By utilizing only e-mail, information could be easily lost, not sent to the correct unit, or remain unopened in an in-box. Any and all of these mishaps could cause issues later, when users searched for an electronic resource that was supposed to be available online, but was not discoverable or contained broken links.

In order to deal with these challenges, a project to create a formalized electronic resources workflow was spearheaded by the Libraries' Electronic Resources Management Sub Group (ERMSG). Including employees from both the Metadata Services and Scholarly Resource Development departments, the ERMSG was formed to ensure efficient and effective management of the Libraries' collection of electronic resources. The project's goal was to improve on the mainly e-mail-based communication used between the different units when setting up trials, purchasing new electronic resources, or approving renewals of electronic resources.

TESTING OF PROGRAM MANAGEMENT TOOLS AND SELECTION OF TRELLO

The ERMSG decided to research, trial, and then select a workflow management tool that would set the units up for better communication and a more efficient workflow. E-mail will always be a tool the Libraries use in this process, but it was hoped a more formalized procedure would help our efficiency and communication. To help us decide which online tool would work the best for our departments, members of ERMSG researched different workflow tools and presented their pros and cons. Two members volunteered to test out and make a recommendation to the group on what would be the best tool for our desired workflow.

The online tools that ERMSG looked at first were Confluence, Trello, and ServiceNow. Our Access & Discovery librarian put together a presentation for the group with notes and screenshots on the three tools, which included information on their pricing, organization, notifications, templates, and other aspects. This allowed the larger ERMSG group to decide what next steps to take in making a selection. Some of the features that ERMSG looked for in the tools that we reviewed were user friendliness and intuitiveness, the availability of free versions of the tool that didn't require any type of paid access, and the ability to add as many staff as needed to access and receive notifications of updates to the tools.

One of the first tools we decided against pursuing was Confluence. Confluence is a workflow/organizational tool, but it has a subscription fee associated with the tool in order to use it. In addition, we did not find Confluence to be as user-friendly as Trello, nor did we have any prior experience using it, as we did with ServiceNow. The latter is also a workflow tool and is one that CU Boulder already pays for. In addition, members of the ERMSG have already had experience using it for service tickets. However, we found ServiceNow to be a more cumbersome tool to keep track of all the information we wanted to collect, and there were conflicts with differentiating the electronic resource access issues already tracked in the tool.

In addition to these three options, the ERMSG also considered Microsoft Planner. This was not included in the original presentation and testing phase because CU Boulder was just beginning to implement Planner on the campus as part of a rollout of Microsoft Teams and other applications in Microsoft Office 365. Planner is a tool Microsoft created that is very similar to Trello, and as CU Boulder already pays for Office 365, this seemed like another option to investigate once we were made aware of it several months later.

After the ERMSG reviewed the information presented, first Trello and later Planner were chosen to test and create workflow procedures for. The unit members who led the selection and testing process were Kimberly Lawler and Erin Block.

Trello

Trello is a collaborative project management tool with both a free and a subscription version. Trello boards are organized into columns, and then cards. Columns are holding places for the cards, thus creating the first organizational structure (see figure 7.2). The columns are laid out from left to right in the web browser, and can be moved in any order by clicking on a column and dragging

FIGURE 7.2
Screenshot of Trello—New resource board

it to where it is needed on the Trello board. Cards are added to the columns vertically and can be moved to any spot on any column by clicking and dragging the card to the desired location. The cards allow for information about the resources being collected in a variety of formats, whether those are checklists, attachments, labels, due dates, and so on.

As discussed previously, our goal was that Trello would be used to keep track of trials, new acquisitions, renewals, and cancellations of electronic resources. Lawler and Block spent time reviewing and testing the tool and creating procedures that would be followed in its use. It was decided to create columns for each of the main library units using the board, as well as cards for "with the vendor" and "year completed." Each new electronic resource receives its own card where information pertinent to the subscription and details relating to access are added and shared across units. As each unit completes its tasks, the card is moved to different columns down the workflow.

Members of the ERMSG group created Trello accounts so they could be notified of new or updated information. This could be done by "tagging" them in a comment, or by adding them as a member of the card. This last was usually done for those responsible for a majority of the workflow from their department. E-mail notifications, based on each user's preference, would be sent so that everyone would be able to track and be reminded of deadlines. After creating guidelines for Trello, the procedure was brought to the group to review and help make further decisions on the finalized process.

Microsoft Planner

After creating procedures and workflows utilizing Trello across all the respective units, the ERSMG used this tool until CU Boulder started advising the use of different Microsoft Office applications and products. Since CU Boulder had already purchased licenses for Microsoft Office, this was a logical step to take. As a result, the two volunteers started to test Microsoft Planner using the workflows we had created for Trello. We also took an additional step and started to use Microsoft Power Automate (previously called Microsoft Flow) in conjunction with Planner. Power Automate offered us the ability to combine different applications and online tools together to make the whole process more efficient.

Deciding whether to move the new resource workflow to Microsoft Planner was a lengthy process, as there was a need to keep track of and maintain the current tasks already implemented using Trello. During this time, work was duplicated and completed on both tools to ensure that daily tasks were not lost in the shuffle. It was decided that Planner would be tested for a month, and then the ERMSG would reconvene to discuss the findings and recommendations.

Planner works in the same fashion as Trello, creating buckets (columns) for each unit, adding tasks (cards) with additional information, and assigning people to work on a resource. Planner resembles Trello visually, with each bucket laid out left to right in the tool, and each task that is created can be moved from one bucket to another (see figure 7.3). Pertinent information is added to the tasks, including checklists and labels. One great attribute Planner has that Trello does not include is statistics. This could be a beneficial addition to allow for data collection and assessment because it would show how many different electronic resources had been trialed, renewed, subscribed to, or even canceled.

As mentioned above, Microsoft also has Power Automate, a tool to automate workflows using different applications, including apps created by different companies outside of Microsoft. This seemed like a great tool to utilize with Planner, and it would give us the ability to bring in Microsoft Forms, thus making the entire process more efficient.

This did not work very well in practice, however, because Planner does not have some key qualities of Trello that we had found to be essential. Specifically, Planner lacked the ability to tag people on cards or tasks, and did not have the functionality to allow the creation of templates to apply across cards as needed. Because of the cross-departmental nature of the workflow, we found tagging to be especially important because it allows us to direct questions to specific people in comments. The templates of tasks for each unit ensure that nothing is forgotten as resources are set up, and they increase efficiency by not having to re-create a list for every card.

Additionally, Automate and Planner did not integrate as well as we'd hoped. Our plan had been to merge the crucial Collection Development forms into Power Automate, which would then generate the most important

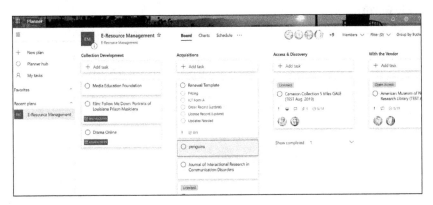

FIGURE 7.3
Screenshot of Microsoft Planner—E-Resource Management board

information from the form and put it into Planner. However, it was found that much of the important information from the Microsoft form wasn't captured and transferred.

After further discussion and practice, the final recommendation was that Trello would be the best tool for our needs, and we would continue to use and adapt the workflow previously created that incorporated Trello into our electronic resource processes.

IMPLEMENTING TRELLO WITH AN IDENTIFIED WORKFLOW

The key deliverable of this project was to create a consistent method of communication between the Collection Development, Acquisitions, and Access & Discovery units. As stated earlier, a historical issue for these teams was new resources falling through the cracks, as the process from purchasing or subscribing to a new resource to finally receiving access can span many months. It was difficult not only to keep track of what needed to be done for new resources, but also to track the resources' progress from subscription to access.

Once other project management software had been eliminated, August 2018 was set aside to test a new Trello workflow for all electronic resources that were either trialed or acquired during that period. The procedures that we developed initially included how to use labels, due dates, and checklists (see figure 7.4).

The first step in creating the workflow was to organize the framework for the New Resource board itself. It was decided that the owner of the board

Trello Workflow for New Resources

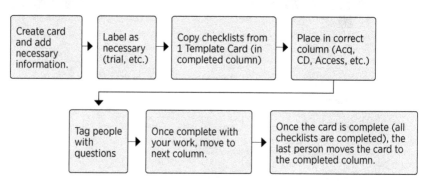

FIGURE 7.4
Chart of the Trello workflow for new resources

should be one of our group e-mail addresses instead of one specific person. This ensured that more than one person could add people to the board when needed, and if someone left the department or libraries, ownership of the board would not need to be transferred.

The next step was deciding how to utilize the board's columns and cards. Ultimately, we designed the board layout to hold seven columns, with an expectation that one new column would be added each year:

- Collection Development
- Acquisitions
- Access & Discovery
- With the Vendor (contains resources waiting on information from the publisher)
- 2020 Completed
- 2019 Completed
- 2018 Completed

Typically, a card is first added in the Collection Development column and then is moved to consecutive columns as the process progresses. However, this is not always the case, and cards are often added directly to the Acquisitions column. This can occur when approval has already been made by Collection Development, if it is a trial request directed toward Acquisitions, or if it is a routine renewal that involves new access details. Particularly in the case of platform updates or trials, cards are added directly to the Access & Discovery column. Any member of our teams can initiate the creation of a card for a new resource, trial, or platform update, but this person is usually the one who receives the request or access details.

When we create a card, we add the name of anyone who is involved with the next steps of the process. This person will then receive notifications based on the preferences they set up in their profile. Notifications can be e-mailed instantly, periodically (which is approximately once an hour), or never. If a person chooses "never," they will only receive notifications when they log in to their account. An alarm bell icon will turn red if someone has new notifications or items that need their attention. We found that some people prefer to receive notifications in real time, others in a daily digest format, and still others prefer to just check the board as needed or when tagged. This flexibility, while providing an underlying consistent frame for a workflow, has been a great part of our implementation of Trello workflow procedures.

Another notification feature is the ability to tag people to alert them that their attention is needed on a certain card or action item. This functions in a manner like that of using the @ feature on social media platforms, and most department members were familiar with this functionality. It is primarily used in comments for tasks such as making a decision about loading MARC records or when access details are active and ready to be implemented. Tagging is heavily relied upon to move communication forward between team members and alert them to column updates.

Labels are used for identifying the type of new resource; for example, trial, licensed, single title, or open access. Labels are also used for marking resources that need MARC records loaded or when there is a platform update. Different colors are used for the different labels, which helps to visually separate and determine what type of resource the card is for and what types of actions are needed.

Cards can be assigned specific due dates as well. Due dates are mostly utilized for indicating the end of trials, but are also set as reminders for those who are working on a card that it is not complete. For example, if a single title journal is not appearing in our knowledge base and we need to check back on its status, we will set a due date for this task.

Another useful function in Trello is that it allows for checklists in each card. A template card was created to house checklists for each unit's tasks. The items on each checklist range from licensing information to EZproxy setup, and to price quotes and branding. As an example, the following are checklist item actions we have identified in the workflow that the Access & Discovery team must complete when setting up a new resource:

- Working URL
- EZproxy configuration
- Create resource record
- Create LibGuide A-Z entry
- Activate in 360KB
- Load MARC records
- Quality check
- Branding

Cards are also used to hold title lists and correspondence from publishers in the form of e-mails. This helps to make information that was often just in the in-box of one person accessible to all members of the team.

Along with facilitating the tracking of new subscription or purchased resources, the New Resource Trello board has also helped to streamline trial requests. Trial requests need to be approved by the head of Collection Development, and subject librarians were often unsure of who to contact to request trials. E-mails were forwarded many times before they reached the correct person, and sometimes the request was submitted to several people who then duplicated work.

This is an area where our investigation of Microsoft Teams paid off, even though we decided to continue using Trello as our main project management tool. Unit members in Collection Development, Acquisitions, and Access & Discovery worked together to create a form in Microsoft Office for a "New or Trial Resource Request." The form asks whether the request is for a new subscription, a one-time purchase, or a trial; and asks for the work's title, the publisher/provider, whether the publisher has already been contacted, their URL, and the work's estimated cost. If approved by the head of Collection Development, the form automatically creates a card on the Trello board and populates the description with information from the request. We hope to further massage this workflow and implement additional elements of automation. However, our initial step toward that goal has been another benefit of implementing the cross-departmental New Resource Trello board.

One downside of the free Trello software is that it does not automatically produce statistics on columns, cards, labels, and so on. While the export of specific statistics is not available with the free implementation of Trello, there is the capability to export data from a Trello board into a JSON file. This is a more technologically complex method and so may not be a good option for every user. It should be kept in mind, however, that the functionality is available and statistics could be gathered by this more complex method. We did find that we are able to gather basic statistics by looking at individual columns, as you can see in figure 7.5, which shows the number of new resources from 2018 to 2020 by their card label.

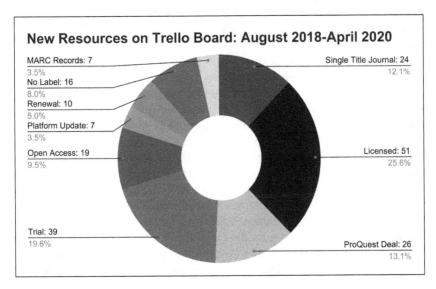

FIGURE 7.5
Donut graph of number of new resources on Trello board

HOW TRELLO HELPS OUR WORKFLOW

Trello allows our units to collect and share as much information as is needed regarding new electronic resources, including descriptions, licensing information, pricing, and communication with publishers and vendors. In the past, before being entered into the catalog, this information only existed in one or two Outlook in-boxes. This was a system that allowed information to be easily lost or forgotten.

The staff's response to the new workflow for acquiring resources has been positive. Change can be difficult and viewed as a criticism of past practices. However, there are several factors that worked in our favor which led to positive acceptance and successful implementation: (1) the existing workflow was not an established procedure, so the new workflow was overwhelmingly viewed as an improvement instead of a change or challenge; and (2) the results are an obvious improvement in workflow and better communication, with the added benefit of our staff being able to follow resources from subscription or purchase through to their addition to our catalog and discovery layer.

The New Resource Trello board creates a level of transparency between departments and also empowers team members to answer questions from subject librarians about the progress on requested trials or new resources. As mentioned earlier, the process from submitting a request for a trial or new resource to its being accessible and discoverable can take from days to even months to complete. Moreover, complications with things such as the wording in the license and configuring EZproxy stanzas can slow the process at various points. Prior to the Trello board workflow, questions about issues like these were often difficult to answer and required many e-mails to different people to track down where in the process a particular resource was. Now, any team member can log into Trello and go to the board to see the status of any trial or new resource. This workflow improvement has greatly simplified our ability to field questions from colleagues outside of our departments.

Implementing Trello in our interdepartmental workflow has also benefited us by giving our colleagues the ability to access stored information about new resources and trials, such as price quotes, communication with vendors, and trial end dates, without needing to identify the correct contact person, which can often vary by resource and be time-consuming to figure out. This new workflow allows us to share collected information with as many colleagues as needed, and allows for flexibility and transparency.

In addition to being unable to provide statistics, there are a few other drawbacks we have found with the free version of Trello. For example, the ability to add people with view-only status is unavailable. Unit members have received requests to make this possible, specifically in the case of subject specialists, as they would like to go directly to the source for information on the progress of their resource requests. However, barring upgrading to a paid Trello subscription, this does not appear to be possible without making the board completely public.

Since creating the Trello workflow, team members have used a similar framework for creatively solving issues in other areas as well. For example, our Electronic Resources Access manager created a Trello board for excessive use cases reported to us by publishers. These are instances where a web crawler harvests articles en masse or a patron's account has been hacked and is being used for gathering articles for nefarious purposes.

A team Trello board was also created for tracking data and security breaches reported to us by publishers. While there are not many of these cases, the publishers' e-mails about them are easily forgotten in in-boxes. In a world moving increasingly online, security breaches are becoming both more common and more of a concern. Patron privacy and trust are crucial, especially for resources where users are required to create an account and log in, or voluntarily do so to save articles and citations. This board will help us track and identify any resources that repeatedly have such breaches, and take the needed action from there.

The more efficient workflow established by using Trello has helped not only with our regular new acquisitions, but also with changes in collections due to unforeseen circumstances. For example, in March 2020, the CU Boulder Libraries moved to remote work and learning due to the COVID-19 pandemic, as did most universities across the country. These unprecedented circumstances caused publishers to offer trial access for many collections and products to facilitate the influx of online teaching and learning. As of May 2020, we had set up thirty-five trials related to access granted by the extenuating circumstances of the COVID-19 pandemic. Without the New Resources board, keeping track of these many trials would have been difficult, inefficient, and prone to error.

As these examples show, the implementation of a workflow with the New Resources Trello board has helped our units manage interdepartmental information and communication about new purchases, subscriptions, platform updates, and trials. And with much of the legwork and structure already in place, it has also helped members of our unit manage other workflows as well.

CONCLUSION

Overall, Trello allows the CU Boulder Libraries' Collection Development, Acquisitions, and Access & Discovery units to better communicate and work together to make new resources accessible to users. It enables us to collect, store, and archive information we input into the program, collating different unit and team members' efforts into one location. This is helpful for our teams in several ways, including looking back on projects by year, retrieving statistics for new resources, and referring back to access or license information. Centralizing the workflow helps our teams work more efficiently through the process of making new and trial resources accessible and discoverable. It has ensured that information is not lost in the process, and that resources move as swiftly as possible through the process from request to access. And as mentioned previously, a great side effect of this new workflow is that the project's success has inspired colleagues across the library to explore using Trello for things like tracking security breaches and excessive use cases. Along with improving the process for team members who are directly involved in the new resources workflow, the Trello board has also improved transparency and the sharing of information with colleagues across the library, and helps trials and new resources become more readily available to our users.

REFERENCES

Collins, Maria. "Evolving Workflows: Knowing When to Hold'em, Knowing When to Fold'em." *The Serials Librarian* 57, no. 3 (2009): 261–71. doi:10.1080/03615260902877050.

Dowdy, Beverly, and Ros Raeford. "Electronic Resources Workflow Using Push Technology: Business Process Manager" (Prezi slides). Duke University Libraries, ER&L, March 18, 2014.

Wells, Amy Grace. "User Test Content before You Start Design." UX Booth, January 22, 2019. www.uxbooth.com/articles/user-test-content-before-you-start-design.

Yue, Paoshan W. "Using Technology to Facilitate Pre-Acquisition Workflows for Electronic Resources." *Proceedings of the Charleston Library Conference* (2016): 480–83. doi:10.5703/1288284316555.

MEGHAN BURKE

8

Communicating E-Resource Access Issues

Marymount University's Steps to Create
Troubleshooting Training for Public Services

Public services staff are on the front lines of helping patrons access library resources. When an electronic resource is unavailable or malfunctioning, it is usually discovered by someone in public services, and often while helping a patron. Unfortunately, there are often barriers that stand in the way of finding a quick solution to an access problem. Follow-up can be difficult, especially with busy college students involved, and as a result, access issues often take longer to resolve or are not reported at all. It is difficult for public services staff to quickly identify the root of the issue if they're not trained in common access problems or are unsure what to include when reporting the problem. Finally, it may be difficult to get in touch with e-resources staff in a timely manner. Marymount University's library has taken several steps to break down the barriers to e-resources troubleshooting and resolution that exist between the front-line public services staff and the technical services staff who resolve the access issues. Implemented in stages, the e-resources troubleshooting infrastructure at Marymount is an inclusive process that involves a local ticketing system and training in troubleshooting for all public services faculty and staff.

BACKGROUND

Marymount University is a small, Catholic, liberal arts university in Arlington, Virginia. Marymount's library is staffed by approximately 21 full-time-equivalent employees, including 8 full-time faculty librarians. The library also employs student workers. Each staff member belongs to a service group with a particular focus:

Collections Services: handles acquisitions, cataloging, and electronic resources management

Education Services: primary responsibilities are teaching and reference service

Technology Services: acts as library IT support

Access and Outreach Services: handles resource transactions, interlibrary loan, reserves, and marketing for the library

In spite of these divisions, there is a lot of overlap among service group duties. In particular, all faculty librarians teach, work on the reference desk, and select resources in their liaison areas.

Within the above framework, there are two people who directly manage electronic resources troubleshooting: the author, the metadata/electronic resources librarian, who handles the management and licensing of databases, packages, e-books, and maintains EZproxy, among other duties; and an acquisitions associate, who works primarily with individually purchased serials and invoicing. The collections management librarian also fills in when necessary.

Libraries use a variety of methods to communicate about e-resource access issues. Many libraries use ticketing systems in order to improve communication, standardize questions, eliminate the use of e-mails that may be missed or answered by multiple people, and track patterns and statistics in a centralized way. In 2016, Kelly Smith of Eastern Kentucky University Libraries conducted a series of interviews with libraries that use ticketing systems to track electronic resources access issues. The libraries reported that using a ticketing system "improved collaboration within and across teams." Smith also found that in libraries that allowed public services staff to view all tickets, such as Virginia Tech, public services staff "develop more technical knowledge so they can do more basic troubleshooting 'on the fly.'"[1]

Other libraries undertake training for both technical services and public services staff to help with identifying e-resource problems, achieve better "on the fly" troubleshooting, and provide more detailed and accurate reporting of access issues. In 2016, Sunshine Carter and Stacie Traill wrote about the complexities of training e-resources staff on troubleshooting in a new technical environment.[2] Kate Hill of the University of North Carolina Greensboro took this training one step further and held a session on e-resource problems and troubleshooting for public services staff.[3]

By adopting a ticketing system, Marymount wanted to combine these techniques: allow all library faculty and staff to see tickets, train e-resources staff in effective troubleshooting, and alert public services staff to common issues that would allow for more robust tickets and the ability to troubleshoot "on the fly." The rest of this chapter will detail the steps we took on the way to our current systematic integration of electronic resources troubleshooting into our public services reference training.

STEP 1: IMPLEMENTING A TICKETING SYSTEM

The author started working at Marymount in July 2016. It was immediately evident that the library would benefit from a central location and a structured form of reporting electronic resource problems. While public services staff were consistent about reporting outages and problems to the metadata/electronic resources librarian, they were not consistent in the way they reported them, or the information they provided. A ticketing system would help with this problem by providing a central place to store e-resource outage information, thus making it easier to track ongoing issues, and by establishing a set of structured questions for those reporting an issue.

An internal e-resources ticketing system was implemented using Google Forms and Google Sheets in the fall of 2016. The system was quickly adopted and expanded to include tickets for other groups and teams within the library, such as IT support. We applied simple coding to the Google sheet to allow us to update and respond to tickets directly from the spreadsheet.

The E-Resources Problems ticket form (figure 8.1) contains a series of questions that can be broken up into three categories: contact information, resource identification, and problem reporting. The questions include radio buttons for more consistent answers, as well as short-answer questions that allow the submitter to describe the problem in detail, and an option to upload a screenshot.

The first two questions ask for the contact information of the person submitting the ticket, which at Marymount is always library faculty or staff. The third question requests the contact information (name, e-mail, and phone number, if desired) of the patron outside the library who encountered the problem, so the e-resources staff can contact them to follow up. (In some cases, the problem is found by a librarian or library staff member, in which case the third question remains blank.) The fourth question asks for the role of the person who originally reported the problem. This question is for record-keeping purposes, and also helps the troubleshooter determine whether or not the person in question *should* have access to the resource. (For example, at Marymount, community patrons only have access to e-resources while they are on-campus.)

The next four questions ask the person submitting the ticket (the "reporter") to specifically identify the resource. Question five asks if the patron is on- or off-campus, which is a crucial piece of troubleshooting information. Then the reporter is asked how the patron originally accessed the resource. This helps the troubleshooter identify where the problem may be coming from, such as a broken link in a catalog record or a problem with a LibGuide. Question seven asks for the type of resource (e-book, e-journal, database, etc.), which is useful in trying to narrow down how widespread the problem is.

Finally, the last two questions ask about the problem itself. The reporter is asked to describe the problem as specifically as possible. If there is an error message, we ask that the reporter include it in the description. The last question on the form allows users to upload a screenshot of the problem. This question was added later since the functionality did not exist when we first launched the ticketing system.

In developing the questionnaire, we recognized that we were asking a large number of questions, but we rationalized that the first four would be easy to answer. We also chose not to make any questions mandatory. If the user was in a rush, their e-mail address would be collected through the Google form, and a quick description of the problem would be better than no response at all. That said, we have not had any complaints about the length of the form or the questions in the nearly four years that it has been in use.

After creating the ticketing system, the next challenge was to get library faculty and staff on board with the new method of reporting. We began by sending a general e-mail to the library personnel in order to introduce them to the system. Because our reference desk is staffed almost entirely by faculty librarians, we started raising awareness with the library faculty first. We demonstrated and discussed the ticketing system in more depth at our biweekly librarians' meeting. We also added both the tickets and the spreadsheet for ticket-tracking to our library's central information portal. Finally, we demonstrated the ticketing system at the library's Fall 2017 Town Hall meeting to introduce it to the entire library. Throughout the process, we continually stressed the simplicity of the system, and encouraged faculty and staff to submit tickets, even if they had originally called or talked to us about an issue.

STEP 2: INITIAL TRAINING SESSION

The e-resources staff felt that the information in the tickets could be more actionable if public services staff understood the tools that are used to

E-Resource Problems Reporting Form

Report and record problems with electronic resources. Please include as much information as you can.

The name, username, and photo associated with your Google account will be recorded when you upload files and submit this form.

Name of person reporting problem _____

Phone number of reporter _____

If you are reporting on someone's behalf, please include their contact information here

_____

Role
- ☐ Library Faculty/Staff
- ☐ Faculty
- ☐ Undergraduate student
- ☐ Graduate student
- ☐ Other

Location
- ☐ On-campus (library, dorms, dining hall, etc.)
- ☐ Off-campus

How are you accessing this resource?
- ☐ Library website
- ☐ Library catalog
- ☐ LibGuide
- ☐ Canvas

What type of e-resource are you reporting?
- ☐ E-book
- ☐ E-journal
- ☐ Database
- ☐ Other

Name of Resource (i.e., Academic Source Premier) _____

_____

Please describe your problem. Be as specific as you can, and copy and paste information about the error message, if possible. _____

_____

_____

_____

_____

Please attach screenshots or related files if needed.

FIGURE 8.1
E-Resources Problem reporting form

manage electronic resources. In summer 2017, we developed a training session to raise awareness and increase the usefulness of tickets for e-resources troubleshooters. The session included information and examples about the circumstances in which access can "break," and the common access issues the staff may encounter while helping patrons. The presentation also covered tips for resolving issues that may be a result of user error. This first training session was inspired by Kate Hill's presentation at the ACRL conference in 2017 in which she describes creating a training to help public services staff identify e-resources problems sent to her team via e-mail.[4]

The one-hour session was tailored to Marymount's needs and borrowed from Hill's presentation and the tickets that had been submitted over the past year. First, it reviewed the e-resources management life cycle (adapted from the "NASIG Core Competencies for Electronic Resources Librarians")[5] at Marymount in order to clarify where and how issues most commonly arise. Next, the presentation went through the seven most common access issues we found through previously submitted tickets. The seven issues are:

- User error and misunderstanding
- Broken links from the catalog or e-resource management system
- An EZproxy problem
- Publisher error (e.g., a journal with coverage to a certain year is missing an interim issue for no apparent reason)
- Vendor issues (e.g., the platform itself is down)
- IP address problems
- Exceeding the simultaneous user limit (for some databases and many e-books)

Each problem was explained, and we allowed time for questions.

Next, we showed a sample library chat as an example of quick, in-the-moment troubleshooting (figure 8.2). This chat details a brief exchange between a librarian and a patron in which the patron was having trouble accessing videos. It turned out that the patron was using an unsupported browser, and a switch to a different browser fixed the problem.

Like the example in figure 8.2, simple troubleshooting techniques, such as asking a patron to switch browsers, clear their browser cache, or reload a page can often solve an access problem without any intervention from an e-resources staff member.

Finally, the session concluded with a series of exercises in which faculty and staff were given a set of access issues and challenged to identify the problem and give a guess as to how they might try to fix it. Exercises included an EZproxy error page, an issue with a mismatch in coverage from the catalog to the vendor, and a broken e-book link. We reviewed the answers and possible solutions as a group, and people were encouraged to ask clarifying questions. Everyone was sent the files and exercises to use for reference in the future.

Patron: Good morning. The videos I want to watch are not playing.

Librarian: Good morning! Let me have a look at that for you.

Librarian: May I ask if you are on or off campus?

Patron: I am on campus in the nursing building.

Librarian: Okay. Are you trying to access them from the library website?

Patron: I am in Canvas. I hit Library Resources . . . and clicked the link to the videos.

Librarian: Okay. Can you try this link for me? *link*

Patron: It opened the page, but the videos all have 00:00 play time listed as if there is no content. But I have used them before.

Librarian: Interesting. They are working for me. Which browser are you using?

Patron: Internet Explorer

Librarian: Could you try a different browser?

Patron: Yeah! That worked. Thank you.

Librarian: Great! Internet Explorer is sometimes a picky browser.

Patron: True. Have a good day. Thanks again. Goodbye.

FIGURE 8.2
Sample library chat of a quick troubleshooting session

STEP 3: INTEGRATION OF E-RESOURCES TROUBLESHOOTING INTO REFERENCE TRAINING

After the success of the workshop, the reference team suggested that we integrate the e-resources troubleshooting training into the reference training. This proved to be a great opportunity to introduce e-resources troubleshooting to all staff working directly with patrons, because the library had recently decided to train all public services staff in reference.

Reference training at Marymount is tailored to the level of support the staff member will be required to provide. Librarians who work at the reference desk receive more intense reference training, while those who work at the circulation desk receive more of an overview. While creating the curriculum, however, we decided that regardless of the level of training, everyone would complete the same e-resources troubleshooting training as a module in the reference training.

Problem	Signs	Possible Cause(s)	Possible Fixes
Patron does not understand the way the resource works	Resource is requesting a login. Login is requested and patron is confused. Layout is confusing (cannot find link on top right of screen, etc.).	Platform has changed. Patron has never logged in off campus before. Patron is not using the library website to access the resources.	Keep up-to-date with changes to platforms. **If problem cannot be solved with standard explanations, contact metadata/ER librarian.**
Broken links	This page does not exist error. Domain does not exist error. Link to incorrect content.	A link has changed or has stopped redirecting—this is especially problematic with freely accessible, open access resources, and links found in catalog records.	Update link resolver (Alma) with correct link. Update catalog records (for individual collections). Update LibGuides links. **Contact metadata/ER librarian.**
Website or host domain has changed and EZproxy needs to be updated.	A message has appeared instructing the user to notify the library to update EZproxy. No off-campus access is available, but on-campus access is working.	A platform has changed. A vendor has updated security protocols (switched from http to https, for example). The access URL has changed. A catalog record is proxied in a LibGuide.	Update EZproxy with the information provided in the message or update the stanza with a new one from the vendor or OCLC website. Remove the prefix from the catalog record URL. **Contact metadata/ER librarian.**
IP address problems	User is forced to login through WRLC while on campus. User is met with a non-WRLC login screen for a resource we should have access to.	Vendor does not have the complete set of IP addresses or has incorrect IP addresses. The University has changed the IP addresses without notifying the library.	Update IP addresses. **Contact metadata/ER librarian.**

Issue	Symptom	Possible cause	Solution
Resource itself is down	Error message is appearing. Database or resource will not load.	Vendor is experiencing an outage. Scheduled maintenance.	Contact vendor (more voices=faster response time). Check listservs and other libraries social media/websites to see if the problem is unique or universal. Wait. **Contact metadata/ER librarian**
Journal access issues: We should have access to X journal from [year] to [year], but an article is inaccessible.	Users are hit with a paywall or asked for a non-WRLC login to access journal content.	The publisher is not providing us with the correct coverage. Our coverage dates in Alma (Journal Finder) do not match our actual subscription. Individual authors are allowed to embargo content for a certain period of time (rare). A journal was dropped from a package and access was not turned off or updated in Alma.	Check EBSCOnet or other order information for correct dates and update in Alma if incorrect. Contact publisher to resolve issue if the problem is on their end. Confirm and turn off access to journal dropped from package. Check journal information and/or with publisher if you suspect content is embargoed by the author. **Contact metadata/ER librarian or serials acquisitions associate).**
Exceeded simultaneous user limit for database	Database is Morningstar or Women's Wear Daily. Users are met with a message saying they have exceeded the number of spots or users on their license . . . or something to that effect.	Too many users. A patron has not logged out after using the resource.	Advise patron to try again later. If teaching the resource, ensure faculty and students know about the user limit. **If problem persists, contact e-resources. Contact liaison librarian for particular resource.**

FIGURE 8.3
E-Resources troubleshooting chart

The training is similar to the initial e-resources troubleshooting session. It includes an overview of e-resource tools, a chart of common e-resource access problems, and several exercises to practice diagnosing a problem and finding resources for the patron in the interim. The chart (figure 8.3) is meant to be a quick reference tool that can be consulted when in conversation with a patron who is experiencing a potential access issue.

There are several exercises the trainee has to complete in the training, and the metadata/electronic resources librarian coordinates with the trainee to go through the exercises together and gives them time to ask any questions. The exercises were chosen based on real-life examples taken from previous e-resource tickets. The trainee is asked what kinds of follow-up questions they may ask the patron to identify the problem, to determine how to help solve the problem, and then give the steps they would take to resolve the problem. The problems include:

1. An EZproxy error screen.
2. A patron is being asked to log in to a resource while on-campus and cannot figure out why they would need to log in.
3. Journal coverage is incorrect in our discovery system, and an embargoed article is coming up as available.
4. A patron is receiving a "link not found" error message when they are trying to access an e-book.

Often, there is more than one correct answer for these problems. For example, in question 2 the IP addresses may be listed incorrectly with the vendor, which is forcing the user to log in to our resource from off-campus. Alternatively, the user may think they need to create an account to access a resource because of a vendor feature, when in fact it is available via IP authentication already. The trainee is encouraged to think of various follow-up questions to ask the patron rather than immediately assume that a problem is as it appears.

The training also asks the trainee to think about alternative ways of providing the patron with access to the resource. For example, if an e-book cannot be accessed from the library discovery system, patrons can be provided with the direct link from the e-book database. Getting public services faculty and staff to provide the resource to the patron gives e-resources staff less anxiety about possible delays when trying to solve the problem. This is especially true if the issue is complex, such as a large-scale bibliographic record update or an issue that requires contacting the vendor.

Thus far, the training has been successful. Faculty and staff have felt more confident helping users troubleshoot access problems, and they provide more detailed feedback when reporting issues.

OUTCOMES

As more public services faculty and staff receive electronic resource trouble-shooting training as part of their reference training, a number of patterns have emerged in their ticket submissions.

Improved Ticket Content

Prior to training, the tickets included minimal information. Generally, submitters included no more than one sentence describing the problem, including simply writing, "cannot access XX database." While this was more useful than no information at all, it was generally not sufficient to solve the problem without substantial follow-up, especially if the problem could not be replicated exactly.

A sampling of tickets from before the initial training session and its subsequent integration into reference training shows that most public services faculty and staff members knew that something was wrong when a patron was having difficulty, but they could not provide details outside of stating what they were seeing. In spite of the prompts of the ticket, the tickets were often unintentionally vague. They might include the title of an e-book, but no indication of how the patron was accessing it. Sometimes they would give the resource as "ProQuest" or "EBSCO" even though we have many databases from these vendors. Occasionally tickets would say, "have not been able to access the database for a few days," with no additional information other than the database name.

Librarians providing reference services were occasionally aware of certain access issues, and sometimes they were able to identify what they thought the problem might be. For example, after our IP addresses were updated, librarians were aware that some vendors might not have been updated, and so they would occasionally include their suspicions that the access issue was related to IP addresses in the problem description.

While these inadequate tickets were better than not reporting the problem at all, they required a substantial amount of follow-up with the ticket submitter. Often, the patron who initially reported the problem also needed to be contacted. This added an additional challenge, because we have found that patrons, particularly students, when provided with the resource they need, do not respond to requests for more information about the problem they experienced.

For example, in a ticket from January 2018, the submitter wrote: "the www.sciencedirect.com link isn't working. I was trying to get the full text article of Threshold concepts and metalearning capacity." As part of the ticketing prompts, the submitter had also included the name of the database (Science

Direct) and wrote that they were accessing it from the library website on-campus. This ticket provided the e-resources team with some useful information, including the name of the article the patron couldn't find, but it was not as useful as it could have been. For instance, the submitter did not describe how the link was not working. Was the full text of the article not available because the link timed out? Was the patron able to access the page and then was met with a paywall? Could the patron get into the database at all? Without this additional information, we needed to follow up with the submitter several times to get to the root of the problem.

Often, when confronted with access issues, the ability to duplicate the problem on the troubleshooter's end is necessary in order to solve it. The more information that is provided by the submitter, the easier it is to duplicate the problem. For the ticket mentioned above, the e-resources team member was unable to fully duplicate the problem. This exchange took three separate updates to resolve, and the problem was likely a cache error in the browser. In another ticket from before we started training, the submitter gave the name of the resource and answered the questions (on or off-campus, etc.), but the only information they gave was "unable to access this database for the last couple of days." This ticket also took three separate messages to sort out. In the end, the faculty member who originally reported the problem never returned our messages for more information, and we were unable to duplicate the error.

These tickets were not intentionally vague. Rather, they represented two issues: a knowledge gap in the ways in which electronic resources can "break," and the types of follow-up questions to ask a patron when confronted with an access problem.

After the training session and integration, the tickets became more robust. Rather than just giving the name of a resource and a quick description of what was wrong, now the tickets also included follow-up questions that the submitters had asked patrons.

More Initial Troubleshooting by Public Services

Prior to the e-resource troubleshooting training for public services faculty and staff, there were relatively few attempts at trying to troubleshoot with the patron outside of ensuring they were accessing the resources through the library website and logging in to the website with the proper credentials. These additions to tickets were very useful, when provided, but they still did not always give the level of detail the e-resources staff needed to solve the problem without substantial follow-up with the ticket submitter and the patron.

After the training, tickets often detailed the steps the faculty or staff member asked the patron to try before submitting the ticket. For instance, now the tickets often say that the patron was asked to try the resource in more than one browser and clear the browser history. The tickets often provide IP address information, and where the patron tried to access the resource—for example, through the library catalog, directly through a database, or from a LibGuide.

Increase in Tickets Submitted

We launched our ticketing system in late 2016, and between the launch and the training session in summer 2017, a total of 28 e-resource tickets were submitted. In the same period after the training, 46 tickets were submitted. While an increase in submitted tickets may not seem like a positive outcome for e-resource troubleshooting training, we were thrilled because it meant the training had accomplished its main goal: raising awareness of e-resource access issues among public services faculty and staff.

Staff who may have been hesitant to submit a ticket in the past became more likely to submit issues. This means a faster turnaround from the time a problem is discovered to when it is reported and ultimately resolved. Before the training, occasionally problems persisted because staff were unclear if an access issue they encountered was a problem that should be reported, a user error, or something that would resolve itself. After the training, staff were better able to identify problems, troubleshoot directly with the patron, and feel confident that their concerns were worth reporting to the e-resources team.

Anecdotally, public services faculty and staff have indicated that they are grateful for the new knowledge and understanding of the functions of electronic resources. Librarians who work the reference desk appreciate having the tools they need to solve many patron-access issues without having to ask e-resources staff for help. They are also pleased that the tickets they do submit are resolved more quickly with less follow-up.

Changes in Overall Resolution Time

There has been a notable reduction in the amount of time it takes e-resources staff to solve e-resource tickets overall. This change can largely be attributed to the results of the training because tickets are more detailed. More detailed tickets lead to fewer follow-ups with faculty, staff, and patrons because the problem can be identified and resolved more quickly. Before training began, the tickets in our ticketing system needed an average of two updates before being resolved. After training, the average ticket took only one update.

In addition to a reduction in the number of follow-ups, the actual time it takes to close a ticket decreased. When we launched the ticketing system, many tickets took over two days to resolve. After the training, most tickets can be resolved on the day they are submitted, with the exception of more complex access issues where communication with vendors may be needed.

CHALLENGES AND NEXT STEPS

The process of training public services staff to understand and troubleshoot electronic resource problems has been smooth overall, but it has come with some challenges. For one, not all staff have completed the e-resources troubleshooting workshop. When the process was integrated into the library's reference training, we had just begun instructing all public services staff in basic reference, including all circulation staff. As a result, circulation staff and librarians hired after the e-resources troubleshooting integration received the training, but librarians who had been working the reference desk for many years did not. Additionally, some librarians never attended the initial session, which was optional. This has left a knowledge gap among some librarians that has yet to be filled.

Our library's switch to Ex Libris's Alma and Primo VE in July 2018 added an additional layer of complexity to e-resources troubleshooting. After a year of training faculty and staff in our old tools, the training needed to be revised to reflect the switch to the new platforms. Additionally, e-resources staff were still learning those new platforms, and it was often difficult to tell if the problem was a result of the system switchover or a problem with the resource itself. We temporarily implemented a second ticketing system to report problems within Primo VE and Alma, and we would transfer tickets over to the appropriate ticket list if they had originally been submitted to the wrong one. About a year later, after the library had adjusted to using the new platforms, we resumed using the e-resources troubleshooting ticketing system for reporting all access issues.

Our initial and continuing success with training public services faculty and staff in e-resources troubleshooting is encouraging. Integrating the troubleshooting training into the reference training ensures that new public services faculty and staff will be trained in identifying and reporting e-resource problems. In addition to training those new to the library, we are also trying to find ways to reinforce and remind those who either did not receive formal training or received it early on of ways to identify e-resource issues.

As a way of bridging the knowledge gap, the metadata/electronic resources librarian has tried bringing tips and tricks to bimonthly librarian meetings, often with a relevant and recent example of a successful or less-successful ticket. We also hope to do a refresher workshop each summer now that most public services faculty and staff have received the initial training. With reminders and reinforcement, we believe we can continue to improve the communication between public services and technical services in a way that will serve our community well.

REFERENCES

Callas, Jennie E., et al. "Transforming Public Services with Technical Services Knowledge." Presented at the ACRL Annual Conference, Baltimore, MD, March 2017.

Carter, Sunshine, and Stacie Traill. "Essential Skills and Knowledge for Troubleshooting E-Resources Access Issues in a Web Scale Discovery Environment." *Journal of Electronic Resources Librarianship* 29, no. 1 (2017). doi:10.1080/1941126X.2017.1270096.

Smith, Kelly. "Managing Electronic Resource Workflows Using Ticketing System Software." *Serials Review* 42, no. 1 (2016): 59–64. doi:10.1080/00987913.2015 .1137674.

Sutton, Sarah, et al. "NASIG Core Competencies for Electronic Resources Librarians." NASIG, January 2, 2019. www.nasig.org/Competencies-Eresources.

NOTES

1. Kelly Smith, "Managing Electronic Resource Workflows Using Ticketing System Software," *Serials Review* 42, no. 1 (2016): 59–64, doi:10.1080/00987913.201 5.1137674.

2. Sunshine Carter and Stacie Traill, "Essential Skills and Knowledge for Troubleshooting E-Resources Access Issues in a Web Scale Discovery Environment," *Journal of Electronic Resources Librarianship* 29, no. 1 (2017), doi:10.1080/1941126X.2017.1270096.

3. Jennie E. Callas et al., "Transforming Public Services with Technical Services Knowledge" (conference presentation, ACRL Annual Conference, Baltimore, MD, March 2017).

4. Callas et al., "Transforming Public Services."

5. Sarah Sutton et al., "NASIG Core Competencies for Electronic Resources Librarians," NASIG, January 2, 2019, www.nasig.org/Competencies -Eresources.

JENNIFER A. MEZICK AND
ELYSSA M. GOULD

9

Investigating Communication Breakdown between Technical Services Departments and Subject Librarians

"What do they spend all their time doing over there?" "Why are they not accomplishing this task with as much urgency as I feel it is due?" These are questions asked in every industry and in businesses big and small. Libraries are not exempt from these questions. Divided into departments or units by the unique services provided, library employees are often siloed by their responsibilities and physical location. Additionally, much of our work is learned on the job, with little cross-training among departments and with processes and procedures varying greatly at each unique institution. Completed work may be visible to those outside the department or unit, but employees outside the unit often have little concept of how tasks are carried out and what is involved in the behind-the-scenes work. This can lead to misunderstandings, miscommunications, and frustrations among employees across the library.

This chapter focuses on the communication about collection development tasks that goes on between technical services departments and subject librarians. It details an initiative to understand why and when miscommunication happens and what can be done to help the two areas work together more effectively, despite their physical distance in the workplace and their often vastly different job responsibilities and career experiences. The resulting takeaway is that training and consistency in communication is an important factor in rebuilding the trust that is essential for successful interdepartmental communication. Improved communication also allows a path for technical services departments to tell their stories.

BACKGROUND

The University of Tennessee, Knoxville (UT) is the flagship campus of the University of Tennessee system. In the Fall 2019 semester, 29,490 students were enrolled there in approximately 900 academic programs. The University of Tennessee Libraries (UT Libraries) comprises one main library and two branch libraries for Music and Agricultural & Veterinary Science. The UT Libraries employ approximately 150 staff and faculty librarians, divided into twenty departments. Four of these departments make up the traditional "technical services" areas: Acquisitions & Continuing Resources (ACR), Assessment Programs & Collection Strategy (APCS), Cataloging & Metadata, and Enterprise Systems. Together these departments employ thirty staff and faculty, with four serving as tenure-track faculty librarians.

The Fall 2018 semester brought many changes to the UT Libraries. A long-serving associate dean retired, and her responsibilities were divided among the two remaining associate deans. Numerous other staff and faculty had retired prior to this, necessitating a reorganization of departments, responsibilities, and workflows. The ensuing reorganization affected approximately one-third of the UT Libraries' employees.

To aid the two remaining associate deans, four new departments and six new middle-management positions were created to shift the management and supervisory load. The Learning, Research & Engagement Department was reimagined as three departments, the largest being Liaison Programs. Individuals from other dissolved departments were moved to new positions within Liaison Programs. This department now houses subject librarians; that is, individuals who have subject-specific knowledge, instruction and engagement responsibilities with specific teaching departments on campus, and collection development responsibilities.

There were other more significant shifts related to collection development and assessment. Research Collections joined with Assessment Programs to create APCS and extend a data-driven approach to collection development. In addition, the UT Libraries' Business Services Office assumed responsibility for the collections budget, which had previously been distributed among individual subject librarians and collections staff. This office coordinates with financial offices across campus, but serves only UT Libraries.

As can be imagined, these changes created some chaos, a bit of anxiety, and a few misunderstandings, as well as a much-needed opportunity for change. Four new departments and six new managers were navigating new roles and responsibilities. Gaps were left by individuals who had moved into new roles, old responsibilities were left vacant or temporarily performed by others while positions were waiting to be filled, and new hires accidentally stepped on toes as they acclimated to their new responsibilities. All of these feelings were understandable (and probably unavoidable), but it had the unfortunate side effect of creating new hurdles as UT Libraries settled into the new normal. A large hurdle emerged between the traditional technical services departments and the Liaison Programs Department, which are areas that work together daily in a collaborative approach to develop and maintain our collections. While the majority of our subject librarians are part of the Liaison Programs Department, other librarians with subject area responsibilities are scattered among other departments. Throughout this chapter we use the phrase "subject librarian" to refer to all librarians with subject collection responsibilities.

FOCUS GROUPS AND FOLLOW-UP SURVEY

In the summer of 2019, we (as the head of ACR and the collection strategist from APCS) decided to address some of the communication issues experienced between subject librarians and the technical services areas. Not knowing where to start or what questions to ask, we conducted focus groups to have guided but open conversations among subject librarians. These focus groups would allow us to listen and learn about the needs, desires, and feelings of our colleagues who were fulfilling subject librarian responsibilities.

The first step was to apply to conduct research through the UT's institutional review board (IRB). After IRB approval, we sent individual e-mail invitations asking subject librarians to participate in our focus groups. Sixteen out of twenty-four subject librarians volunteered to participate. We grouped the participants based on perceived similar experiences in order to have more focused conversations that would inform our perspectives and understanding. Those groups were arranged as follows: subject librarians who have extensive collection development experience through decades of librarianship; subject librarians who are newer to librarianship and collection development; subject librarians who have significant librarianship experience, but perhaps not as much collection development experience as those in the first group; and subject librarians whose primary responsibilities are outside Liaison Programs but are assigned as a subject librarian to one or more academic departments.

The questions we asked were intentionally broad because this was an exercise in gathering information:

1. What does collection development mean to you?
2. How do you go about developing and managing your collections?
3. In your experience with the acquisitions process here at UT Libraries, what do you like about the process and what do you not like about it?
4. How confident do you feel with collection development?
5. In a perfect world, how involved would you be with collection development?
6. When it comes to communication related to collection development and acquisitions (information about submitting orders, the status of orders, the status of our budget, vendor visits, etc.), what is going well and what is not?
7. Is there anything else you would like to share about this topic?

After the focus groups, we anonymized the notes and uploaded them to NVivo, a software for analyzing qualitative data. This helped produce our findings and takeaways by allowing us to tag discussions and view those discussions in an organized and analytical way. In our analysis, we tagged, or labeled, statements from the notes as they related to recurrent topics discussed, such as the acquisitions process, time management, selection, and anticipating patron needs. Certain themes emerged after several readings of the notes when organized by topic. The overarching themes that emerged from the NVivo analysis were training and processes, communication, and collection development, as illustrated in figure 9.1. Training and processes and related

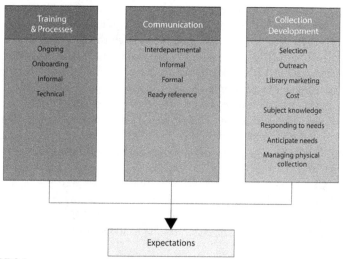

FIGURE 9.1
Diagram showing themes with sub-themes that came out of focus group discussions. Only training and processes and communication are discussed in this chapter.

sub-themes, as well as communication and its related sub-themes, are discussed in some detail in later sections of this chapter.

The need for shared expectations emerged as the major underlying theme and an important takeaway from our research. Shared expectations in this context refer to a common understanding of each department's workflows and activities. Expectations were not specifically discussed in any focus group, but they were clearly a missing element that was expressed through sentiments, such as a reference to collections as a "black box," and general uncertainty or lack of confidence in the skills and activities related to collection development. For example, the focus groups revealed that subject librarians don't often know who to ask questions of or what roles technical services staff now perform. The reorganization likely contributed to a lack of expectations when many roles and responsibilities for collection development changed and new expectations were not formally established. This appears to have greatly contributed to a lack of communication between different areas of the library. Expectations are repeatedly discussed in the sections that follow because we believe that establishing expectations directly affects the success of the activities discussed.

In spring 2020, we followed up the focus group research with an online survey. The survey was created using QuestionPro and was sent to all librarians with subject responsibilities for collection management, regardless of their participation in the focus groups. Eleven librarians completed the survey of thirteen questions (see Appendix A at the end of this book). Each question was informed by the focus group findings and was meant to help ACR and APCS clarify their discussions and prioritize their efforts for planning training and communication activities. Based on the focus group discussions and survey results, we identified several actions that might help establish expectations and mend broken communication. These actions are described in the sections below.

PROCESSES AND TRAINING

Many of the focus group discussions tagged using NVivo could be grouped under technical services processes. Technical services workflows and acquisition processes can be complicated and are constantly evolving due to changes in acquisition methods, university requirements, and technical systems. We concluded that many subject librarians lack a contextual understanding of most technical services processes, as most of them have never worked in library technical services areas or had an opportunity to learn about those processes. We also found that most subject librarians have little understanding of what is expected of them at any moment related to technical services processes, as well as what to expect of technical services staff. This lack of understanding was feeding subject librarians' confusion and communication errors. Subject librarians don't need to be experts in the technical services areas or know what goes into every step of technical processes and workflows, but having an idea of how these processes unfold and their role in the processes can help establish expectations. Acquiring this contextual knowledge may also help subject librarians feel more confident in completing procedural tasks, and better understand their responsibilities related to these tasks. To accomplish this, we felt that some form of training was needed to provide a foundational-level of understanding. Furthermore, the training could help manage expectations by establishing what subject librarians need and can expect from technical services departments, as well as what technical services departments need and can expect from subject librarians. Creating this framework might positively influence successful communication between these areas.

We define *training* from Robertson's 2018 article on human resources literature as something that is "short-term in its focus and is provided when employees need specific knowledge, skills, and attitudes to perform their jobs successfully."[1] This is in contrast to "staff development," which is "long-term in focus" and is more appropriate for building collection development skills related to theory and critical thinking.

Informal training was discussed by the focus group participants as exchanges between peers and as the preferred method of training, despite its inconsistent nature. The advantage is that it happens at the point of need. The disadvantage is that it can be difficult to physically access a peer in our current environment. Subject librarians who were employed at UT Libraries ten years ago fondly remember shouting out questions in their cubicle-filled office area and receiving a response from a handful of people. Unfortunately, that is not the case today. Subject librarians were displaced from their office area for a little over a year while renovations transformed the space into rows of chic offices with bright white walls and sliding glass doors. The displaced librarians became accustomed to working remotely during that period of time. Also, their roles continue to change in a way that increasingly keeps them out of the library and in front of faculty and students. The reorganization, retirements, and new hires may have further contributed to a change in camaraderie. Nowadays, the Liaison Programs office area is silent and lacks the informal sharing of information that previously occurred. Adding to this is two floors of distance between the liaison and technical services office areas and the physical separation of subject librarians who are located in different departments or branch libraries.

Considering these factors, we wondered if a librarian or staff member from one of our technical services departments would be a better informal contact for most collections advice because they have the most up-to-date knowledge of processes, procedures, and acquisition trends, and they interact with ordering processes and vendors on a daily basis. This may be truer at the UT Libraries than at other institutions because APCS is grouped with technical services departments rather than with subject librarians. Also, allowing different technical services staff the time to provide training throughout the year, informally or formally, might help establish relationships between those staff and subject librarians. Since subject librarians often have a difficult time knowing who to ask for help and many have never met the acquisitions staff member in-person who they communicate with regularly through e-mail, allowing a face-to-face connection through training could help establish relationships. This might be particularly useful in a large organization like the UT Libraries where there are thirty people working in the technical services departments.

Despite their expressed preference for informal training, the focus groups also uncovered a strong desire for onboarding training, with suggestions for incorporating a scaffolding type of learning so as to introduce procedures and tools over the course of a subject librarian's first year. Accordingly, we have been experimenting with a formal onboarding process that allows new subject librarians to meet with collections and acquisitions staff and faculty. This gives them a general context for collection development procedures, tools, and processes, as well as knowledge of who is responsible for different parts of the acquisitions cycle. The onboarding also gives technical services staff and faculty an opportunity to become familiar with the new librarian and their experience with collection development, and to identify and plan the next steps for training based on the experience of the new librarian. Though we are still testing and improving onboarding, we have found it so successful in establishing good communication that we now also provide an altered version for new librarians who don't have any subject librarian responsibilities.

Ongoing training opportunities were discussed by the focus group participants as a way to provide refreshers for uncommon tasks, as well as updates to procedures and workflows as they change. The focus group discussions about technical training mostly involved the systems used for collection development at UT Libraries, such as Alma and GOBI. This technical training could be best fulfilled with both a formal onboarding process and ongoing training. Of note in these discussions was the expressed need for terminology training. Libraries have a particular jargon that varies at each institution. It can take some time to learn the meaning of words used in technical services departments, even for librarians who come to the UT Libraries with an understanding of processes from another institution. Some terms have lost context over decades of time but linger as the commonly understood terminology among staff. Technical services departments began hosting an annual fiscal year kick-off meeting in 2017 that provides an opportunity to highlight major changes to acquisitions procedures and workflows. The follow-up survey showed that subject librarians find this meeting very useful. We hope to provide this type of ongoing training more often in the future and are currently developing outlines for topics to start a full training program. We also believe that some sessions we have provided to new librarians can be open to all subject librarians to attend, such as a popular session on using Alma Analytics.

As we work towards developing a full training program, sustainability and responding to the needs expressed in the focus group discussions are in the forefront of our minds. One important consideration is lack of time. In planning we want to be mindful that everyone is spread thin. Keeping sessions as short and to-the-point as possible by focusing on specific topics in ongoing training sessions and scaffolding onboarding sessions will help to maximize time. We can also incorporate remote sessions that can be recorded so subject librarians who are unable to attend in person can view sessions later or as a refresher when the information is needed. Point of need was discussed in focus groups as the preferred training method by some subject librarians. Those subject librarians would also like to see the recorded sessions in one central location to avoid digging through e-mails.

In addition to imparting the knowledge needed to carry out tasks, we think that a formalized training program can bring shared understanding and respect by establishing expectations and relationships across departments. Establishing relationships may also provide increased comfort in communications, which can have a positive effect overall. Anecdotally, we currently experience better communication with those subject librarians with whom we have established relationships through formal and informal interactions. Informal feedback from our current efforts around training shows that we are on the right path to improving subject librarians' expectations and understanding, but we still have a way to go.

CONSISTENCY IN COMMUNICATION

Mohammed M. Aman observes that "library work relies on human interaction as it is a people-oriented profession. The ability of the librarian to communicate with fellow workers and the general public is of utmost importance."[2] We anecdotally found that good communication is at the root of many successful interactions in the library, including training. Training contributes to good communication by establishing shared expectations and processes, as described in the section above. Technical services workflows are especially dependent on good communication and training to successfully complete the process of acquiring, cataloging, and making available materials for research and learning. Adding other departments into the workflow, such as subject librarians who make the purchasing recommendations, makes clear and consistent communication all the more important.

Aman goes on to summarize research that describes two types of communication: formal and informal. Formal communication is written, whether in policies, procedures, or e-mails.[3] Informal communication is spoken, whether in meetings, training sessions, or hallway conversations. This classification does not include all twenty-first-century communication, such as more casual communications through texting or Slack messages, but it does cover a large part of communication within the UT Libraries' workplace. Our culture is very e-mail-heavy, where formal communication can be time-consuming to write and read, as well as easy to misunderstand if shared understandings don't exist between the message-sender and message-recipient. Informal communication also occurs frequently at UT through in-person meetings, where information may be shared but is not recorded, and therefore is easy to forget.

Good communication, whether formal or informal, is key for organizational effectiveness. The time period around the UT Libraries' reorganization was marked by limited formal communication and increased informal communication in the form of grapevines. Grapevines are the spoken conversations through which information, either faulty or legitimate, can travel.[4] The reorganization prompted significant changes to positions and departments, which were understandably disruptive to existing workflows. As individuals struggled to adapt to new tasks and increased workloads, formal communication was used less often. Unfortunately, a side effect of these trends was a loss of trust. Increased misunderstandings occurred between departments, workflows did not run smoothly, and authority was questioned.

In an effort to regain trust and bring some consistency to our library-wide communications, the four technical services departments implemented a regular "Collections Updates" e-mail in 2019 (an example is available in Appendix B). Three adjacent departments were also invited to contribute. The draft e-mail lives in a shared SharePoint document where key individuals from the departments can input information as it is relevant. The most common entries are related to newly acquired collections, changes in our existing online resource platforms, MARC record information, trials for potential online resources, and a collections budget update. Every other week, a designated person reviews the content and sends an e-mail to the all-staff discussion list. If there are limited updates, the e-mail is sent only once a month. The focus group discussions indicated that these update e-mails were quite useful. The follow-up survey found that 72 percent of the respondents found these e-mails to be very helpful, while only 9 percent of respondents reported that they didn't read the updates at all. However, the problem with sending e-mails is that they are very easy to lose within an e-mail in-box, and they also contribute to our organization's e-mail overload.

The focus group study also revealed that subject librarians desired a "ready reference" tool—something they could refer to that had current procedures for ordering various kinds of materials, reminders about the pros and cons of various e-book platforms, a list of who to contact in the technical services departments, and more. Most of this information was already kept on an internal LibGuide for subject librarians, known as the "Liaison LibGuide." However, the focus group discussions revealed that many subject librarians did not know that this guide existed. A coordinated effort occurred between the Liaison Programs and APCS staff in Spring 2020 to revamp this LibGuide and provide more direct, detailed information on collections workflows and procedures in a way that subject librarians can use to quickly locate an answer.[5] The information was streamlined for readability, verified by all relevant departments, and was made live in April 2020.

The focus groups also revealed or highlighted a number of known barriers to communication within the UT Libraries: the size of the library, the nature of outreach and engagement responsibilities, e-mail overload, the use of jargon, and an absent shared foundation. Some of these barriers are out of the control of technical services, as nothing can be done about the size of the library or the nature of librarians' responsibilities. However, we can consider the last three barriers as we work to improve internal communications. With the revised Liaison LibGuide, we hope to provide a static location for basic information that can help subject librarians perform their collection development tasks. Research also shows that consistency is key, so while the Collections Updates e-mails remain e-mails, they arrive in an expected format and on a relatively regular schedule. Future areas of improvement in consistency and communication will include:

- APCS and ACR staff regularly attending subject librarian meetings to share news and updates
- Working with the Liaison Programs Department head to solidify subject librarians' responsibilities for collection development as a way to establish formal expectations, which will in turn assist communication efforts
- Sending consistent updates to subject librarians about purchase requests in progress
- Continuing timely communication with all relevant parties about any changes in technical services' processes and workflows

Communicating that we share the same patron-centered goals has helped us have conversations that increased our shared understanding. By creating resources where the technical services departments can share information together, such as the Collections Updates e-mails and the Liaison LibGuide, we demonstrated a shared understanding among the four technical services departments. Proactively sending the Collections Updates e-mails on a regular basis shows transparency and consistency in our activities and has continued to build trust with the subject librarians. It is rare that a month goes by without the e-mail sender receiving a "thank you" e-mail from a subject librarian.

Training that is offered on a predictable schedule (e.g., an orientation when a librarian attains subject collection duties) also builds trust.

We hope that the regularly shared information from technical services departments will lead to an increased and steady flow of information from the UT Libraries to those we serve. Regularly sharing information about our activities allows us to demonstrate the hidden value provided by technical services staff in upholding the best cataloging standards, facilitating discovery and access, and helping users to solve access issues. In technical services departments, we are not often in the position of demonstrating the library's value directly to faculty members, so we have to count on subject librarians to do it, and they can better do that if they feel more confident and are more informed about technical services processes and activities. Consistent communication about these activities may help subject librarians feel more confident when speaking with faculty about certain topics, such as acquisition timelines, instead of being completely unfamiliar and feeling out of context. A better understanding of technical services roles and impacts may also assist our subject librarians in providing more support for the UT Libraries as a whole.

CONCLUSION

The focus groups and follow-up survey were eye-opening and instrumental in our data-driven approach to improving interdepartmental communication between the technical services departments and the Liaison Programs Department at UT Libraries throughout 2019 and 2020. Once the chaos of the Fall 2018 reorganization died down and individuals had settled into their new roles, the communication gaps were obvious. By coalescing around collection development processes, we were able to create buy-in around one area where we all have strong beliefs: getting the best materials for our faculty, staff, and students' research, teaching, and learning needs. The focus group study and follow-up survey sought to identify a shared foundation of collection development expectations at the UT Libraries, which we hope will develop into a shared foundation for all communication about collection development. We are hopeful that the small steps taken in 2019–2020 and the areas identified for future improvement will reestablish the trust between the technical services departments and subject librarians that was broken during the reorganization. After we have addressed all of the areas for improvement, we will develop assessments to verify if these actions have achieved the desired outcomes of successful communication, shared foundational knowledge, and widely understood expectations.

In the end, by seeking to improve interdepartmental communications between technical services departments and subject librarians, we are intrinsically illustrating our story. When the context of what we do and what others do is widely understood, successful outcomes are produced for the whole organization. We are better able to communicate internally because we have a fuller understanding of those with whom we communicate and how they receive the information we are providing. Our mutually understood expectations and vocabulary reduce miscommunication, and contextual learning opportunities cultivate shared understanding across departments. When we deliver information to those with whom we communicate in a way that is easy for them to receive it, communication will be more successful.

NOTES

1. Sabina Rovertson, "Exploring the Efficacy of Training and Development for Liaison Librarians at Deakin University, Australia," *Journal of Higher Education Policy and Management* 40, no. 2 (2018): 107–20, doi:10.1080/13600 80X.2018.1426370.

2. Mohammed M. Aman, *Academic Library Management Issues and Practices* (Mequon, WI: Global Information Company, 2010), 84, https://dc.uwm.edu/sois_facbooks/1.

3. Aman, *Academic Library Management Issues and Practices*, 84.

4. "5 Challenges of Grapevine Communication [and 5 Solutions]," Status.net, https://status.net/articles/grapevine-communication.

5. University of Tennessee, Knoxville, "Collections Ready Reference," University Libraries, https://libguides.utk.edu/CDM_ReadyReference.

PART III

COMMUNICATION OUTSIDE THE LIBRARY

ANNA SEIFFERT

10
Collections as a Campus Conversation

The Colorado School of Mines' Approach
to Collection Development

A t the Colorado School of Mines, a familiar tale has been playing out. The library's collection budget was falling hopelessly behind the skyrocketing pace of journal costs, and instead of collection building, it was merely maintaining. The administration, from the library's perspective, seemed to be turning a cold shoulder to funding requests; and the faculty, tired of hearing "no" to their requests for new journal subscriptions, had simply stopped communicating their needs to the library. The Colorado School of Mines is certainly not alone in needing to bridge this communication barrier surrounding the library's materials budget and its understanding across campus, especially at the administration level. This lack of understanding and accompanying dialogue can lead to frustration, and can even become a hindrance to the library's mission to support instruction and research. Research has shown that, no matter how the current crisis in materials costs is resolved, libraries will continue to need to find ways of making compelling arguments for budget increases.[1] This chapter will show how the Arthur Lakes Library was able to break free from a cycle of collection stagnation, which had been perpetrated by a lack of effective communication. The result was that the library was able to tell a story with data in order to communicate a message, as well as strengthen its partnerships with faculty regarding collection management.

BACKGROUND

The Colorado School of Mines (more commonly known as Mines) is a public university focused on science and engineering, dedicated to pioneering research that addresses the significant challenges society faces today—particularly as they relate to the Earth, energy, and the environment—and is committed to educating students who will do the same. Located in Golden, Colorado, Mines has a current enrollment of just under 6,000 full-time equivalents (FTEs). The Arthur Lakes Library supports the campus and has thirteen academic faculty and nine administrative faculty and staff members. The library has two librarians who focus on outreach; however, there is no formal liaison program. The library has an annual materials budget of $2 million, with 92 percent of it allocated for subscription-based resources. The addition of new academic programs over the years has not come with monies earmarked for spending on library resources. Overall, the library materials budget has increased at an average annual rate of 3.6 percent over the past decade. For perspective, there has been a 6 percent average price increase for serials since 2012.[2]

The library's collection budget was not keeping pace with rising journal costs, and instead of collection building, it was maintaining at best. The faculty, frustrated with the lack of positive action from the library, had simply stopped communicating their needs to librarians, and the administration was not responding to annual budget request submissions with meaningful dialogue. The library needed to reset the information flow with faculty and with the administration, and the first step in that process was to find out the history of this situation.

GAINING A HISTORICAL PERSPECTIVE

The first analysis looked at the history of collection management and assessment within the library. The Arthur Lakes Library owned 858,000 books and maintained 169,000 journals and 141 database subscriptions at the beginning of the 2016–2017 academic year. The library participates in a regional consortial sharing project that allows for quick access to 13 million titles.[3] Most print books were acquired via a robust print-preferred approval plan, as well as firm order requests that were honored as funds allowed. The journal subscriptions were mainly legacy and were primarily the direct result of individual faculty requests. The database subscriptions were also long-standing and were a mix of consortial and direct from the vendor. Almost all subscriptions were handled by a subscription agent and were all auto-renewed; these subscriptions have gradually impinged on the one-time budget items, until they reached 92 percent of the budget in 2016.

With regard to faculty interactions, previously, the library had inadvertently been putting the pressure of collection development decisions onto faculty, by requesting that an equal cancellation accompany any new subscription requests. This policy was perceived as an acceptable solution to the cost of supporting new acquisitions during years of flat budgets. The aim was to involve faculty members in dialogue about high-need resources and collaborate on nonessential items that could be canceled. However good these intentions were, the reality was that the faculty did not have enough information to make these decisions, and so they eventually became frustrated and stopped communicating their needs to the library. Petitions for new undergraduate and graduate courses include a line item asking if any new library resources are needed to support the course. Faculty members, being cognizant of the fact that there weren't any funds for new library resources, always answered this question with a resounding no. There was a fear that admitting that resources were needed would hinder the approval process, and because the faculty were not speaking up, the library had little ability to justify its new funding requests.

When communicating its annual budget requests to the administration, the library had been using general inflation index reports, such as EBSCO's annual serials price projection report,[4] as a justification, with only mixed success. The library's requests for new funds were tied to the growth in research and instructional programs on campus, but its requests were, for the most part, denied. In early 2017, the administration instead requested the library to justify its current subscriptions as well as all historical cancellations at the title level, and provide granular cost-per-use data in order to substantiate the annual materials budget request. While the library appreciated the thinking behind the request, in its attempt to contextualize and gain insight into annual budget requests, the library did not believe that the type of data requested was appropriate or ultimately informative for the administration. The library felt that this data, which had never been systematically tracked before, was useful, but that it was more appropriate for internal library use, with higher-level results passed on to the administration. The library politely declined to provide that level of granular data to the administration, and the result was only a 4 percent increase to the materials budget instead of the 7 percent increase that had been requested to cover inflation (6 percent based on EBSCO) and to provide additional funds to grow the collection (1 percent). This incident was a primary driver for modifying our local practices.

FOUNDATIONAL DATA AND COLLECTION DEVELOPMENT

Based on the historical analysis recounted here, it was decided that collection decisions, both additions and cancellations, needed to be reframed with data. The library wanted data to be the foundation of its collection and budget decisions and thought it prudent to inform not only itself but the faculty about its overall budget, materials allocation, holdings, usage, and the subscription publishing landscape. We started by first compiling and summarizing ten years of historical data for the materials budget (table 10.1).

TABLE 10.1

The Arthur Lakes Library's historical materials budget

Fiscal Year	Budget	$ Increase	% Increase
2008	$1,250,000		
2009	$1,250,000	$ -	0
2010	$1,250,000	$ -	0
2011	$1,250,000	$ -	0
2012	$1,312,500	$62,500	5
2013	$1,351,875	$39,375	3
2014	$1,426,875	$75,000	5.55
2015	$1,486,875	$60,000	4.2
2016	$1,548,292	$61,417	4.13
2017	$1,700,423	$152,131	9.83
2018	$1,770,990	$70,567	4.15
	10 year average	$52,099	3.58%

This analysis was compared to the actual inflation rate in journal prices during a five-year period (table 10.2), and we observed that the average projected inflation range over ten years had been 5.5–7.5 percent annually, with a 6.5 percent average overall.

TABLE 10.2

EBSCO five-year journal price increase history (2015–2019)

Five Year Journal Price Increase History (2015 - 2019)														
This report shows price fluctuations over the last five years for typical library lists invoiced in U.S. dollars. Data for each library type is based on a merged list of titles ordered by representative libraries purchasing in U.S. dollars.														
			2015	2016		2017		2018		2019		%		
Library Type	% of Total Titles	% of Total Expenditure	Avg. Title Price	Avg. Title Price	% Increase	Avg. Title Price	% Increase	Avg. Title Price	% Increase	Avg. Title Price	% Increase	Increase 15-19		
ARL														
US Titles	38.0%	31.8%	$1,065.33	$1,126.88	5.78%	$1,186.74	5.31%	$1,257.90	6.00%	$1,328.75	5.63%	24.73%		
Non-US Titles	62.0%	68.2%	$1,390.41	$1,466.10	5.44%	$1,545.96	5.45%	$1,625.87	5.17%	$1,721.77	5.90%	23.83%		
Total Titles	100.0%	100.0%	$1,269.61	$1,340.05	5.55%	$1,412.48	5.41%	$1,489.13	5.43%	$1,575.72	5.81%	24.11%		
College & University														
US Titles	37.5%	32.2%	$1,167.01	$1,235.80	5.89%	$1,300.53	5.24%	$1,382.28	6.29%	$1,460.81	5.68%	25.18%		
Non-US Titles	62.5%	67.8%	$1,436.98	$1,516.39	5.53%	$1,598.02	5.38%	$1,678.30	5.02%	$1,777.03	5.88%	23.66%		
Total Titles	100.0%	100.0%	$1,340.68	$1,416.31	5.64%	$1,491.90	5.34%	$1,572.70	5.42%	$1,664.23	5.82%	24.13%		

Next, we looked at the library's overall materials budget as compared to peer institutions with regard to their historical materials budget increases, and with a spending breakdown per student (table 10.3).

TABLE 10.3

Comparative 2016–2017 materials budget data for Mines' peer institutions according to Integrated Postsecondary Education Data System (IPEDS)

Institution Name	FTE	Total	Per Student
California Institute of Technology	2,240	$3,272,525	$1,461
Massachusetts Institute of Technology	11,247	$11,390,802	$1,013
New Mexico Institute of Mining and Technology	1,805	$1,180,000	$654
Michigan Technological University	6,666	$3,024,338	$454
Worcester Polytechnic Institute	6,136	$2,612,410	$426
Rensselaer Polytechnic Institute	7,747	$2,496,880	$322
Georgia Institute of Technology-Main Campus	26,625	$8,241,935	$310
Colorado School of Mines	**5,897**	**$1,709,502**	**$290**
Missouri University of Science and Technology	7,383	$1,576,394	$213
South Dakota School of Mines and Technology	2,475	$442,360	$179
New Jersey Institute of Technology	9,123	$1,462,494	$160

We wanted to know where we stood compared to current and aspirational peer institutions. It was essential to create a baseline of knowledge based on quantitative instead of qualitative data. The result of the analysis was that if the Arthur Lakes Library's materials budget had increased by 6.5 percent annually over the past ten years, its 2018 materials budget would be $2,170,113 ($399,123 or 22.5 percent higher), an amount that would have enabled Mines to be on a par with its peers.

The next data points to be collected and evaluated were usage statistics for subscriptions, as they represented the majority of the materials budget. Instead of automatic renewals, every subscription was evaluated for renewal based on its support of the current academic curriculum or faculty research, the strength of the existing collection in the resources' subject area, the current or projected future use of library resources in that discipline, and the cost of the subscription. The need for multiple formats, such as print and online, was evaluated as well. A sustainable threshold was set for annual inflation increases in journal prices, and negotiations were initiated with vendors when that threshold was crossed. In order to meet the inflation threshold, multiyear agreements, consortium deals, and other tactics were utilized. Simply changing how purchases were made and actively involving library faculty members with renewals created substantial savings.

The resulting data provided a clear picture that enabled us to see patterns in usage. We were able to identify low-use resources, which were then evaluated by library faculty to provide context and qualitative information that gave us a complete picture of each resource. For example, was this a resource that should be retained despite low usage because it was critical for a small department? Cancellations of low-use items were made for the academic year 2018–2019 and were based on the following considerations:

- The resource's support of the present academic curriculum or faculty research (specific or interdisciplinary)
- The strength of the existing collection in the resource's subject area
- The existing or projected future use of library resources in that discipline
- The cost of the resource's subscription

The resulting savings more than covered inflation, and hence many new subscriptions and purchases were able to be made. These additions were based on historical feedback from faculty collated onto a "wish list" spreadsheet, under-supported program growth, high turnaways (as calculated by vendor-provided usage statistics reports), and interlibrary loan data on titles that had reached copyright limits.

ANNUAL BUDGET REQUESTS

We took the time to view with a critical eye our communication strategies with the administration. In years past, there had been no dialogue between the administration and the library. The annual budget cycle began with an e-mail early in the spring semester from the administration requesting that the library submit its annual materials budget request. This e-mail was an open request with no detailed instructions or criteria. In response, the library would put together a memo requesting an inflationary amount citing the EBSCO projections report, and would list new resources and their approximate cost for funding approval in the new fiscal year. Months later, the library would be informed of its final budget allocation. There were no clarifying questions asked in the interim, nor was any rationale provided in explanation of the resulting allocation. The library's annual budget requests did not roll over, and so any historical request information was not captured by the administration.

With a fresh outlook and understanding, our new goal was to provide contextual, relevant, and accurate information to back up our materials budget request. The information was chosen to provide a holistic picture of the factors affecting the library's materials collection budget. We realized that we should not assume that the administration would understand the library materials landscape, especially with regard to serials inflation. The library's revised response to the annual budget request in early 2018 was to provide a detailed Excel spreadsheet as documentation for its inflationary request for the materials budget. The report provided a nearly comprehensive list of subscription titles, the current fiscal year's cost, the renewal increase dollar amount, and the percentage change. The report also included whether the subscription item was part of a multiyear agreement or was consortial.

The materials budget request in 2018 was based on actual inflation rates, as well as exact subscription costs for the new funds requested. Outlining the annual request in this way satisfied the administration's requirements for transparency and proved the request to be justifiable. The library views the management of library resources as a faculty conversation and, as such, fully appreciated the need to show responsible stewardship. Additionally, the administration also needed to understand what the library is dealing with in regard to inflation, as well as the importance to the faculty of specific resources to support their research and instruction. Thus, having national data as well as peer data was relevant. It was also important to remind the administration of what the library's materials budget has been historically to help frame where it needed to go in the future. Part of the goal was to show that the library is not a cost center, but a strategic investment that will help the university grow and thrive. The new budget request process was accepted by the administration, and we were then able to move forward with communicating with the rest of the campus.

COMMUNICATING WITH DATA

We felt that a critical component for successful communication was employing a mix of different channels: some mass media channels that would rapidly dispense the information, as well as more interpersonal channels that would be more effective in forming and changing attitudes toward a new idea.[5] The communication channels utilized were a dedicated LibGuide, departmental e-mails, in-service sessions on the collection, campus announcements via the daily newsletter, and updates to the Faculty Senate via a newly established

Faculty Senate Library Committee, which also included student representative members from the Undergraduate Student Government and the Graduate Student Government.

A driving consideration in the library's communication planning was that faculty input should be central to collection decisions. The library needed to show the campus a broad overview of where the collection budget stood and its relation to the overall landscape of academic publishing in order to lay the groundwork for a healthy dialogue with the campus faculty and staff. It was also determined that the existing channels of communication were ineffective at facilitating pertinent information exchange across campus. It was hoped that interaction and engagement in faculty conversations would help faculty members see what the library does in a new light and also aid the library in understanding faculty needs. The library also wanted a better understanding of the current instruction and research processes; in this way, it could better support these critical missions of the university. The ability to have one-on-one conversations with faculty members demonstrated to the library that more such conversations were needed to facilitate genuine understanding and participation.

These personal dialogues appeared to help to ease the hard conversations with faculty members when journal cancellations needed to be made. Also, having collection decisions rooted in data helps ease the sting, and allowing faculty to have a voice and respond to the data helps complete the picture. This feedback is then powerful messaging to relay, in an anonymized fashion, to the administration the importance of supporting instruction and research with library-funded resources. Communications of this type also helped uncover those hidden personal libraries and the usage of particular resources at the department or even instructor level that would have otherwise been undiscovered and, therefore, unsupported by the library and thus the broader campus level.

After several e-mail exchanges, personal conversations, and in-service sessions, it became apparent that this was an active and productive style of communication that should be explored in order to move into being a partner and working with faculty to provide for their needs within the mutually understood constraints of the budget. The library's experience was that this communication style also has the advantage of providing faculty with information that empowered them to advocate to department heads and the administration on behalf of the library. In order to keep this communication channel open and aid in the strategic initiatives of the library, the library, led by the university librarian, worked with the Faculty Senate to establish a standing Library Faculty Senate Committee. The committee is chaired by a member of the Senate who is appointed each academic year by that body. The committee's additional membership is comprised of three members of the academic faculty, appointed by the Senate to serve three-year terms; the university librarian, with no term limit; one additional library member of the academic faculty recommended by the university librarian and appointed by the Senate to serve a three-year term; one member of the undergraduate student body, recommended by the Undergraduate Student Government to serve a one-year term; and one member of the graduate student body, recommended by the Graduate Student Government to serve a one-year term. The functions of this committee are (1) to serve as a channel of communication between faculty, students, and the library; (2) to serve as an advisory body on matters related to the development of library resources and services, and policies and procedures related to the operations and facilities of the library, and the allocation of library funds; and (3) to report on and advocate for the needs of the library and the impact of library services to the Mines' academic community. The committee regularly reports to the Faculty Senate, making recommendations as appropriate.

While the administration was not excluded from the other communication channels, it was evident that different mechanisms needed to be employed with the administration regarding the library's annual materials budget request. An engineering school inherently responds to numbers, and indeed was requiring them, so for the next year, actual inflation rates were calculated, as well as exact numbers for the new funds requested. The benefit was that this provided a transparent mechanism to support budgetary requests. Collection decisions for acquisition or cancellation were already being discussed at the campus level, having already been framed as a faculty conversation. However, the administration needed to understand what the library was dealing with in regard to inflation, as well as the importance to the faculty of specific resources, so having a variety of data, including national and peer data, was critical. Ithaka's S+R Library Survey 2019 shows that "library directors continue to perceive the value of their roles—and the roles of their libraries—as declining in the eyes of their supervisors and other higher education leaders."[6] In response to this trend, the library also framed the dialogue with the administration in this light in order to help them understand the critical role of the library in moving the mission of the institution forward. It was also important to remind them of what the historical library materials budget has been because memories are short, and the now is what they are thinking about.

How collection decisions are made was reframed as a campus conversation that would be based on data and decided only after thoughtful qualitative analysis. The library initiated cancellation suggestions, instead of requesting them from faculty, and these suggestions were rooted in cost-per-use data. This process ensured a comprehensive analysis that could be reviewed holistically. New acquisitions were offered as options based on data such as interlibrary loan requests, turnaways, academic program growth, and the number of purchase requests. In order to better facilitate purchase requests, a dedicated online form was created. The benefit of this is that the form has built-in tracking and statistics capabilities. Interlibrary loan has come a long way from decades past, when it involved mailed physical copies or poorly reproduced faxes. It is a service that will become increasingly relied upon to provide post-cancellation access to pertinent articles, but also to build a case for future acquisitions when loan requests exceed what the service can provide, and a subscription becomes evident and necessary.

The LibGuide has proven to be a useful tool for explanations as well as for soliciting feedback. Our usage shows that it has been most effective when combined with campus announcements and departmental e-mails that incorporate a call for action. Most feedback has been in the form of e-mail or personal interaction. This feedback is shared anonymously with librarians to aid in their decision-making for final cancellations. The current practice is to archive feedback to ensure that follow-up notifications are made personally once final decisions are made. This follow-up piece has proven effective and has elicited positive interactions.

CONCLUSION: SUCCESSES AND CHALLENGES

The results of implementing these new collection strategies have been encouraging, but not perfect. In the initial year, the library made modest journal cuts, which freed up funds to start many new journal subscriptions and several new databases. The feedback from the faculty about the cancellation process and their subsequent use of the new resources has been positive. The second year of implementation saw a 9.8 percent increase to the materials budget and the purchase of many more needed resources. The current, third year saw only a 4.2 percent increase, which was less than requested, but it was a less robust financial year all around on campus. Even with the inadequate budget allotment, there was a marked difference in the annual request process, as well as in cancellation cycles from years past. It was a very collaborative process between the administration, the library, and the faculty, with a healthy dialogue and greater understanding all around. There were, of course, both successes and challenges in developing the Mines Library collection communication program, including choices made when framing the budget request and collection decisions. The program combined background elements of data-driven collection assessment and data visualization with foreground elements of marketing and communication strategies. One of our successes was educating the administration that collection decisions are appropriately made as a dialogue between the faculty and the library. While granular data was provided to justify the library's inflationary budget requests and to strengthen those requests, title-level and usage data were not included. That data was instead the focus of faculty communications, especially when determining cancellations. This strategy led to approved budget requests for inflation as well as new funds, both continuing and one-time. Different strategies and tools were developed, including a LibGuide and an online request form that were integrated into the library's website, and the creation of a Faculty Senate Library Committee.

After nearly three years of collaboration and development, the dialogue between the faculty and the library has dramatically increased, which has led to resource needs being better met, creating a healthier collection. The challenges that persist include getting a baseline inflation factor approved for the materials budget, as well as a dedicated budget line item to support new academic programs on campus, and eliciting valid resource requests from faculty members during the New Program approval process.

The Arthur Lakes Library has gained valuable insights from this entire process by leveraging national data and data from peer institutions, as well as local quantitative data, in order to support its materials budget requests. Moreover, the library has begun considering the campus dialogue holistically. It is hoped that we can continue to learn from this experience, building and strengthening our communication channels in order to treat collection management as an ongoing campus conversation.

BIBLIOGRAPHY

Bosch, S., Barbara Albee, and S. Romaine. "Deal or No Deal: Periodicals Price Survey 2019." *Library Journal* 144, no. 3 (April 2019).

Colorado Alliance of Research Libraries. "Prospector Bib and Item Quarterly Statistics, April 2017." April 2017. www.coalliance.org/old-prospector-statistics.

EBSCO. "2019 Serials Price Projections." 2019. www.ebscohost.com/promoMaterials/2019_Serials_Price_Projections.pdf.

Gerber, Kent. "Conversation as a Model to Build the Relationship among Libraries, Digital Humanities, and Campus Leadership." *College & Undergraduate Libraries* 24, no. 2-4 (June 8, 2017): 418–33. https://doi.org/10.1080/10691316.2017.1328296.

Lynden, F. "Library Materials Budget Justifications." *Book Research Quarterly* 5, no. 4 (1989). https://doi.org/10.1007/BF02683802.

Rogers, Everett M. *Diffusion of Innovations*. 5th ed. New York: Free Press, 2003.

Wolff-Eisenberg, Christine, and Jennifer K. Frederick. "Coalition for Networked Information." Coalition for Networked Information. March 2020. www.cni.org/wp-content/uploads/2020/03/Jennifer-Frederick-Ithaka-SR-Library-Survey-2019-CNI.pdf.

NOTES

1. F. Lynden, "Library Materials Budget Justifications," *Book Research Quarterly* 5, no. 4 (1989), https://doi.org/10.1007/BF02683802.

2. S. Bosch, Barbara Albee, and S. Romaine, "Deal or No Deal: Periodicals Price Survey 2019," *Library Journal* 144, no. 3 (April 2019).

3. Colorado Alliance of Research Libraries, "Prospector Bib and Item Quarterly Statistics, April 2017," 2017, www.coalliance.org/old-prospector-statistics.

4. EBSCO, "2019 Serials Price Projections," 2019, www.ebscohost.com/promo Materials/2019_Serials_Price_Projections.pdf.

5. Everett M. Rogers, *Diffusion of Innovations*, 5th ed. (New York: Free Press, 2003).

6. Christine Wolff-Eisenberg and Jennifer K. Frederick, "Coalition for Networked Information," Coalition for Networked Information, March 2020, www.cni.org/wp-content/uploads/2020/03/Jennifer-Frederick-Ithaka-SR-Library-Survey -2019-CNI.pdf.

HILARY HARGIS AND
JENNY NOVACESCU

11
What Difference Does It Make?

Marketing in Technical Services at a Special Library

"Give us your thoughts on marketing in libraries, Hilary."

I was sitting in a conference room with a group of librarians and administrators, including Jenny Novacescu, the current chief librarian, to interview for a cataloger position. I was well prepared to discuss my qualifications—knowledge of cataloging standards, experience with original and copy cataloging, understanding of Library of Congress classification. A marketing question, however, took me by surprise. Nothing in my background spoke to library marketing or prepared me to address it proficiently. I had been an assistant cataloger at the Chemical Heritage Foundation (now the Science History Institute) and a junior cataloger at a large Midwestern public library. In both cases, the technical services department had been located behind closed doors, completely separate from anything public-facing. What happened to the books after I cataloged them had been someone else's concern.

In the interview, I answered on the fly. "I believe marketing should recognize the different ways people process information. Think about learning styles, for example. I would make sure to hit each channel. A poster by the elevator for visual impact, or a meeting announcement for people who learn by hearing, or an e-mail for those who prefer reading." The interviewers jotted down some notes and moved on to the next topic.

The interview was a mixed bag, though it must have had some redeeming qualities: I received an offer of employment as associate librarian at the Space Telescope Science Institute (STScI) in Baltimore, Maryland, and was installed in the position within a few months.

The STScI serves as a prime contractor to NASA for the purpose of supporting the science operations of the Hubble Space Telescope and both the science and flight operations of the James Webb Space Telescope. The institute is also actively engaged in the concept and development of future and proposed missions, including the Nancy Grace Roman Space Telescope, and in supporting worldwide access to astronomical data. The STScI Library, a resource for the institute's staff of 800, was founded with the institute in 1982. Its collections were initially built from discarded texts from other astronomical institutions, but have grown to encompass approximately 21,500 unique bibliographic entries, with a slight majority represented as electronic resources. The chief and associate librarians are the only staff dedicated to library work, though the library also includes two archivists and a bibliographer assigned to other projects.

With such a small staff size, I knew I would have to pitch in as needed. So, when the chief librarian asked me to assist with some basic promotional activities, I prepared displays, wrote for the library's newsletter, and created signage. However, I saw these tasks as tangential, not essential to my work in technical services. This was the same mindset I had had all along: what happens with the materials after cataloging is, or should be, someone else's job.

The 2018 "Computers in Libraries Conference" started to shift my thinking. The chief librarian and I agreed that attending the conference would be ideal for my professional development, due to its focus on marketing as well as technical services and future trends. Amidst the sessions on search techniques and linked data were some speakers who demonstrated a new outlook. The first were Brendan Howley and Daniel Lee, cofounders of Icebox Logic, in their keynote address on tightening a library's connection to its community. Partway through their address, they argued that libraries are not about circulation but about user experience. "What stories will resonate with your audience?" they asked.[1] The next day Rebecca Jones, a managing partner of Dysart and Jones Associates, spoke on ruthless prioritization, developing ideas from the product management expert Brandon Chu.[2] Expounding on Chu's prioritization framework, she echoed his push to focus on the value being created for the client or customer.[3]

On the train ride home, I found myself entertaining a new set of questions. How, as a technical services librarian, am I creating value for STScI staff? How are the staff experiencing that value? And what are the staff at STScI actually trying to *do*? If we could tell a story about the goals of STScI staff, what would those stories be? How could these narratives and values guide our communication?

When I got back to work, I felt better prepared to collaborate with the chief librarian in the library's marketing efforts—not just checking promotions off the list, but taking a hard look at our users and ourselves, and working to frame our communications in a way that demonstrated the library's value to our users. Throughout this chapter, we describe how we have gone about this work: learning more, seeing where marketing plays out in the rhythms of our work, and pivoting communication from *what* resources and services the library provides to *why* those resources and services are essential offerings for our community.

WHAT DID WE LEARN?

Now that the chief librarian and I had a shared vision, one of our first steps was to educate ourselves more fully on library marketing concepts. We cast a wide net in our search for information—participating in national library conferences, attending online trainings, and following up on books, articles, and white papers we encountered along the way. This gave us a good view of library marketing basics, as well as the specific relationship that marketing can have to technical services and the expression of marketing through communication.

At its core, marketing encompasses "the long-term planned activities and communication strategies an organization engages in so they can connect their products and services with their intended users."[4] Marketing is characterized as a multi-step, recurring process where one iteration of marketing activities informs another. The stages of the library marketing cycle have been described in various ways across the field. Kathy Dempsey is well known for her Cycle of True Marketing—an eleven-step process emphasizing goal-setting, planning, and measurement.[5] A more concise summary of the library marketing cycle is presented by Emily Hauser in her 2019 *Choice* white paper. Hauser identifies the four key elements of library marketing as research, or gathering information; segmentation, which divides a library's users into logical groupings; promotion, the communicative activities that people tend to think of most readily when it comes to marketing; and assessment, noting lessons learned for the next round of marketing.[6]

Apart from the stages of the marketing process, another high-level model is the marketing mix or Four Ps. These focus on *product*, *price*, *place*, and *promotion* and are commonly discussed in marketing across many disciplines. In her book *Fundamentals of Collection Development*, Peggy Johnson situates the Four Ps in library discourse. She describes the concepts as:

Product—library collections (on-site and online) and services
Price—the accessibility and convenience of the library's offerings to its
    users

Place—any location where products or services are accessed
Promotion—a library's "liaison and outreach activities."[7]

All of these elements are typically codified in a library's marketing plan, a document that outlines who is marketing what to whom, for what purpose, and which explains how the library will measure the success of its efforts.[8]

The question of who performs marketing, or who is involved in forming and executing marketing plans, is indicative. Two recent surveys show how the majority of public and academic libraries rely on existing library staff to carry out marketing for their communities. Specifically, 73 percent of public libraries reported that marketing is carried out by staff with library rather than marketing backgrounds,[9] and 55 percent of academic libraries indicated that marketing tasks are juggled by staff who also have other areas of responsibility.[10] Could technical services librarians be among the staff contributing to marketing alongside their other work? Lynda Duke and Toni Tucker make the assertion that effective marketing is the result of full buy-in across the library's staff. They argue that *everyone*—which presumably includes technical services—should participate in or endorse the library's formal marketing efforts in some way, even by making the most of off-the-cuff "encounters" that happen naturally throughout the course of a workday.[11]

Our research helped fill in the picture of what it could look like for technical services to have a role in marketing. To start, Peggy Johnson makes explicit ties between marketing and the activities that technical services already typically performs. In the Four Ps, she puts *product* and *price* firmly in the camp of technical services. It is the responsibility of technical services to select, acquire, and catalog our library collections—the *product*. Likewise, technical service departments contribute to the accessibility of those collections—the *price*—through value-added cataloging, electronic resource management, and other services. "Developing and modifying the collections and services the library provides are what librarians do constantly," Johnson writes, "though they seldom think of these as marketing activities."[12] *Place* is also an important consideration for technical services, because format dictates how and where library users will access the materials. Online tools and resources are available outside the library's building and allow patrons to engage with content in essentially any *place* of their choosing.[13]

What about the concept of *promotion*? Does technical services have any role to play there? Promotion is "how organizations communicate their value to their customers,"[14] where value is understood as the ability of the library to satisfy its users' needs.[15] In doing promotion, libraries are articulating *why* their resources can be meaningful to a particular set of patrons. Technical services can help connect these dots through their knowledge of the value of a resource for a given audience—because, in the process of delivering a product, technical services librarians have become familiar with *why* those particular products were selected in contrast to other options available. So even if librarians with more forward-facing roles are the ones executing entire promotional campaigns, technical services librarians can make a significant contribution to the planning of promotions[16] through these elements.

It is worth taking a closer look at the language that goes into promotion because promotion is so communication-focused. An important factor to note is that there is no one-size-fits-all approach to messaging in promotion. In fact, at her 2018 ALA Annual Conference talk, Kathy Dempsey emphasized shaping the message for each individual target audience,[17] as each audience has its own *why* or motivation for engaging the library. Not only should the audiences be considered individually, but the types of *whys* that they possess can be broken down as well. According to Chris Foster, the vice president of business development at Modern Postcard, and Robert Storer, director of marketing for SirsiDynix, three main categories of *why* can be distinguished: a functional *why*, which addresses a practical need for "tools" or information; an emotional *why*, which seeks intangible personal benefits such as connection with other people; and a moral *why*, which focuses on big-picture elements such as advancing human knowledge.[18]

All this is illustrated beautifully by the ALA's Libraries Transform campaign, a "public awareness campaign . . . advocat[ing] the value of librarianship" and providing tools for libraries to do the same.[19] The central features of this campaign are "Because" statements that communicate, directly and succinctly, how libraries meet an audience's need. As library marketing proponents would advocate, no two of these statements are the same. Rather, they play out differently based on the audience and the category of *why* that has been identified. For instance, the ALA's statement "Because 5 million students can't access broadband at home" is a functional *why* for the target market of student learners; "Because superfans are welcome here" is an emotional *why* for the devoted enthusiast; "Because blue state or red state, everyone benefits from an enlightened state" is a moral *why* for activists and citizens.[20] Each statement gets to the heart of what someone cares about, showing a path to meaningful engagement or change. Or, as Foster and Storer would put it, each statement frames a person's *why* as "a story."[21]

Just as technical services has a marketing role through the Four Ps, it also has a part to play in the marketing cycle—particularly as relating to research and market segmentation. As noted, technical services selects and prepares resources, basing its decisions on an understanding of the user community. In other words, technical services uses the library's *research* about its community to deliver resources supporting various market *segments*. Johnson frames it this way: "The library examines the needs, demands, and wants of all segments of its public and the long-term requirements of the communities it serves, then designs a product—library services and resources—to meet those needs."[22] Technical services is essentially acting on research to select resources for target markets, a function echoing the definition of marketing above with its emphasis on "connect[ing]" products and users.[23]

HOW HAS THE STScI LIBRARY EMBRACED MARKETING PROCESSES AND CONCEPTS?

When the authors of this chapter started at the STScI Library, there was no marketing plan already in place for the library. After a few sit-down sessions, we went from no plan to a "somewhat well organized" and "loose" plan, in line with 46 percent of academic libraries having active but informal marketing efforts.[24]

In her *Choice* white paper, Hauser acknowledges that a lot can stand in the way of putting marketing ideas into practice: "budget, staff size, and existing time constraints may seem like non-negotiable obstacles to investigating and implementing marketing principles."[25] At the STScI Library, staff size and existing time constraints are the dominant factors keeping our planning and execution at an informal rather than a formal level. The library has only two dedicated staff, as noted above, and neither of us is fully allocated to marketing. The breadth of our responsibilities does not afford us the time to produce extensive documentation or elaborate plans. But by the same token, our staff size allows us to function without them; as a small team, we can coordinate meetings and keep each other abreast of developments more naturally than larger teams that must rely on formalized plans to keep their efforts cohesive.

Day to day, our informal marketing efforts tend to play out as follows: the technical services librarian often chooses which print books, e-books, and booklists we will market to the institute's staff. Ordering and cataloging our newest acquisitions has made technical services familiar with the library's materials, which makes it easier to identify which works will appeal to different demographics. From there, the chief librarian does most of the execution—sending library updates, maintaining physical displays and signage, and speaking at meetings requiring the library's presence. This is very much in line with the way Johnson situates technical services in marketing,[26] with technical services staff helping to provide content (the *product*) and knowledge of the audience (*market segment*) to more publicly oriented staff.

The informality of our efforts extends to the assessment phase of the marketing cycle as well. One contributing factor is that we are not required to submit marketing reports inside or outside the library. Consequently, assessments can be more ad hoc: for example, a quick check of usage statistics for an online resource or an attendance count for a training class, shared between library staff. The important thing in marketing assessment is that "conclusions are drawn,"[27] and we can continue to do this conversationally even if we don't conduct formal assessments such as marketing reports.

At the STScI Library, we have found that assessments conducted in this way—informally, conversationally, as the need arises—can still have a significant impact. This is particularly true in renewals season and during the budgeting process or the change of fiscal year, when the concept of marketing assessment coincides with the evaluation that we are naturally doing to prepare for the coming year. Our subscription to the Optics InfoBase Premium (OIB) journal package from the Optical Society of America provides an interesting example here of assessment, as well as of the entire marketing cycle at the STScI Library. One of the first assignments given to the new technical services librarian was to ensure that all our online holdings from OIB were accurately represented in our catalog and e-journal portal. Once all the descriptions were accurate, the chief librarian highlighted the resources in a library newsletter. During the next two renewal seasons, we tracked usage for the OIB package and concluded that some of the materials remained low-use. From there, the chief librarian consulted key stakeholders at the institute and worked with the publisher to shift our subscription to a lower-cost package of journals, including only the most highly used resources. Then it was back to technical services to update our catalog and e-journal portal so we could communicate the changes and highlight the remaining resources again.

The most formal of our marketing efforts so far has been the survey we administered to STScI staff in 2018. The survey was a conscious effort to engage in the research portion of the marketing cycle and to better understand our users' needs. Responses came in from across the institute and served as the basis for a change to the access models for staff in satellite buildings. One of the most interesting aspects of the survey, however, was its role as a communication tool between the library and the institute's staff, which leads us to how our adoption of a marketing mentality is expressing itself in our communication.

WHAT HAS BEEN THE OUTGROWTH FOR OUR COMMUNICATION?

As we became more familiar with marketing concepts and their application at our library, we began to see our library's communication through new eyes. In particular, we revisited the list of the STScI Library's core services that we circulated on our internal website, included with our newsletters, and distributed to new patrons (see figure 11.1). A rereading showed that the list was heavy on functional details, answering the question *what* resources and services were offered by the library.

Summary of CORE Library Services

- Telescope bibliographies
- Journal and book acquisitions: Our collection includes both research and support staff interests:
  - » Astronomy, physics, optics, and engineering
  - » Procurement and government purchasing
  - » Organizational management
  - » Scholarly publishing and scientific communications
  - » Software engineering/programming
  - » Public outreach and data visualization
  - » Careers, coaching, mentoring, and performance recognition

- Targeted classes on a variety of topics in information services and scholarly publishing
- Interlibrary loan services—most resources from other libraries can be obtained in less than one week
- Assistance with citation formatting
- Literature searches (ADS and more)
- Bibliography tracking for professional development (PaperTrack/ProPer)/OR-CID implementation (forthcoming)
- Institutional (non-data) archiving
- Instrument paper submissions to ADS
- Online access and print checkout available 24/7

FIGURE 11.1
BEFORE: The STScI Library's core services as a continuous list, uncategorized

Yet we now understood that by focusing on *products*, we were missing key ideas: our messages were generalized instead of tailored to specific audiences, and they did not address what users actually gained from the products. Could we illuminate the *whys* and the *to whoms*? To draw these out, we looked for areas of resonance between our core services and the various target markets at the institute. This required some groundwork, as there was no breakdown of STScI's target markets already in use at the library. Fortunately, we were also formalizing the library's collection development plan around this time; a formulation of our target markets would be applicable in both areas.

Considering our target markets, we started with the question, "What are STScI staff actually trying to *do*?" An obvious answer was research, for the 200 or so scientists at the institute whose paid work includes their own research programs. These programs require a variety of activities, from keeping up with the achievements of colleagues to drawing conclusions from astronomical data or simulations and publishing results—all in ways that advance the scientists' careers and demonstrate the meaning of their accomplishments.

Another obvious answer was "functional work," which at the institute has a broad meaning. Scientists perform their own research, but they also support

Engage Your Field of Inquiry

- Research assistance and ADS queries/troubleshooting
- Journal and book acquisitions
  - » astronomy and astrophysics
  - » optics
  - » engineering
  - » chemistry
  - » programming, agile development, and other technical topics
  - » management, communications, public outreach
- Interlibrary loan and info about JHU libraries
- Online access and print checkout available 24/7

Leverage on-the-Job Skills

- O'Reilly Learning for technical and staff development
- Skillsoft and Project Management resources
- Resources on careers, coaching, and mentoring

Communicate Your Work

- Proposal and grant writing resources; writing for engineers
- Resources on scientific communication and scholarly publishing
- Instrument and proposal submissions to ADS
- ORCID and bibliography tracking for professional development

Evaluate Your Impact

- Telescope bibliographies
- Institutional (non-data) archiving
- Metric analyses for institutions, individuals, or research topics

FIGURE 11.2
AFTER: The STScI Library's core services grouped into user narratives, based on the aims of market segments at the institute

one of the institute's missions, such as the operation of the Hubble Space Telescope. Beyond the functional work of the scientists, there are numerous staff keeping the institute running through their professional expertise in areas such as information technology, project management, public outreach, human resources, and business operations. These are functional areas of work as well, where staff have concrete goals to reach using a defined skill set and drawing on the professional resources of their fields for support.

We started to see certain themes emerging. All workers at the institute are engaged in one discipline or another, whether that be astronomy, finance, or graphic design. All have a job to do relying on their specific competencies. Communication is a relevant competency across the board, with teams working together, individuals sharing results, and scientists having the added responsibility of publishing. With this in view, we started rearranging the library's core services into related groups, and we brainstormed category names that would answer the question of *why* those resources or services would be useful to STScI staff (see figure 11.2).

A strength of the four narrative categories we came up with is that they tap into the types of *whys* described by Foster and Storer. "Leverage on-the-job skills" and "Communicate your work" are the clearest examples of functional *whys*, leading to concrete outcomes. "Engage your field of inquiry" has functional aspects, as there are particular tools and resources that assist staff as they work within their disciplines. However, this category also has a strong moral component, given the inspiring nature of the astronomical discoveries supported by the institute. Similarly, there are functional considerations for "Evaluate your impact" such as specific reporting measures, but the broader context is an emotional one that ties into the concept of legacy for the institute and the individual.

Now that we had divided our services into four broad categories of user motivation, where did we go from there? We used these narratives to help us tailor our messages and focus on values—shifting from *what* we have and do to *why* those resources and services benefit our users—for both our external and internal communication.

For external communication between the library and the institute staff, we are at the beginning stages of using our four narratives for promotional language. One of our first projects was to create new materials for Human Resources (HR) to use while onboarding staff. We worked with HR to produce a very brief introductory slide about the library to be incorporated into a first-day orientation (see figure 11.3). The first-day slide is well-grounded in our guiding narratives, using *why* language to lead the conversation about the library. It still allows the library's *products* to shine through, giving exposure to the resources contributed by technical services. The difference is that the products are being framed in terms of bigger goals, not presented as ends in themselves.

We were also conscientious about the language used in the survey that we administered to institute staff in 2018. For example, in asking respondents to rank the library's services in order of importance, we included a *why* statement with the description of each service—such as "so I can get the info I need to perform my work and increase my skill base," "so I can focus on science and/or functional work," or "to demonstrate impact in the community." The wording of the survey highlighted the library's ability to provide value to its users. Technical services may deliver resources from behind the scenes, but the purpose and impact of those resources was emphasized by the survey language.

While our narratives are beginning to shape the communication between the library and STScI staff, they have had an even greater impact on our communication within the library about our internal projects. This has been

STScI LIBRARY

Learn, Engage, Discover

- STScI Library is located on 4th floor (Muller)
- 24/7 digital/remote access and print check outs
- Access to JHU Libraries, interlibrary loan, and worldwide astronomical library network

Advance Your Research and Technical Skills

- Journal access and training on ADS and ORCID
- O'Reilly Learning digital platform for software developers, coders, IT, project managers, researchers

Evaluate Your Impact

- Customizable staff bibliographies
- Institute and observatory productivity metrics

FIGURE 11.3
Introductory slide for use in first-day orientation for new STScI staff

particularly true in technical services for our deaccessioning project and our search for a new library services platform (LSP).

The STScI Library's current deaccessioning project is its first comprehensive collection assessment since the library's founding. As we assess our print collections, we are using our narratives as guiding principles for retention or deselection. Is this item an accurate, timely representation of a field of inquiry engaged at the institute? Does this item help the staff sharpen their functional or research skill sets? Does it support their scientific, technical, or business communication? Does it demonstrate the long-term contributions of the institute and its staff? Other criteria are certainly at play, but the answers to these questions can help us make a first cut—with *noes* to be examined for possible removal and *yeses* shortlisted for retention—and give us confidence that we are aligning our collection with the motivations of our patrons.

Weeding with these big-picture criteria in view also allows us to answer the question of *why* we are or are not keeping something. Why are we retaining materials on data science, for example? Because our data archive staff rely on it to skillfully perform their daily work, and because many of our researchers employ big data concepts in their scientific inquiries. Likewise, why are we divesting CD-ROMs? Because data in this format is no longer timely and is not actively used by our researchers and staff in their various fields. As such, we have the language we need to discuss our weeding choices with concerned staff members or administrators who are seeking visibility into our processes.

Our search for a new LSP is also of interest when considering these communication narratives. Our library catalog is a key portal for staff to access or locate the resources they need for any purpose—whether that be research, skill-building, supporting their writing and presentation efforts, or seeing their or the institute's work in context. One of our main reasons for replacing our legacy integrated library system is to make it easier for staff to achieve their goals via our catalog. For example, we would like institute staff to have a state-of-the-art user experience, and we want our electronic resources to be accessible seamlessly from the catalog. These objectives relate to the marketing concepts of *price* and *place*, which seek to reduce barriers and increase the convenience and accessibility of the library's offerings. We are still early in the process of system migration. As the process continues, we will have a tremendous opportunity to communicate what our system migration means to the institute's staff: easier access to the resources they care about, helping them achieve their most important goals, and so on. Our four narratives lay the groundwork for this campaign.

CONCLUSION AND FUTURE DIRECTIONS

The STScI Library, and technical services in particular, have come a long way on our marketing journey. We have gotten a sense of the marketing landscape and codified our marketing plans at a level that makes sense for a library of our size. Technical services is making a significant contribution to our marketing efforts through the identification of resources, or *products*, to be highlighted for specific groups. All of this is culminating in a revision of our communication, which now uses *why* language to mirror the motivations of various target markets at the institute. This *why* language has been applied in the library's onboarding materials and survey, highlighting the value of *products* provided by technical services in both cases. The concept of *why* also permeates our projects in technical services, driving how we understand our collection evaluation and our search for a new LSP.

We are also aware of next steps that would help us along on our marketing journey. We plan to design targeted marketing for new hires, emphasizing resources specific to their divisions. This communication will be sent about a month after new hires join the institute, to allow them time to learn about their projected duties and future information needs. We intend to evaluate our online presence and reframe the offerings on our website. We also plan to focus on reducing the *price* or difficulty of access for e-books coming from various suppliers. Likewise, we could do more to hone our communication on individual resources or products, making sure the *why's* are clear at that level as well. Fortunately, we have a foundation for these projects, understanding why they are important and having the language to bring them to fruition.

Whenever my next interview happens, will I be surprised by a marketing question? No, I will be expecting it—and I will have much to discuss on the topic of *why*.

REFERENCES

American Library Association. "Libraries Transform." ilovelibraries. www.ilove libraries.org/librariestransform/.

Breed, Liz, Mary Stein, and Kathy Dempsey. "Marketing Strategy, Marketing Plan, and Marketing Tactics: Why You Need All 3!" Presentation at the American Library Association Annual Conference, New Orleans, LA, June 2018. www.eventscribe .com/2018/ALA-Annual/fsPopup.asp?Mode=presInfo&PresentationID=352590.

Chu, Brandon. "Ruthless Prioritization." *The Black Box of Product Management* (blog). March 5, 2017. https://blackboxofpm.com/ruthless-prioritization-e4256 e3520a9.

Dantus, Sabine, and Jennifer Park. "Marketing Academic Library Resources and Services." *Choice*, 2018. http://choice360.org/librarianship/whitepaper.

Duke, Lynda M., and Toni Tucker. "How to Develop a Marketing Plan for an Academic Library." *Technical Services Quarterly* 25, no. 1 (2007): 51–68. https://doi.org/ 10.1300/J124v25n01_05.

Foster, Christopher, and Robert Storer. "Marketing 102: Tackling Misconceptions That Prevent Effective Library Marketing." SirsiDynix Library Marketing Series. http://go.sirsidynix.com/Marketing-102-Tackling-Misconceptions-That-Can -Prevent-Effective-Library-Marketing.html.

Hauser, Emily. "Implementing Marketing Plans in the Academic Library: Rules, Roles, and Definitions." *Choice*, 2019. http://choice360.org/librarianship/whitepaper.

Howley, Brendan, and Daniel Lee. "Digital Transformation & Libraries: Participatory Culture Hubs." Keynote presentation at Computers in Libraries, Arlington, VA, April 2018. http://computersinlibraries.infotoday.com/2018/Sessions/Digital -Transformation-and-Libraries-Participatory-Culture-Hubs-11644.aspx.

Johnson, Peggy. *Fundamentals of Collection Development*. 3rd ed. Chicago: American Library Association, 2014.

Jones, Rebecca. "Ruthless Prioritization." Presentation at Computers in Libraries, Arlington, VA, April 2018. http://computersinlibraries.infotoday.com/2018/ Sessions/D302-Ruthless-Prioritization-11699.aspx.

OCLC. "Public Libraries: Marketing and Communications Landscape." 2018. www.oclc.org/content/dam/research/publications/2018/216084_2018_Public _Library_Marketing_Report.pdf.

Polger, Mark Aaron. *Library Marketing Basics*. Lanham, MD: Rowman & Littlefield, 2019.

NOTES

1. Brendan Howley and Daniel Lee, "Digital Transformation & Libraries: Participatory Culture Hubs" (keynote presentation, Computers in Libraries, Arlington, VA, April 18, 2018).

2. Brandon Chu, "Ruthless Prioritization," *The Black Box of Product Management* (blog), March 5, 2017, https://blackboxofpm.com/ruthless-prioritization-e4256e3520a9.

3. Rebecca Jones, "Ruthless Prioritization" (presentation at Computers in Libraries, Arlington, VA, April 19, 2018).

4. Mark Aaron Polger, *Library Marketing Basics* (Lanham, MD: Rowman & Littlefield, 2019), 16.

5. Polger, *Library Marketing Basics*, 20–21.

6. Emily Hauser, "Implementing Marketing Plans in the Academics Library: Rules, Roles, and Definitions," *Choice*, 2019, http://choice360.org/librarianship/whitepaper.

7. Peggy Johnson, *Fundamentals of Collection Development*, 3rd ed. (Chicago: American Library Association, 2014), 257, 259.

8. Lynda M. Duke and Toni Tucker, "How to Develop a Marketing Plan for an Academic Library," *Technical Services Quarterly* 25, no. 1 (2007): 51–68.

9. OCLC, "Public Libraries: Marketing and Communications Landscape," 2018, www.oclc.org/content/dam/research/publications/2018/216084_2018_Public_Library_Marketing_Report.pdf.

10. Sabine Dantus and Jennifer Park, "Marketing Academic Library Resources and Services," *Choice*, 2018, http://choice360.org/librarianship/whitepaper.

11. Duke and Tucker, "How to Develop a Marketing Plan," 56.

12. Johnson, *Fundamentals*, 258.

13. Johnson, *Fundamentals*, 259.

14. Polger, *Library Marketing Basics*, 24.

15. Johnson, *Fundamentals*, 256.

16. Johnson, *Fundamentals*, 272.

17. Liz Breed, Mary Stein, and Kathy Dempsey, "Marketing Strategy, Marketing Plan, and Marketing Tactics: Why You Need All 3!" (presentation at American Library Association Annual Conference, New Orleans, LA, June 24, 2018).

18. Christopher Foster and Robert Storer, "Marketing 102: Tackling Misconceptions That Prevent Effective Library Marketing," SirsiDynix Library Marketing Series, http://go.sirsidynix.com/Marketing-102-Tackling-Misconceptions-That-Can-Prevent-Effective-Library-Marketing.html.

19. American Library Association, "Libraries Transform," ilovelibraries, www.ilovelibraries.org/librariestransform/.

20. American Library Association, "Libraries Transform."

21. Foster and Storer, "Marketing 102."

22. Johnson, *Fundamentals*, 257–58.

23. Polger, *Library Marketing Basics,* 16.

24. Dantus and Park, "Marketing," 8.

25. Hauser, "Implementing Marketing Plans," 14.

26. Johnson, *Fundamentals*, 257–58, 272.

27. Hauser, "Implementing Marketing Plans," 12.

HEATHER JEFFCOAT,
MARLEE GIVENS,
SOFIA SLUTSKAYA, AND
KAREN E. VIARS

12

Continuous Improvement

Using Collaboration between Technical Services,
IT, and Public Services to Make an Impact

Through a multiyear transformative effort known as Library Next, the Georgia Tech Library underwent a significant organizational restructuring, offering the authors of this chapter the opportunity to engage in cross-functional teams and actively participate in projects outside of their "traditional" areas.

Georgia Tech is a public research university in the metro Atlanta area. It enrolls 32,722 students in undergraduate, graduate, and doctoral programs. With an eye to supporting the shifting needs of our campus community, the Library Next initiative began in 2013 and aimed to radically change the traditional academic library model. The former dean of libraries, Catherine Murray-Rust, stated: "The biggest challenge to our transformation was organizational." To achieve this transformation, the library adopted "techniques used in disciplines such as supply chain thinking and portfolio management to radically restructure the way we operate."[1]

According to the Project Management Institute (PMI), "organizational leaders initiate projects in response to factors acting upon their organizations."[2] At the Georgia Tech Library, three factors led to the initiation of Library Next:

1. Dwindling use of print collections
2. Rising use of electronic collections
3. Decreased in-person visits to the library

Realizing the growing need to respond to these trends, the library moved its physical collections off campus and turned its focus to virtual collections and services. In 2019, 99.6 percent of collections use was electronic, averaging 4.89 million downloads of more than 1.97 million e-journals and e-books covering virtually every conceivable topic of scholarship. The infographic,

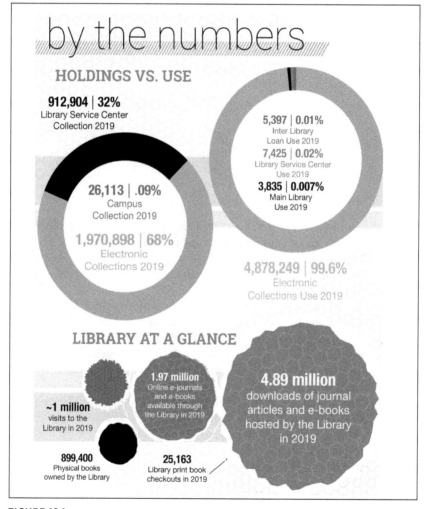

FIGURE 12.1
Infographic showing the shift in both the composition of the Georgia Tech Library's collection and the use of library resources

included in the library's "2019 Impact Report" (figure 12.1), was created to explain the physical collection move and provides a good visual representation of a tremendous shift in both the composition of the library collection and the use of library resources.[3]

A MODEL FOR COLLABORATION

To help envision next-generation library services, the library collaborated with Brightspot Strategy on a multipart user research study. Brightspot facilitated the user research process and enabled the library to develop a new vision for the twenty-first-century research library. This vision required the reimagining of the library's spaces and services. Among these were virtual browsing environments for exploration and the serendipitous discovery of materials for research and scholarship; an online presence that meets users where they are, both on and off campus; and an increase in self-service options for users. The new services, coupled with no traditional physical collection in the library building, required a new organizational structure and management strategies that emphasized cross-functional collaborations. To succeed, library faculty and staff who work with patrons would rely more heavily on their colleagues in technical services and information technology (IT) to help users navigate to the resources they need. Likewise, the faculty and staff who work behind the scenes to maintain collections and support the digital environment would depend on their peers in public services to facilitate feedback-gathering and educating library staff and users on new technologies.

Following this work with Brightspot, the library partnered with Georgia Tech Strategic Consulting (GTSC) to implement a portfolio management process. This process helped cultivate collaboration throughout the organization and facilitated the successful implementation of new services.

The methodology of portfolio management is defined by the PMI as a centralized management system where the portfolio is a collection of "projects, programs, subsidiary portfolios, and operations managed as a group to achieve strategic objectives."[4] Library Next portfolio projects followed a similar arc from start to finish, through a distinct set of phases:

Need identified—the initial need to embark on a project, defined by the organization's leadership in response to factors such as a request from external stakeholders, an opportunity to improve business processes, or an external change such as a new technology. Often the need is defined through a systematic needs analysis.

Project charter—this document defines the scope of the project, the project team, the timeline for deliverables, and any identified risks or issues that might complicate the project, along with supporting information such as a business case, goals, and objectives.

Data gathering—during the planning phase, data-gathering techniques such as brainstorming, focus groups, interviews, surveys, and so on can inform the outputs of the project.

Data analysis—subject-matter experts analyze the data gathered and offer recommendations.

Implementation—the project manager and team act on the recommendations and perform work to produce deliverables and meet the objectives of the project.

Communication—communication planning can address the numerous communication needs for a project: upwards, from the project to the portfolio; outwards, from the project to stakeholders; and within, between the project manager and the team. Communication planning addresses communication methods, technologies, strategies, and methods.

Feedback gathering—near the completion or at the close of the project, feedback from the project team, stakeholders, and organizational leadership can provide information such as lessons learned, recommendations, remaining issues, and plans to monitor the post-project phase of work.

Identify new needs from feedback (and start again from the top)—any new needs identified at the close of one project can inform subsequent projects.

The library's portfolio process focuses on the tactical, daily execution of library and Georgia Tech strategic initiatives. This process has fostered consistency, accountability, and the efficient implementation of new ideas for improvement and innovation. The library's "2019 Impact Report" offers a visual representation of the library's involvement with the portfolio framework and the level of staff engagement with portfolio projects (figure 12.2).[5]

The Library Next projects are prioritized based on strategic alignment, resource availability, and overall value. All of them require a cross-functional team of people with expertise in different areas for successful completion. The projects discussed in this chapter were only three out of the more than sixty initial projects in the portfolio. In all three projects, the librarians with technical services and IT backgrounds combined their project management expertise with the outreach and instruction skills of their colleagues in public services in collaborative endeavors to introduce improved online services to users. The projects are:

1. Virtual browsing of print and electronic books in the library catalog with Syndetics Unbound
2. Enhancements to the discovery interface (Ex Libris Primo) to help students more easily locate resources for their classwork and scholarship
3. A single sign-on authentication for licensed content through OpenAthens

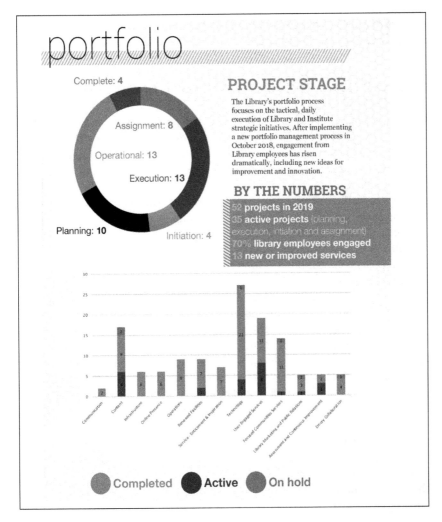

FIGURE 12.2
Infographic illustrating the Georgia Tech Library's involvement with the portfolio framework and the level of staff engagement with portfolio projects

These projects share:

- The use of the portfolio management framework described above
- The active participation of cross-functional teams consisting of technical services, public services, and IT staff in all stages of the projects
- The active gathering of user feedback to recalibrate project goals and deliverables

All participants agree that combining these elements leads to successful projects with the most positive impact on user services and the library's operations.

LIBRARY NEXT PROJECT 1: VIRTUAL BROWSING

One of the first key Library Next project collaborations between technical services, IT, and public services was the virtual browsing initiative. The exploration of a virtual browsing solution began in late 2014 after the announcement that most of the library's physical collection would be moved to an off-site storage facility.

As a commitment to the Georgia Tech faculty, the library was tasked with figuring out a way for users to simulate browsing the shelves in an online environment, since the ability to browse the physical shelves would no longer be available. A virtual browsing task force consisting of librarians, IT, and technical and public services staff was formed. The task force polled peer institutions and researched projects that were tackling the problem of serendipitously discovering library materials in an online environment. The work of the task force was also informed by the publication of a student research paper on virtual browsing that addressed the changing user expectations of discovering library resources and discussed alternatives and implementation options. The paper concludes that "with all of the changes and evolution that will come to the Georgia Tech Library, virtual browsing is arguably one of the most influential, affecting students both in and out of the library." The paper goes on to state that "it will once again be possible to achieve serendipity when browsing, although the mode of access may be different."[6]

By late 2016, the Library Next portfolio had launched, and a virtual browsing project was officially initiated as part of the portfolio. The research and recommendations compiled by the task force served as key inputs for the project. The project started with a conceptual white paper and internal library discussions about the role of browsing in a primarily digital library. The paper's abstract reads: "in order to recreate one of the qualities of collection browsing that is lost by relocating the physical collection off-site, the Library should provide a recommendation service that can provide the kind of serendipitous search results that patrons have identified as critical-to-quality in their browsing."[7]

With the needs identified and the data gathered and analyzed, it was time to identify and implement a technical solution. Developing an in-house platform utilizing Georgia Tech's own engineering and computer-programing expertise was briefly considered, but true to portfolio management principles, based on the available human and budgetary resources as well as the desired timeline, the library decided that the implementation of an existing commercial product would be a better path forward.

During phase 2 of the project, a group of librarians from technical services and IT evaluated a variety of products from different vendors, using the following criteria established in the data-gathering from phase 1:

- Affordability
- Support
- Ease of implementation
- Integration with Primo
- Ease of maintenance
- Similarity to traditional physical browsing
- E-books integration

The evaluation resulted in the selection of Syndetics Unbound for a trial subscription. The team used the trial to collect user feedback (see Appendix C) by facilitating focus groups with undergraduate and graduate students to gauge their satisfaction with the selected virtual browsing platform and to inform enhancements. The sessions were facilitated by the library's IT librarian and the metadata strategist, who were both heavily involved in implementation. They were able to immediately translate users' questions and comments into setup adjustments and enhancement requests, resulting in an improved user interface. The Syndetics Unbound team was also a truly collaborative partner, as they were able to update their code to the specifics of the library's bibliographic descriptions to more effectively incorporate e-books into virtual browsing. The user feedback received was overwhelming positive, prompting the library to select Syndetics Unbound as the provider of the virtual browsing solution.

Observing graduate and undergraduate students experiencing virtual browsing and discussing their impression during feedback-gathering sessions gave us a better understanding of what users' expectations are for the virtual browsing platform and how it is used. These observations shaped the communication strategy to advertise and promote the new service. After the implementation, a subject librarian used focus groups' feedback and the implementation team's insights to create a video tutorial to introduce the service to users.[8] As the library continues the project life cycle, the project team routinely gathers feedback to identify new needs and enhance the service as updates become available.

LIBRARY NEXT PROJECT 2: ENHANCEMENTS TO THE DISCOVERY INTERFACE

In many libraries, the pursuit of information literacy is a long-term and vital library instruction goal. As discovery tools become increasingly critical to libraries' functioning, it is worthwhile to examine how library instruction and discovery work together. As part of the Library Next five-year renewal process, the Georgia Tech Library implemented Primo as both a catalog interface and a discovery tool in 2016.

For this project, the humanities & science fiction librarian, who instructs introductory English classes, and the metadata strategist, who works directly with Primo and Alma, collaborated. Through their combined expertise, they were able to assess first-year students' experiences with the newly implemented discovery tool to make improvements both in teaching and to the interface itself.

Starting with the intention to learn how students use the tools available to them, and how the library can help support those efforts through interface improvements and instruction, the need for a project based on users' assessments in library instruction classes was identified. This project began in January 2016 and coincided with many other changes at the Georgia Tech Library, including the removal of much of the physical collection to a shared repository with Emory University, a major renovation of both library buildings on the Georgia Tech campus, and new services to complement the new physical spaces. Due to these additional changes, the library's Primo implementation was minimally customized, making it ideal to collect user feedback early in the process.

We selected first-year English classes as the focus group to evaluate Primo and Alma for several reasons. A review of the literature demonstrated that students early in their college experience often overestimate their comprehension of information literacy.[9] These students had not experienced the Georgia Tech Library's previous search interface; thus their feedback would be focused on their experience with Primo, rather than on a comparison of Primo with the earlier catalog. Also, like many libraries, the Georgia Tech Library's strongest teaching partnerships are with introductory humanities classes. The Marion L. Brittain Fellows, recent PhD graduates who refine their teaching and research during a three-year fellowship at Georgia Tech, are the instructors for English 1101 and 1102. They are creative teachers who utilize a multimodal curriculum represented by the acronym WOVEN (written, oral, visual, electronic, and nonverbal communication) and were ideal collaboration partners for this project.

The research design sought to illuminate students' experiences with the Primo discovery tool, as well as inviting them to share their opinions about it. Using Qualtrics software to record their responses, the project team asked students to complete these six tasks in Primo (see Appendix D):

- Search for a book by title.
- Search for works by a specific author.
- Search for a journal by name.

- Find a newspaper article on a specific topic.
- Search for works on a specific topic.
- Search for a DVD by title.

While the goals remained the same from class to class, the team was able to customize these tasks to fit the class's research topic to make the experience more relevant to students and to increase instructors' buy-in. The students were also asked to complete the following survey questions:

- How often they use the catalog and for what purposes
- Their overall impressions of the interface
- What they like best about the interface
- Suggestions for changes
- How comprehensible the language on the interface was to them
- Whether they have requested items from the library service center
- Ratings for:
  - » Ease of searching
  - » Organization of search results
  - » Relevance of search results
  - » Aesthetic appearance of the website
  - » An open response field for any additional comments

Both the tasks and the survey questions were distributed to students in a single assessment instrument (i.e., Appendix D). Students could choose to stop participating in the research at any time, and none of the questions were required to complete the survey.

This research was conducted in the Spring semester of 2017 and provided three different English 1102 classes the opportunity to participate. Of the pool of 104 students present in class on those days, 84 completed the assessment instrument. Because none of the questions were mandatory, the total number of responses to each question was used when analyzing the results.

The project team developed a rubric to grade the tasks, and for questions with multiple parts they evaluated each part separately. The students were most successful at finding physical items using Primo, especially books and DVDs. The students found locating a digital newspaper article challenging, as well as determining the availability of electronic journal titles. In the survey questions, students reported low library usage, and a general favorable impression of the Primo interface (see figure 12.3). Many also commented that they found Primo easy to use.

In addition to adopting changes to instruction to guide students more effectively through search scopes, the team shared the results of its research

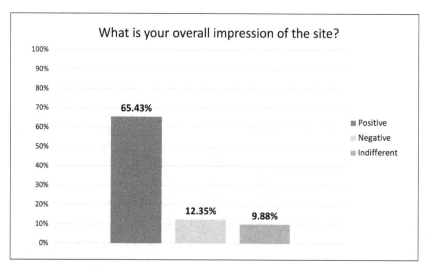

FIGURE 12.3
Chart showing students' satisfaction with the Primo interface

with the library's Content Discovery Group, which manages the library's discovery interface and is responsible for making changes to it to ensure a positive user experience.

The results of the research were also shared with the head of Campus Engagement and Scholarly Outreach and with the associate dean for Learning and Research Services. In order to continue to strengthen the relationship with the first-year English program, the results and changes forthcoming from the research were also shared with the Brittain Fellows whose classes participated, with the director of the Writing and Communication program, and with the chair of the School of Literature, Media and Communication.

The results of the students' in-class exercises and comments, combined with the feedback from meetings with librarians, library staff, and library undergraduate, graduate, and faculty advisory boards, provided guidance on valuable improvements to the interface. Technical services and IT librarians summarized the feedback and prioritized and implemented the updates, resulting in a more intuitive discovery interface. The team used Trello, a project management tool, to translate the users' feedback into an actionable list of catalog interface enhancements (see figure 12.4) and to determine the order of priorities based on articulated user preferences and the complexity of implementing changes.

This case study is a particularly good example of the importance of identifying all stakeholders early in the process and creating a communication plan that is specific to each internal and external stakeholder group. Through this project we taught undergraduate students about the library's catalog and

FIGURE 12.4
Trello board used to translate users' feedback into an actionable list of catalog interface enhancements

resources, and instruction librarians were able to gain insight into students' use of the catalog, adjust their teaching strategies, and develop new training and promotional materials. The communication between the teaching faculty and the library helped to show faculty the impact of their feedback on the library's systems and services. Technical services and IT librarians developed a better understanding of how to communicate system changes and limitations to their public services colleagues, and this communication translated into better teaching and easier troubleshooting.

LIBRARY NEXT PROJECT 3: SINGLE SIGN-ON AUTHENTICATION

Of the three Library Next projects highlighted in this chapter, the migration to a new, single sign-on authentication solution (OpenAthens) appeared to require the least feedback from end-users. Instead, technical services and IT staff relied on their public services colleagues' expertise to provide the project with training and insight into end-users' behavior and expectations. Two sub-projects were initiated due to the diverse requirements for migrating to a different remote authentication system. The two sub-projects involved separate project teams, each with its own goals, charter, and timeline, yet focused on the same outcome: the successful implementation of a single sign-on authentication system.

The first project team evaluated the available technologies, collaborated with the selected vendor on the implementation, and completed the technical side of the migration process. It was apparent at the end of this first process that the success of the migration and the acceptance of the new authentication system by library stakeholders (faculty and students) required a good communication strategy and the training of library front-line staff.

The second project team identified the training needs, created the training and communication plan, and produced patron-facing documentation. To ensure the success of the project, it was imperative to collaborate with a colleague who had experience in training and explaining difficult technical concepts to the library staff who have minimal technical experience. A public services librarian with a knowledge of instructional design principles was an ideal choice.

The training strategy implemented by the team was twofold. First, the library faculty advisory group was offered a preview of the new technology, including an overview of the advantages of using it both to simplify the authentication process and to be able to collect more robust and granular usage data. For the initial meeting with the faculty stakeholders, we implemented a few resources on the new system so we could offer them a real-life experience and hands-on demonstration of the system. Involving library patrons early in the experience of the new technology helped to develop a staff-training strategy because it highlighted the steps of the process that were not clear and were confusing to patrons. Conducting the training with different groups also helped with developing the communication plan and documentation. The frequently asked questions (FAQ) became a dynamic document that was updated after each training session.

Implementing the OpenAthens solution highlighted the importance of developing and executing a realistic project timeline, with ongoing collaboration between project team members, the project team, and end-users. The initial negative response from patrons helped the project team to reevaluate the project timeline and analyze the shortcomings of the preliminary planning. For example, the project team hadn't fully considered user behavior and pathways to library e-resources when they made decisions about implementing and introducing the new authentication system.

To mitigate the situation, the project team requested that a public services librarian develop a short video explaining the reasons for migrating to the new technology and how to overcome the most common technical issues accompanying its use.[10] This project experience underscored the need for constant collaboration between technical and public services staff, where front-end staff contribute a knowledge and understanding of user needs and behavior and an ability to explain technology in simple terms, while the technical services staff provide expertise to identify and implement the improvements to the system.

CONCLUSION

Collaboration creates unique and valuable opportunities for continuous improvement spanning departmental lines, as identified in the Library Next use case. As we implemented new services in newly renovated buildings after the physical collections had been moved off-site, we also learned the benefits of cross-functional collaborations in new ways. Our success depended on learning different ways to work together to support library users as they navigate the Georgia Tech Library's new physical and digital landscapes.

As this use case demonstrates, there is something to learn from every project. In the virtual browsing project, technical services and library IT made the library's collection accessible in an entirely new way. Making enhancements to the discovery interface allowed a liaison librarian and technical services to tailor the new catalog and discovery interface based on student feedback. And working together to implement OpenAthens, the single sign-on authentication, involved the collaboration of technical services, a public services librarian, and library staff members.

Communication and information-sharing are key elements of these cooperative efforts, demonstrating how common goals led not only to increased efficiency, but also to greater team efforts and improved morale. Ultimately, collaboration is the key to implementing improved services for library users in the twenty-first century.

NOTES

1. Catherine Murray-Rust, "Radical Restructuring," *American Libraries*, 2017, https://americanlibrariesmagazine.org/2017/09/01/radical-restructuring-library-renovation/.
2. Project Management Institute, ed., *A Guide to the Project Management Body of Knowledge: PMBOK Guide*, 6th ed., PMI Global Standard (Newtown Square, PA: Project Management Institute, 2017), 7.
3. Georgia Tech Library, "2019 Impact Report," n.d., http://hdl.handle.net/1853/64271.
4. Project Management Institute, *A Guide to the Project Management Body of Knowledge*, 15.
5. Georgia Tech Library, "2019 Impact Report."
6. Alex Akins et al., "Virtual Browsing: The Georgia Tech Library in the Digital

Age," 2015, Georgia Tech, https://smartech.gatech.edu/handle/1853/62875.

7. Charlie Bennett and Seth Porter, "Virtual Browsing: A White Paper," May 2017, Georgia Tech, https://smartech.gatech.edu/handle/1853/62874.

8. Georgia Tech Library, "Using Virtual Browsing," 2019, https://youtu.be/cNX3cByYrvU.

9. Zahid Hossain Shoeb, "Information Literacy Competency of Freshman Business Students of a Private University in Bangladesh," *Library Review* 60, no. 9 (October 11, 2011): 762–72, https://doi.org/10.1108/00242531111176781.

10. Georgia Tech Library, "How to Use OpenAthens," n.d., https://youtu.be/6-TLL OUZD1o.

MAGGIE DULL

13

Expand Your Reach, Empower Your Community

Implementing a Metadata Outreach Service Program

In 2018, staff at the University of Rochester's River Campus Libraries (RCL) began a three-year project to formalize and launch a new service called Metadata Outreach. Focused on the broader university community, Metadata Outreach leverages the experience and expertise held by Metadata Services staff, particularly in information organization, metadata schemas, and controlled vocabularies, to empower our community to recognize and tackle their information-based or metadata-based challenges, enhance their research, and reimagine their worlds. A consultation-based service, Metadata Outreach expands the ability of Metadata Services (RCL's Cataloging and Metadata Department) to support the teaching, learning, and research activities at the University of Rochester beyond our traditional library collections-focused work. From developing research data management workflows and consulting on effective and consistent tagging for digital humanities projects, to collaborating on definitions and conceptual models for the university's data governance work, Metadata Outreach's impact on the university community powerfully communicates the value of technical services and technical services practitioners to the library's stakeholders and users.

This chapter will define what the author means by Metadata Outreach and how it emerged as a concept and possible service through ad hoc consultations with faculty and university staff and through collaborative projects with more forward-facing library staff. Readers will learn how this "proof of concept" phase informed the development of Metadata Outreach into an articulated library service—a phase that included defining roles and stakeholders, user needs and service offerings, and a collaborative service model. The chapter will conclude with a discussion of the RCL's launch of Metadata Outreach as a library service, with a focus on strengthening relationships and communication and lessons learned. Ultimately, readers will be provided with the tools and concepts they need to identify Metadata Outreach opportunities at their own institutions and to develop and define their own Metadata Outreach service.

METADATA OUTREACH: DEFINITION AND ORIGINS

Located in Rochester, New York, the University of Rochester (UR) is a private research university that has about 12,000 students and 3,000 faculty across three major campuses: the River Campus, the Eastman School of Music, and the University of Rochester Medical Center.[1] The River Campus Libraries is one of three main libraries that support the educational and research mission of the University of Rochester. Though we collaborate with and share systems with our colleagues at the Sibley Music Library and the Medical Center Libraries, the RCL focuses on supporting research, teaching, and learning at the university's School of Arts & Sciences, Hajim School of Engineering, Simon Business School, Warner School of Education, and the Laboratory for Laser Energetics.[2] The RCL thus engages with a wide range of departments and disciplines in developing its collections and services. Currently, the RCL has more than 100 staff members, six of whom are members of Metadata Services.

Metadata Outreach emerged at the RCL as an opportunity to make more visible the expertise and experience contained within Metadata Services, the department responsible for cataloging and metadata activities. Metadata and cataloging work, along with the rest of technical services operations, are at the core of library services but aren't often seen by our colleagues within RCL and across the university. Even though they are a core component of the library infrastructure, when metadata or cataloging efforts are successful, they don't intrude into the user experience. By this, I mean that their work facilitates a smooth and seamless journey through discovery interfaces and library collections. The enrichment of bibliographic records with table of contents information, the consistent application of subject vocabularies, and the careful encoding of material types all help to readily and easily connect users with the materials they need. Users will only consider what is happening behind the scenes when something goes wrong—a bad link, a missing item, a failed search. While library users and stakeholders benefit from cataloging and metadata work, they never need to consider who is making that experience possible. Metadata Outreach allows Metadata Services staff to communicate what they do, why they do it, and how their work positively impacts the university community.

The core work of Metadata Services is to make things findable in ways that are consistent, intuitive, and standards-driven. Typically, the "things" that Metadata Services makes findable are library resources and collections, such as monographs, serials, e-books, media, and digital collections. We rely on long-standing standards such as MARC and the Library of Congress Subject Headings. A critical aspect of Metadata Outreach is that the focus of the staff's expertise and efforts is not on library materials and information problems, but rather on the collections, data, and research challenges confronting the wider university community. While technical services staff may hesitate to move beyond their familiar collections and standards, this movement towards collaborating with library users to solve metadata problems aligns with the natural progression of the field. As library collections evolve through changes in media and technology and in user needs, Metadata Services staff adapt to these changes by leveraging their current expertise and growing their skills as needed. This adaptation may mean learning new platforms or standards, such as our migration to Alma or the shift from AACR2 to RDA. The staff may also need to research new solutions, such as when tasked with cataloging a video game collection, or new standards, such as when selecting appropriate subject vocabularies for digital collections. In addition to expertise, technical services staff have a long history of collaborating across different departments and supporting a variety of disciplines. This rich history of practice leaves Metadata Services staff uniquely able to tackle a wide range of information-based problems and to seek out new or emerging solutions.

Perhaps most importantly, working alongside the community to solve metadata problems is not at all a new concept in librarianship or technical services. There are numerous examples of metadata and technical services staff supporting faculty and researchers on metadata projects, especially within the digital humanities.[3] While these projects are more faculty-driven and may involve materials from outside library collections, many digital humanities platforms and projects rely on the same standards used in library digital projects, such as Omeka's use of Dublin Core and other controlled vocabularies, and share similar approaches to connecting users with resources through improved discovery. As described in the next section, Metadata Outreach pushes beyond the usual library standards and platforms to assist and empower our communities, reaching a more diverse group of faculty as well as connecting with university staff. Metadata Outreach is simply the next logical step in expanding the impact of technical services work.

While the RCL and Metadata Services continually work to communicate the value of metadata and cataloging work, Metadata Outreach as a solution emerged from a chance connection in spring 2018. The RCL's then director of Research Initiatives, Lauren Di Monte, wanted to assist a faculty member with a research data management problem. As part of her work on this project, she thought to reach out to the author, the director of Metadata Strategies, for advice. The problem involved the best way to organize and manage versions of linguistics research data, in this case, audio recordings. The author and Di Monte met with the faculty member for a conversation about the challenges that she faced. We asked questions to better understand the faculty member's needs and the nature of her research data, very much in the vein of a reference interview. The results were ideas and suggestions for how to approach organizing the data in a manner that reflected the research process, clarified the relationship between versions, and allowed for regular backups. The faculty member thought the suggestions to be helpful and soon began work on reorganizing her data, occasionally reaching out to the author for advice. With this first consultation, Metadata Outreach was born.

METADATA OUTREACH: PROJECT PHASES

Building upon that first consultation, the development of Metadata Outreach at the RCL occurred in three distinct phases. Phase One focused on "pilot projects" and the iteration of services to feel out and determine what Metadata Outreach could, and should, look like at the River Campus Libraries. Phase Two focused on conceptualizing and describing Metadata Outreach in such a way to allow it to be managed and marketed as a fully realized, ongoing library service. This included defining roles and responsibilities, service offerings, and a conceptual service model. The final phase, Phase Three, is concerned with the launch of Metadata Outreach as a service, including communication and a website, and is ongoing at the time of writing. The different phases are described below and detail how this work evolved at the RCL. This case study approach will allow cataloging and technical services departments at other academic institutions to develop their own Metadata Outreach program. That being said, there is no "one size fits all" method of doing Metadata Outreach. Each institution will need to reflect on the expertise and capacity of its metadata and cataloging staff and the needs of its users in order to define a sustainable program scope. The goal of this chapter is to provide a framework for metadata and technical services staff to sustainably implement their own Metadata Outreach service in a way that best serves and empowers their community.

Phase One: Pilot Projects and Iteration

Metadata Outreach as a service emerged from the aforementioned consultation as an ad hoc, project-based program that was managed with varying levels of formality. Phase One, which lasted about six months, focused on assisting members of the university community with a variety of projects to which Metadata Services staff felt they could contribute. At this point, Metadata Outreach was still a vague concept. While the overarching goal of leveraging the expertise of metadata staff to help our users solve their metadata quandaries could be articulated, specific elements such as the "how" and "why" needed refining. The process as a whole felt somewhat makeshift, and the required expertise and service boundaries were still unclear. By working through these pilot projects, the author hoped to gauge the needs of the university community and discover how metadata staff could sustainably meet those needs.

The pilot projects can be roughly grouped into three categories: digital scholarship, faculty research support, and data governance. Each category relies on the strong relationships with external stakeholders held by other members of the RCL's staff and generously shared with Metadata Services. This sharing of relationships and contacts by other library staff is a key element to making Metadata Outreach viable. As discussed above, metadata and cataloging work tends to occur behind the scenes, and the staff in those departments don't interact with the community to the same extent as departments that are focused on services such as reference and outreach, research support, and digital scholarship. In addition to bringing together users and metadata staff, collaborating with patron-facing colleagues allows metadata staff to understand the kinds of information-based problems their communities face and the range of solutions already available. As will be discussed in Phase Three, the successful launch of Metadata Outreach relied on collaboration from patron-facing colleagues, who maintain a connection with the broader community and who have the capacity to direct users toward the service.

Digital Scholarship

The RCL's Digital Scholarship Lab (DSL)[4] was an early supporter of Metadata Outreach. Beginning in 2018, Emily Sherwood, director of Digital Scholarship, reached out to Metadata Services staff at the start of any of the lab's faculty projects that needed metadata support or had information organization elements. The metadata staff's assistance has ranged from advising on metadata schema and standards selections for Omeka-based digital collections, to working through questions involving the organization of project elements or research materials. By including metadata staff at the start, the

DSL ensures that projects are not bogged down later by problems and that faculty are empowered at the start to discover and work through any metadata questions. The first project that emerged as part of the DSL's collaboration with Metadata Outreach was *Sekuru's Stories*, a multimedia book coauthored by Sekuru Tute Chigamba and Dr. Jennifer Kyker.[5] *Sekuru's Stories* is "a public digital humanities project featuring the renowned Zimbabwean mbira player, oral historian, and ritual specialist Sekuru Tute Chigamba."[6] As an interactive, multimedia-rich digital monograph developed on WordPress, this work presented a number of interesting metadata challenges for the DSL and Kyker. A key issue was that Kyker did not want the metadata to be obvious or intrusive. The work is a digital monograph, not a collection of records. Metadata wasn't the focus of the project, but rather an element that needed to work to support the overarching narrative of the book.

Over the course of several meetings and a one-on-one consultation, the author provided suggestions and possible solutions for ensuring that related entity and subject relationships could be leveraged throughout the digital monograph, as well as how to connect different versions of the same work (e.g., audio recording, transcription, translation, etc.). While some of the solutions were actionable steps in the creation of the digital monograph, most of the value provided by Metadata Outreach was asking questions and articulating the impact of metadata in such a project. What kind of user experience does the metadata need to facilitate? Where can the metadata reside? How can you ensure that the metadata is consistent? By listening to Kyker's needs and by illustrating the kinds of questions that needed to be considered at the start of a project, the author empowered Kyker to use metadata to bring her vision to life.

Faculty Research Support

A long-standing and key service in academic libraries is supporting faculty research and teaching. This support often comes from externally facing library departments, such as reference and outreach, and can range from assistance with research queries, to instructional support for individual classes, to collection development. Across the RCL, staff are at work building new services to address emerging faculty and researcher needs. This includes, but is not limited to, open pedagogy support, scholarly profile management, and research data management. Metadata Outreach aligns with these new services, many of which are still developing, by providing the faculty with new approaches and tools to address the challenges posed by researching and teaching in an increasingly digital environment. One notable pilot project was planning a repository for student-generated linguistics data. The staff from RCL's Research Initiatives, Data Outreach, Digital Initiatives, and Learning Initiatives came together to help a professor develop an alternative repository for her students. Depositing research data in an extant disciplinary repository is a common practice for linguistics scholars; however, students face some barriers in participating in this practice. The primary barrier to participation is that the two major archives for depositing, archiving, and preserving linguistics research data, the Endangered Languages Archive at the University of London's School of Oriental and African Studies, and the Language Archive at the Max Planck Institute, will not accept research data collected by students because this is beyond their scope. A local solution would allow the students more flexibility as they learned to navigate the same data management questions faced by established scholars in the field. Metadata Outreach provided feedback and suggestions on the metadata in the repository and prepared programming to instruct the students on the value of metadata and developing metadata within their data and within the repository. Due to IRB challenges, this project is currently on hold. However, the experience of bringing a variety of expertise to the table to support a new, faculty-generated project proved the value of this approach and the added value provided by metadata staff in the process.

Data Governance

The third and most unique category of pilot projects consists of those related to the University of Rochester's data governance efforts. In addition to the proliferation of research data, the focus of institutions on leveraging institutional data in their decision-making creates a clear need for the metadata and information organization expertise found within technical services departments. At the University of Rochester, data governance "sets the standards and protocols for the definition, exchange, integrity, and security" of data generated by the university community and "enables accurate analytics and reporting, which generate answers to key questions and inform decision-making by leadership, internal audiences, and external agencies."[7] San Cannon, the university's chief data officer, reached out to the RCL to establish relationships with staff from several departments. The author was asked to join as a consultant on one of the university's first data governance projects, the revision of academic job codes. These job codes are used in the university's human resources system to identify and manage faculty and related positions. In November 2018, a working group convened to address the challenges that the current job code structure presented to managing faculty data, and to develop a solution.[8] The author advised on metadata best practices and worked with a core group to workshop the different elements that make up an academic position and thus an academic job code, such as teaching and research, and to capture structural elements of these positions such as rank and tenure eligibility.[9] After approval from across the university, the new codes were implemented in the summer of 2019.

The conversations begun in this project, particularly conceptual questions around data unique to a faculty member versus a staff member versus an employee, have continued in a university-level data-modeling project. Currently ongoing, this project develops definitions and an overarching structure that inform the various aspects of data governance, such as people data, location data, and so on. Metadata Outreach participates in this project as requested. Another key pilot project that originated from data governance is the RCL's participation in the University of Rochester's Love Data Week. In February 2019 and February 2020, staff from across the RCL presented on topics relating to data management and data governance. The author presented two sessions on metadata essentials for faculty, students, and staff.[10] This provided a unique opportunity to connect directly with users in order to begin a dialogue on metadata and metadata needs.

The Metadata Outreach pilot projects provided valuable insights into how Metadata Outreach should function at the University of Rochester. This review of user needs and Metadata Services expertise and capacity generated the following conclusions:

- *Focus on consultations and education, not generating metadata.* The real value of Metadata Outreach comes from showing community members how to identify metadata problems and how to ask the right questions of their research and their materials. Empowering the university community to tackle its metadata questions will allow the community to work without constant intervention by Metadata Services staff, thus expanding the overall capacity for Metadata Outreach work.
- *Collaborate with colleagues who steward community relationships.* Metadata Outreach relies on the relationships established by library colleagues with faculty, students, and staff. Metadata Outreach is not designed to replace library staff who maintain those relationships. Working through metadata problems should include relevant library staff whenever possible, which has the bonus of providing colleagues with metadata troubleshooting skills of their own.
- *Integrate Metadata Outreach in established or emerging library services.* There are many opportunities to add Metadata Outreach into other library services or to serve as a referral from other library services. The pilot projects identified the RCL's data management service, digital scholarship services, and instructional design services as potential areas for referrals, in both directions.
- *Create a website or other virtual space where the community can learn more about Metadata Outreach, as well as the basics of*

metadata. The pilot projects surfaced a need for a centralized space where the university community could go for information on what Metadata Outreach provides, the basics of metadata, and who to contact. This website could serve as the first level of support and could clearly articulate how Metadata Outreach provides value.

Phase Two: Developing Metadata Outreach as a Service

The pilot project experience fed directly into Phase Two of the development of Metadata Outreach. The goal of this second phase was to conceptualize and describe Metadata Outreach in such a way as to allow it to be managed and marketed as a fully realized, ongoing library service. Per standard practice at RCL, this service model project was managed through a written project plan[11] that included the following milestones:

- Brainstorm and describe the resources, skills, and perspectives that Metadata Outreach can provide.
- Define and articulate the roles and responsibilities of participants and stakeholders in Metadata Outreach, including Metadata Services staff, liaison librarians, Research Initiatives staff, and so on.
- Design a conceptual model of Metadata Outreach as a service.
- Create a Metadata Outreach website and draft a communication plan.

Originally, the project plan's milestones started with delivering the conceptual model of the service. However, it became readily apparent that the model would only emerge after developing an understanding of the resources, skills, roles, and responsibilities that the staff could provide to Metadata Outreach. Phase Two also incorporated the author's experience collaborating on the creation of a service model for active research data management at RCL, a cross-departmental service designed to aid researchers at a specific point in their research data life cycle. This project demonstrated the importance of centering user needs in the service model, clearly defining how users would enter and navigate the service, and the sustainability of a program focused on consultation and education to enable users to identify and solve problems before calling on the experts again.

Because Metadata Outreach relies on the expertise and experience of Metadata Services staff, the first step in creating a service model for Metadata Outreach was to brainstorm and describe the resources, skills, and perspectives that staff could provide. This is a key step for all institutions looking to launch such a program and will vary due to the nature of a department's staff. When brainstorming, it is important not to get bogged down in a list of specific standards, technologies, or systems. Rather, this list should touch on the "bigger picture" skills or experiences that metadata staff can provide. Consider, for example, the difference between "a knowledge of LCSH, AAT, FAST, and MeSH" and "identifying, selecting, and developing controlled vocabularies for information organization projects." At this stage, the notion of scope must also be considered. What is a reasonable level of service when taking into consideration the size of the user base, the potential use of the service, and the current capacity of Metadata Services staff? As revealed earlier in the process, services that emphasize conversation and education are far more sustainable and impactful than the custom-made creation of metadata or metadata standards.

This brainstorming resulted in an "Offering Inventory," a document that included the name of the offering, a description, the audience for the service, and its impact on the community. An example of this inventory is shown in figure 13.1.

The Offering Inventory is a living document that will be edited and updated as departmental expertise evolves and as new offerings emerge. For example, the notion of advising on keywords and abstracts for publications and other research outputs joined the list of offerings after a faculty member specifically requested this assistance. The Inventory is also intended to be an

Offering	Description	Audience	Impact
Consultation on information organization problems or questions.	Provide assistance to those facing an information organization problem(s). You have "stuff" and you need to address how you are organizing, arranging, and/or describing that stuff so as to support discovery and sharing. Includes discussing file paths/directory structure, developing file names, internal or external metadata descriptions, selecting schemas and controlled vocabularies. May include existing systems/solutions as well as brainstorming new options or choices.	Faculty ; Staff ; Student	Empower the University community to tackle their metadata problems and roadblocks. Improves your work and your ability to describe, share, and discover said work. Supports and improves business processes across the University.
Developing and selecting keywords and abstracts for publications and other research outputs	Assisting researchers in thinking through how they would describe their outputs so as to improve retrieval, align their outputs with related materials in repositories and collections, provide keyword enrichment for discovery, etc.	Faculty ; Student	Improves the discovery of and thus impact of research outputs.
Identifying, selecting, and developing maetadata schemas for information organization projects.	Provide assistance in selecting or augmenting an existing metadata schema or developing a new metadata schema for a variety of projects. Working with the individual, develop an understanding of the information objects being described, the users accessing said objects, and how these objects will be managed/curated. Research and recommend extant schemas, if available, or develop new schemas as needed.	Faculty ; Staff	Improve the management and discovery of information objects. Support the management of information objects. Support the sharing and reuse of metadata surrounding the information objects with an eye towards interoperability.
Identifying, selecting, and developing controlled vocabularies for information organization projects.	Provide assistance in selecting or augmenting an existing controlled vocabulary or developing a new controlled vocabulary for a variety of projects. Working with the individual, develop an understanding of how the controlled vocabulary will be used and how and with whom the metadata using this controlled vocabulary will be shared. Research and recommend extant vocabularies, if available, or develop new vocabularies as needed.	Faculty ; Staff	Improve the management and discovery of information objects, particularly the gathering together of like objects. Support the sharing and reuse of metadata surrounding information objects with an eye towards interoperability.
Support and advise on conceptual data modelling projects.	Provide assistance in developing conceptual data models for a variety of domains.	Faculty ; Staff	Improve and support complex business processes across the University. Improve the flow of information or the description of complex information systems in research projects.

FIGURE 13.1
Metadata Outreach's Offering Inventory

internal document that guides the implementation of the program. The offerings themselves will be shared with the community, but information such as impact and audience are more geared toward RCL internal stakeholders.

Once the services were established, the next step was to define and articulate the roles and responsibilities of participants and stakeholders in Metadata Outreach, including Metadata Services staff, liaison librarians, Research Initiatives staff, and so on. This step also helped define the scope of the program by clearly identifying the user base and collaborators. Roles were broken up into three main stakeholder groups: RCL staff, UR staff, and UR users. Essentially, these three groups are RCL staff who may participate in or recommend Metadata Outreach as a service; external UR staff whose work may make them potential collaborators with Metadata Outreach; and the UR users of Metadata Outreach. These categories and thus roles are not mutually exclusive. For example, UR staff may be called on to support a Metadata Outreach consultation, such as providing data governance assistance, and may also take advantage of the service to support their work.

The outcome of this process was a "Roles and Responsibilities" document outlining specific users and user groups and defining their roles and how they connect to Metadata Outreach as a service (figure 13.2).

RCL Staff	Role in Metadata Outreach
Metadata Services	Provide Metadata Outreach Services. Includes all members of Metadata Services based on their skills, schedule, and inclination.
Outreach and Science Librarians	Provide a connection between the wider university community, particularly faculty and students, and Metadata Outreach Services. Helps the university community identify that they have a "metadata problem" and direct them towards Metadata Outreach staff.
Data Outreach Librarian	Provide a connection between the wider university community, particularly faculty and researchers, and Metadata Outreach Services. Helps researchers leverage Metadata Outreach Services in managing their research data and related outputs.
Research Initiatives	Provide a connection between the wider university community, particularly researchers and university research services, and Metadata Outreach Services. Helps researchers and research-focused departments leverage Metadata Outreach Services in managing and understanding research data and related outputs.
IDT	Provide support for Metadata Outreach Services that rely upon the systems and services managed by IDT. This includes, but is not limited to, UR Research, Alma, etc.

FIGURE 13.2
Metadata Outreach roles and responsibilities

With the services and players defined, a conceptual model of Metadata Outreach as a functioning service readily emerged (figure 13.3). This model is a visual representation of how Metadata Outreach flows. The service model includes the users of the service, collaborators, and Metadata Outreach staff. It also includes resources, such as the Metadata Outreach website and Metadata Outreach programming. Throughout the model, relationships are defined and many go in both directions. As with the Offerings Inventory, this is an internal document that will guide the implementation of Metadata Outreach as a service, and it is intended to evolve and change.

The last elements to launching Metadata Outreach as a functioning service were to craft a Metadata Outreach website and a communication plan, in order to facilitate sharing the service with users and stakeholders. Though Metadata Outreach's online presence had originally been conceived as a LibGuide, the recent revamp of the RCL's website provided a space for Metadata Outreach under "Services."[12] The "Metadata Outreach" subsection there features three main areas. The first is a general introduction to Metadata Outreach that defines the service for the university community and explains why metadata matters to them. Next is a page on "Understanding Metadata and Metadata Resources," which provides the university community with materials to help them understand the basics of metadata, how it connects to their

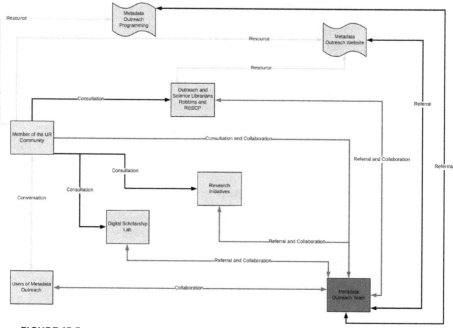

FIGURE 13.3
Metadata Outreach service conceptual model

work, and resources to help them start solving metadata problems. The final page outlines "Projects and Services," providing user-focused descriptions of the offerings from the Offering Inventory and a summary of the work already undertaken as part of the service. The Metadata Outreach content on the RCL's website launched in May 2020, and will evolve as the service develops.

The "Metadata Outreach" part of the RCL's website is a key aspect of a Communication Plan drafted to assist in the launching of Metadata Outreach. The plan will facilitate sharing with the RCL and University of Rochester community the basic ideas of Metadata Outreach as a service, including its purpose, how it can help, and how to get in touch with it. The Communication Plan outlines the audience for the plan (users, RCL stakeholders, and UR stakeholders). Most importantly, the plan defines the overall message about Metadata Outreach that needs to be communicated, which includes what the service can do and who it is for. Metadata Outreach is for everyone at the university. Beyond faculty teaching and research, the service can help university staff improve their business processes and better understand how their work relates to data governance, and help students manage, describe, and understand their research data and outputs. The plan outlines how this message will be communicated, mainly through the relationships stewarded by the author and her colleagues at the RCL. It includes a list of conversations to be held and meetings to attend. It concludes with thoughts on evaluating the effectiveness of the plan, such as measuring an increase in consultations, hits to the website, and so on.

Phase Three: Launching Metadata Outreach as a Service

With the Phase Two milestones achieved, the RCL was poised to launch Metadata Outreach as a service. As mentioned above, the Metadata Outreach web content went live in May 2020, and the author began implementing elements of the Communication Plan. The formal launch of Metadata Outreach was originally planned to occur in early spring 2020. However, this timeline was delayed due to the impact of the COVID-19 pandemic, and the consequent movement of library operations, teaching and learning, and research to remote work. During this time of working from home, Metadata Outreach is still supporting the campus community, particularly through the Digital Scholarship's digital pedagogy programming and the RCL's support of faculty research projects. It is hoped that the resources offered on the new "Metadata Outreach" subsection of the RCL's website will also help support the community in continuing their work from home.

Work continues on implementing the Communication Plan. Before the web content went live, the author reached out to colleagues in the RCL whose services overlap with or include Metadata Outreach, such as the Digital

Scholarship Lab and Research Initiatives, and colleagues who work closely with graduate students and faculty, such as the director of the Rossell Hope Robbins Library and the Koller-Collins Center for English Studies. Meetings are planned between colleagues from Learning Initiatives, which will feature an activity on identifying and diagnosing metadata issues in a variety of teaching and research settings. The author continues to work through this communication plan, focusing on marketing and assessment efforts.

MOVING FORWARD

Through conversations, collaborations, and education, the RCL's Metadata Outreach service empowers the university community to tackle their metadata challenges, while also ably illustrating the value of technical services staff. The development of the program at RCL provides a straightforward model that any institution can adapt to suit its users' needs and staff's expertise. You should begin by reaching out to library colleagues to help identify potential users and institutional needs. Data and metadata problems are universal, and cataloging and metadata departments are uniquely suited to wading into the fray. Your efforts may also reveal new or unfamiliar library services and offerings that align with Metadata Outreach. You should identify collaborators throughout the institution. One of the biggest proponents of Metadata Outreach at the University of Rochester has been San Cannon, the chief data officer, and she continues to endorse and refer colleagues to this service. You should consider your institution's needs, as well as the capacity of the metadata department. What needs can be met, and how can your library meet them while still supporting its collections and regular activities? Finally, you should focus on communication and education. This will ensure that users will learn to identify a metadata problem and think of the library's metadata department first.

ACKNOWLEDGMENTS

Metadata Outreach and this chapter would not be possible without the support of colleagues at the University of Rochester, including Adrienne Canino, San Cannon, Cynthia Carlton, Lauren Di Monte, Maggie Graham, Nadine Grimm, Kim Hoffman, Zary Kamarei, Rochelle Mazar, Joyce McDonough, Sarah Pugachev, Emily Sherwood, and Anna Siebach-Larsen.

REFERENCES

Bair, Sheila, and Sharon Carlson. "Where Keywords Fail: Using Metadata to Facilitate Digital Humanities Scholarship." *Journal of Library Metadata* 8, no. 3 (2008): 249–62.

Cannon, Sandra. "Academic Job Codes." Office of the Provost, University of Rochester. www.rochester.edu/provost/academic-job-codes/.

Digital Scholarship Lab. "DSL." January 2, 2019. https://dslab.lib.rochester.edu/.

Kyker, Jennifer, and Sekuru Tute Chigamba. *Sekuru's Stories*. https://sekuru.org/home/.

McFall, Lisa M. "Beyond the Back Room: The Role of Metadata and Catalog Librarians in Digital Humanities." In *Supporting Digital Humanities for Knowledge Acquisition in Modern Libraries*, ed. Kathleen L. Sacco, Scott S. Richmond, Sara Parme, and Kerrie Fergen Wilkes, 21–43. Hershey, PA: Information Science Reference, 2015.

Sherwood, Emily. "Sekuru's Stories." Digital Scholarship Lab. January 3, 2019. https://dslab.lib.rochester.edu/sekurus-stories/.

Stewart-Marshall, Elizabeth. "Extending the Role of Library Technical Services to Metadata Outreach: An Interview with Martin Kurth." *Library Hi Tech News* 19, no. 9 (2002): 20.

University of Rochester. "About the University of Rochester." www.rochester.edu/about/.

———. "Libraries at Rochester." www.rochester.edu/libraries/.

University of Rochester, Office of the Provost. "Data Governance." www.rochester.edu/provost/data-governance-overview/.

University of Rochester, River Campus Libraries. "Metadata Outreach." www.library.rochester.edu/services/metadata-outreach.

Wilson, Emma Annette, and Mary Alexander. "When Metadata Becomes Outreach: Indexing, Describing, and Encoding for DH." dh+lib (dh+lib, July 29, 2016). https://acrl.ala.org/dh/2016/07/29/when-metadata-becomes-outreach/.

NOTES

1. University of Rochester, "About the University of Rochester," www.rochester.edu/about/.
2. University of Rochester, "Libraries at the University of Rochester," www.rochester.edu/libraries/.
3. Sheila Bair and Sharon Carlson, "Where Keywords Fail: Using Metadata to Facilitate Digital Humanities Scholarship," *Journal of Library Metadata* 8, no. 3 (2008): 249–62 ; Lisa M. McFall, "Beyond the Back Room: The Role of Metadata and Catalog Librarians in Digital Humanities," in *Supporting Digital Humanities for Knowledge Acquisition in Modern Libraries*, ed. Kathleen L.

Sacco, Scott S. Richmond, Sara Parme, and Kerrie Fergen Wilkes (Hershey, PA: Information Science Reference, 2015), 21-43; Elizabeth Stewart-Marshall, "Extending the Role of Library Technical Services to Metadata Outreach: An Interview with Martin Kurth," *Library Hi Tech News* 19, no. 9 (2002): 20; Emma Annette Wilson and Mary Alexander, "When Metadata Becomes Outreach: Indexing, Describing, and Encoding for DH," dh+lib (dh+lib, July 29, 2016), https://acrl.ala.org/dh/2016/07/29/when-metadata-becomes-outreach/.

4. Digital Scholarship Lab, "DSL," January 2, 2019, https://dslab.lib.rochester.edu/.

5. Jennifer Kyker and Sekuru Tute Chigamba, *Sekuru's Stories*, https://sekuru.org/home/.

6. Emily Sherwood, "Sekuru's Stories," Digital Scholarship Lab, January 3, 2019. https://dslab.lib.rochester.edu/sekurus-stories/.

7. University of Rochester, Office of the Provost, "Data Governance," www.rochester.edu/provost/data-governance-overview/.

8. Sandra Cannon, "Academic Job Codes," Office of the Provost, University of Rochester, www.rochester.edu/provost/academic-job-codes/.

9. Cannon, "Academic Job Codes."

10. The RCL's 2020 presentation for Love Data Week can be found online at www.library.rochester.edu/sites/default/files/documents/202002_Metadata_LoveLetter_Final.pdf.

11. The written project plan is available by contacting the author.

12. University of Rochester, River Campus Libraries, "Metadata Outreach," www.library.rochester.edu/services/metadata-outreach.

JAMIE HAZLITT AND
GLENN JOHNSON-GRAU

14

Hope for the Best, Prepare for the Worst

A Case Study for Engaging Faculty and University
Administration with a Multiyear Deselection Project

S pace limitations are a ubiquitous problem for libraries, but each library must work within its institutional context and constraints to fashion an acceptable solution for keeping a collection current and providing room for growth. When librarians at the William H. Hannon Library at Loyola Marymount University (LMU) foresaw the eventual limit of space for expansion of their physical collections, the authors looked widely at deselection projects at other libraries in order to seek out best practices and pitfalls before undertaking our initiative. Through reviewing the literature and talking with colleagues at other institutions, we began to consider the risks inherent in deselection projects. Public relations and political firestorms can be set off when faculty are caught off guard by "dumpsters full of books," and protracted projects can bog down when there are too many cooks in the kitchen. We sought to devise a deselection process and corresponding communication plan that was "not too hot, nor too cold," with full transparency to the university community and carefully structured faculty consultation that would still allow us to keep the project moving.

In this chapter, we introduce our comprehensive print monograph deselection plan, our experience with faculty engagement, and the results from the first two semesters of the project, along with lessons that we learned along the way. Readers will take away a concrete example of a time-intensive but effective model for engaging the library administration, faculty, librarian liaisons, and the university administration with a multiyear deselection project.

UPSTAIRS, DOWNSTAIRS

Loyola Marymount University is a Roman Catholic institution grounded in the Jesuit and Marymount traditions. Located in west Los Angeles, California, the university serves a population of 6,600 undergraduates in 60 majors and 55 minors across 43 academic departments, as well as 2,000 graduate students in more than 50 master's programs and one doctoral program.

When the William H. Hannon Library opened in 2009 after fifteen years of planning—it was only the second new library in the university's entire 100-year history—it was designed to meet the current and future needs for library collections and to provide much-needed spaces for collaborative learning. The library was built with open stacks for nearly 200,000 circulating volumes, and a closed-stack basement storage area to hold the remainder of the collection, including the return of over 150,000 volumes of low-use monographs and bound periodicals that had been stored in an off-site storage facility. This basement area contains over 400,000 circulating books, bound journal volumes, and other parts of the collection; a separate secure vault holds the entirety of materials maintained by Archives & Special Collections.

The basement has substantial capacity; however, it was not optimized for efficient storage. The shelving units in the basement are standard utility shelving, not that different from those at a storage warehouse. This initial configuration had standard-height shelving, with more recent materials stored in open cardboard totes arranged by call number and older materials stored in Bankers Box-style containers.

As the collection grew and the existing shelving filled up, library staff began looking seven to ten years into the future for when we would be out of space. The relatively small size of the open-stacks area means that for each new book acquired, an older, lower-use book must be moved to the basement: one in, one down. In 2014, the library implemented a high-density storage arrangement using Generation Fifth Applications (GFA) software. With reconfigured shelving and GFA in the basement, we could shelve books by size, greatly increasing the capacity of this closed-stacks space. Upon implementing GFA, the first couple of years were dedicated to moving recent and high-use materials from the open stacks on the upper floors into the high-density configuration, but inevitably it came time to deal with older and low-use books. Because every item to be moved into the high-density system would be touched, the authors began planning the first comprehensive deselection project in decades for these low-use items, with the goal of not relocating books we did not want to keep.

LMU had never engaged in a thorough deselection project for reasons common to many libraries, including competing priorities, a distributed liaison model of subject selectors who often lack deep subject expertise, and a lingering perception from an earlier era, particularly among faculty and administrators, that a large book collection is a marker of a good library. Additionally, because a substantial portion of the collection had been in off-campus storage with limited access for nearly ten years, the lowest-use books, which were prime candidates for deselection, had been the most difficult ones to withdraw. Add to that a general faculty and academic community hostility to "weeding," and the result was inertia.

THE "WEEDING" MINEFIELD

Concerns about the repercussions from a library deselection project are well-founded. Community outrage can take multiple forms: it can focus on principle (some variant of "books are sacred"), process (anything less than complete faculty control is "too secretive"), or both. Whatever the line of argument, however, a deselection project is almost always accompanied by incredulity that librarians would ever willingly remove a book from a collection. This attitude often reflects a lack of understanding of the realities of library work and the professional practice of librarians and collection management.

The cautionary tale of a journal withdrawal project at the University of California, Santa Cruz, figured prominently in our planning. In Scott, Troy, and Cowell's presentation[1] at the Acquisitions Institute at Timberline Lodge, they outlined their challenges, even when the library seemed to be doing everything right. UCSC's thoughtful, data-driven project with ample outreach to university administrators, academic departments, and faculty partners went off the rails when a small number of faculty members protested, including a scathing op-ed in the local press,[2] after which campus support for the project seemingly disintegrated. One key handicap in the UCSC project was outside their control: the immediate need for space mandated by the university administration made the timeline too short to give the library the luxury of time to win over resistant faculty members.

If the Scylla of insufficient faculty buy-in is one hazard, so is the Charybdis of overconsultation. DeMars, Roll, and Phillips[3] at California State University, Fullerton, outline how their project bogged down with a process that allowed faculty members to make individual retention decisions electronically. Even after adjusting the project guidelines to curb the impulse of certain faculty members to save everything, the project's design gave too much authority to faculty to retain titles. The authors state that a project that could have taken "one year was stretched out to three years to meet the desires of the faculty and library administration" by an overly complex process that did "nothing more than make additional work" for both library staff and a small subset of the faculty.[4] This precisely echoed a failed LMU project in the 1990s, when we consulted faculty before we moved books into off-campus storage. In that effort, when we distributed Excel spreadsheets to faculty to invite what we hoped would be thoughtful and measured subject expertise to help us create more room in the stacks, the faculty members most vehemently opposed to the project quickly realized that they could easily drag the "retain" value down a whole column. And once the faculty had been "consulted," it became untenable to then overrule their decisions.

Going into this current project, we sought to preserve our hard-won trust and positive relationships with the campus community and to make sure that insufficient planning did not derail or stall this strategic priority. We also wanted the deselection project to move forward on our timeline, where we could adjust the physical processing of materials into GFA or for withdrawal based upon our staff's capacity.

A HYBRID APPROACH

In fall 2017, the authors set out to plan a multiyear project to review our print monograph collection for potential withdrawals. Our participation in the SCELC Shared Print Program, a collaboration of thirty-five libraries in the western United States to build a regional collective collection of retained titles, bolstered our confidence in undertaking a substantial deselection project without losing access to the scholarship once held in our collections. Through SCELC Shared Print, we also had access to the sophisticated collection analysis tools provided by OCLC's GreenGlass software.

Unlike many libraries, we were not under a looming deadline, but we were working against longer-term space constraints and the need to maintain a steady flow of volumes to be retained and moved into our GFA system.

Our review of the recent literature on weeding projects led us to consider several key areas of concern. One of these is that faculty have very different perspectives on the value of the library's book collections; this often but not always breaks down by academic discipline. Building a consideration of these sensibilities into the planning process can increase the odds for success. An article by McAllister and Scherlen[5] was influential in reinforcing our thinking about how to structure the project in order to recognize the deep connection that scholars in the humanities and the arts have with print collections. We could not, however, assume that scientists or social scientists would be indifferent either. In the UC Santa Cruz case, the newspaper opinion piece that blew things up was authored by an emeritus mathematics professor.

We recognized that the faculty would be our partners in a deselection project. Although we are fortunate to have a strong relationship with our faculty, that relation is not simply the result of good luck. LMU librarians have cultivated this relationship over many years and the faculty have in turn been our champions, not least in the long effort to build the "new" library. We did not want to squander that relationship; in fact, we knew that it had the potential to make the project more successful. Agee's analysis[6] of the psycholinguistics of faculty responses to deselection underscores the value in recognizing the strong emotions that accompany this kind of work. But with transparency, clear communication, and steps that empower faculty, even when their requests seem excessive, libraries can complete deselection projects successfully.[7]

Armed with these insights, the authors, with the support of our dean, developed what amounted to two plans: an internal operational deselection plan, and an external outreach and communication plan for the campus community. We started with a white paper titled "William H. Hannon Library Sustainable Collection Growth Proposal."[8] This document provided the first public discussion of our concerns about the room for future collection growth, which we knew would surprise many in the campus community who thought that our "new" library would have solved any space problems once and for all. The white paper explained the proposed project in order to both address our concerns and dispel any mistaken assumptions about the library's future capacity. This document emphasized deselection as an essential component of stewardship of university resources and a key feature of the library's strategic plan. We also noted that LMU's recent participation in the SCELC Shared Print Program provided a "safety net" for titles removed from the local collection. The specific audience for this document was the provost, who we suspected would be supportive. Since he would approach the project from an institutional-level perspective, the white paper could frame the issues for the whole campus before we needed to address the more specific concerns of faculty at the departmental and individual levels.

The white paper outlined the problems the library faced, provided context on deselection as a standard practice across academic libraries, and elucidated our goal as the long-term sustainability and stewardship of university resources. We also noted the differences between disciplines and proposed a three-part project divided by broad academic disciplines (table 14.1).

TABLE 14.1
Deselection targets by discipline

Aggressive	Moderate	Conservative
STEM, business; est. 80–90% withdrawal	Social sciences; est. 50% withdrawal	Arts and humanities; highest level of retention

Simultaneously, we developed the actual plan for the review and processing of titles under consideration. This project would cut across library departmental lines and involve many staff members (and student workers). Therefore, the plan needed to incorporate a steady and sustainable workflow that would be designed to minimize bottlenecks and backlogs across technical services units.

Our process began with creating spreadsheets of low-use, pre-2000 copyright books in GreenGlass—books for which LMU is not the retaining library for our shared print project. We worked by LC classification, but used our GOBI approval profile, which already is mapped to our department structure, in order to pick up all relevant areas of the classification for each academic discipline. Our library liaisons then gave a cursory review to each spreadsheet, sending obvious retentions directly to GFA and obvious withdrawals on for removal. Next, the books were pulled for physical review, and again the liaisons were asked to spend a few hours looking for easy keep/withdraw decisions.

The last step is where we tried to strike a balance on faculty consultation. We did not send the faculty spreadsheets to review, even when we were requested to do so. Instead, over a two- to three-week window, the faculty in affected departments were encouraged to come to the library by appointment or to just drop in to review the books in person. They had the option to fill out a flag to insert in the book, with their contact information and a brief justification for retention, if they thought we should retain it in the collection or if they would like to receive it for their personal collections after withdrawal.

This faculty review step, while clearly slowing down the process, achieved several ends. It was real and meaningful consultation, but only with faculty members who were engaged enough to make the effort. The physical review revealed to faculty that many of the proposed withdrawals were not classics but instead the lower-tier works of earlier eras, as by definition books that had been used at LMU were not weeding candidates. Because much of the emotional resistance to withdrawing books is the hope that each book will be valued, giving faculty members the option of retaining books for themselves made it clear that if they loved a particular book, they could keep it.

AN (OVER)COMMUNICATION PLAN EMERGES

The provost endorsed the project and process as outlined in the white paper, and the two-and-a-half-year clock for what was officially named the Sustainable Collection Growth Project (SCGP) began ticking. We expanded upon the white paper to develop a presentation for the Faculty Library Committee, an interdisciplinary committee of the Faculty Senate with representation from each of LMU's six schools and colleges. In this presentation, we shared the proposed project timeline and our careful disciplinary approach to reviewing the materials, introduced the consortial shared print program that would enable the library to withdraw materials while remaining confident that the works would remain accessible through interlibrary loan, and introduced the in-person process for faculty review.

The resulting discussion yielded feedback that ranged across a spectrum from complete trust in the process (one professor expressed surprise that we were sharing this information with them at all and deferred to our expertise in the matter) to a request that the faculty be invited to review digital lists of every book under consideration, in addition to in-person review. With the plan for faculty engagement firmly situated in between the two responses highlighted above, the Faculty Library Committee unanimously endorsed the project. The range of diverse responses underscored the importance of developing and committing to a consistent and transparent outreach plan for such a politically sensitive initiative.

The communication plan for the SCGP started with the development of a comprehensive LibGuide to serve as "home base" for the project, and a strategy using broad and targeted communication to inform and invite faculty participation (table 14.2).[9]

TABLE 14.2
Communication Outlets for the Sustainable Collection Growth Project

Broad Communication Outlets	Targeted Communication Outlets
School/college e-mail newsletters	E-mail to university deans from library dean
Library e-mail newsletter	Faculty library committee updates
Library blog/website	Librarian liaison network—e-mail to individual departments
Library social media	Department meetings
Open forums	

Using a disciplinary approach for the in-person review process meant that we needed to have a method for making sure that faculty members who might be interested in a particular subject area outside of their academic department could still be informed of upcoming review dates. For example, historians do not work exclusively in subjects covered through the D, E, and F ranges of the Library of Congress Classification system. We did not, however, want to bombard the History Department with e-mails each time a new set of books was up for review. Combining a broad approach that reaches all faculty members through a couple of touch points each semester with targeted communication through the liaison network for departments allowed us to be thorough without overbearing or redundant messaging. The success of this communication plan relied on partnership with our outreach and communication librarian, who in turn has a close working relationship with the communication managers embedded in academic units across campus. Because these networks were already in place, we could focus on our messaging.

As an example, the outreach and communication schedule for one of the departmental review cycles from Spring semester 2019 went as follows:

- December 7, 2018: Dean's network e-mail introducing the project, the LibGuide, and the review schedule for Spring 2020 (broad)
- January 7, 2019: School and college e-newsletter communication containing the LibGuide, the review schedule, and RSVP links for open forums (broad)
- January 7, 2019: E-mail invitation through the liaison to the Physics Department, cc'ing the department chair, sharing the LibGuide, review instructions, and upcoming three-week review dates for their discipline (January 13–31). This is the call to action. (targeted)
- January 14–18, 2019: The SCGP project is highlighted in the library's communications, including featured space on the library's website, blog, and social media (broad)
- January 25, 2019: E-mail reminder sent through the liaison to the Physics Department about one week remaining in the review period (targeted)
- January 28, 2019: If applicable, follow-up communication with the Physics faculty thanking them for their engagement in the project and sharing information about when to expect withdrawn books that they requested for their personal collections to be delivered (targeted)
- February 15, 2019: Update to the Faculty Library Committee at their first meeting in the Spring semester (targeted)

During the period of time the physics books were on the shelves for in-person review, we started the process of engaging with the departments that were next in line. We repeated this cycle each semester—skipping summers—for each LC call number range and corresponding academic department(s); this will continue until the project's completion. We also designed a parallel process for internal training and regular communication with the library liaisons, who we relied upon for pre-screening book lists and communicating with the faculty in their subject areas. We created an internal Gantt chart for project management, developed a suite of e-mail templates, and scheduled reminders for each touch point to ensure consistent messaging and to keep the project moving (see figure 14.1).

Throughout its development, we affectionately referred to the communication plan as "overkill by design." This strategy attempted to forestall complaints from stakeholders who might feel that they had learned about the

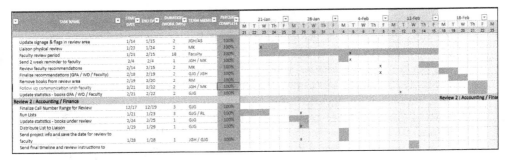

FIGURE 14.1
Excerpt from Gantt chart to track SCGP timeline and tasks

project too late to participate. Although it is impossible to completely elimi-nate the likelihood of an irate faculty member who missed all of our messag-ing, this method has so far been effective for this project.

SO FAR, SO GOOD

From January 2018 through December 2019 we kept the SCGP moving, meet-ing our desired targets for both faculty and campus communication and the deselection process itself. In this section we will share the outcomes of our efforts in both areas. Note that the results to date do not include the academic disciplines that were up for review in Spring semester 2020, which was inter-rupted by the campus closure due to the COVID-19 pandemic.

Over the first two semesters of the SCGP, we enlisted the support of ten of our library-liaison colleagues to review book lists and conduct outreach to 20 of LMU's 43 academic departments, including all STEM disciplines, busi-ness, education, and certain social sciences. Some disciplines (such as biology) had thousands of books in the queue and accordingly had stand-alone review dates. Other disciplines with smaller lists were grouped together. Nonethe-less, the targeted outreach and invitation to participate in the review was individualized by each liaison for each academic department. We also used the liaisons' knowledge of individual faculty research areas to identify faculty members who might have an interest in disciplines outside of their depart-ment, and we sent these individuals invitations to participate in the review.

Our communication plan relied on the assumption that our e-mails would reach every faculty member who might wish to participate in the review pro-cess, and more importantly, that the e-mails would be opened and read. We know that this does not happen, but the introduction, the invitation, and the reminder e-mails all reflected our commitment and good faith efforts to inte-grate complete transparency into the deselection project.

How did it go? Not surprisingly, even with consistency in our messaging throughout, the faculty's engagement and response to the project was uneven, often in unexpected ways. Based on the anecdotal experience of colleagues at other universities, we expected a higher degree of interest in the project (either positive or negative) from colleagues in the humanities and the arts, with lesser engagement from faculty in less book-reliant or historically focused disciplines. We assumed that because we were reviewing pre-2000 books, science and business faculty members would be less interested in those older materials. Additionally, we expected the various departments' engagement to align with the typical patterns of faculty engagement that we track through our liaison program.

The first few semesters of the project yielded a couple of surprises. For example, the Physics faculty at LMU did not typically have much connection with the library through instruction, programming, feedback on collection-building, or other measures of faculty engagement. Yet, six out of the seven tenure-line faculty in the department accepted the liaison's invitation. They reviewed the books as a group—other departments did so as well—and we had the opportunity to discuss the project with them in person while they were in the review area. The professors understood and respected the methodology through which we identified the candidates for deselection and subsequently requested that every book under review (nearly 700) be delivered to the department after withdrawal. On the other side of the spectrum, the faculty in the five departments in the School of Education have a more integrated connection with the library through library instruction and collaboration on course material adoption, but only one professor chose to participate in the in-person review. Individual faculty members surprised us with both enthusiastic, understanding support and disgruntled resistance. Some departments where we would have expected more engagement were silent, but the project also opened doors to developing relationships with faculty in departments that lacked strong preexisting connections to the library.

During the first two semesters of the SCGP, librarian liaisons sent targeted invitations to approximately 200 tenure-line faculty members (and an even wider distribution, depending on how the invitations were distributed, to clinical and part-time faculty) across 20 academic departments to participate in the review process, in addition to the broad promotion through other library and university channels. We scheduled and broadly promoted a series of open forums about the SCGP at the beginning of each semester, but a disappointing total of only two faculty members have attended these forums to date. As we move into the final year of the project, the authors may record a version of the forum presentation for departments to view asynchronously (if they desire). We received an invitation to three individual department meetings to answer questions about the project (including one in a department where the liaison has had little success with faculty engagement), and

32 unique faculty members across 9 departments visited the library to review books in their area(s).

The faculty members who chose to participate were all respectful of the space problem that we needed to solve through deselection and the methodology through which we identified the materials for review. Over the course of two academic semesters, after the liaison review had routed approximately 3 percent of the books identified in GreenGlass to GFA and another 23 percent of them to be withdrawn, we pulled 15,831 books for the faculty review process. The faculty only requested that we keep 25 books in the collection. As a private institution, our ability to give withdrawn books to our faculty members certainly might have been a factor in the faculty's acceptance and participation in the project. In all, we delivered 812 books (including those that were sent to the Physics Department) to individual faculty members for their personal collections.

To date, the high-touch process we designed to inform (at least) and engage (at best) the LMU faculty with the SCGP has been successful. It required a great deal more time and outreach than a deselection process based solely on data would have required, but we had the time, and we also felt that the investment in our existing strong relationship with the faculty was worthwhile. Two-thirds of the way through the project, we have not received any overtly negative feedback about the project. In this case, no news really is good news. We may never know whether the faculty's reaction (or lack of one) is due to their inherent trust in our professional judgment, their earned trust after learning more about the project, or a general ambivalence about communication from the library. It is probably a combination of all three. The coronavirus notwithstanding, we have met all of our deselection goals to date, we have consistently and transparently communicated with our faculty about the project, and we are cautiously optimistic that we have a road map in place for a review of the books in the humanities and arts (and for concluding the project) whenever we are able to return to campus.

REFERENCES

Agee, A. "Faculty Response to Deselection in Academic Libraries: A Psycholinguistic Analysis." *Collection Management* 42, no. 2 (2017): 59–75. doi:10.1080/0146267 9.2017.1310069.

DeMars, J. M., A. Roll, and K. Phillips. "Deep in the Weeds: Faculty Participation in a Large Scale Deselection Project." *Collection Management* 44, no. 1 (2019): 21–34. doi:10.1080/01462679.2018.1544956.

Hazlitt, J., and G. Johnson-Grau. "Hannon Library Sustainable Collection Growth 2018–2021." William H. Hannon Library LibGuides. http://libguides.lmu.edu/ sustainablecollections.

McAllister, A. D., and A. Scherlen. "Weeding with Wisdom: Tuning Deselection of Print Monographs in Book-Reliant Disciplines." *Collection Management* 42, no. 2 (2017): 76–91. doi:10.1080/01462679.2017.1299657.

Montgomery, R. "On UCSC's Outrageous Mass Destruction of Books." *The Mercury News*, December 24, 2016. www.mercurynews.com/2016/12/24/montgomery-on-ucscs-outrageous-mass-destruction-of-books/.

Scott, K., S. Troy, and M. E. Cowell. "Culture Clash in the Collision Space." Presentation at 2017 Acquisitions Institute at Timberline Lodge. https://drive.google.com/file/d/0Bwz2gOFBtGKVcGJQZXd3d1FHVjQ/view?authkey=CJmfl-AI.

NOTES

1. Scott, Troy, and Cowell, "Culture Clash in the Collision Space."
2. Montgomery, "On UCSC's Outrageous Mass Destruction of Books."
3. DeMars, Roll, and Phillips, "Deep in the Weeds."
4. DeMars, Roll, and Phillips, "Deep in the Weeds," 33.
5. McAllister and Scherlen, "Weeding with Wisdom."
6. Agee, "Faculty Response to Deselection in Academic Libraries."
7. Agee, "Faculty Response to Deselection in Academic Libraries," 68.
8. Hazlitt and Johnson-Grau, "Hannon Library Sustainable Collection Growth 2018–2021."
9. Hazlitt and Johnson-Grau, "Hannon Library Sustainable Collection Growth 2018–2021."

APPENDIX A

Follow-Up Survey Questions

1. How well do you feel that you understand your job responsibilities related to collection development and management?
   - ☐ Very well
   - ☐ Somewhat
   - ☐ Not at all

2. What percentage of your total liaison activities are spent on collection development activities and tasks?

3. Of the time spent on collection development, what percentage is spent on the following collection development tasks:
   _____ Reviewing data that informs collection development and management
   _____ Reviewing slips/GOBI notifications
   _____ Providing input to Collection Strategy for renewals and new resource decisions (not including time spent on Collection Committee activities if you are a current Committee representative)
   _____ Ordering materials requested by faculty and students
   _____ Ordering materials you select (not requested by faculty and students)
   _____ Communicating with faculty and students about order requests
   _____ Professional development related to collection development
   _____ Other:

4. Which of the following do you feel is a good use of your time?
   - ☐ Reviewing data that informs collection development and management
   - ☐ Reviewing slips/GOBI notifications
   - ☐ Providing input to Collection Strategy for renewals and new resource decisions (not including time spent on Collection Committee activities if you are a current Committee representative)

(continued)

☐ Ordering materials requested by faculty and students
☐ Ordering materials you select (not requested by faculty and students)
☐ Communicating with faculty and students about order requests
☐ Professional development related to collection development
☐ Other:

5. When do you devote the most time to collection development:
☐ Fall
☐ Spring
☐ Summer
☐ Equally spread throughout the year
☐ Other:

6. What types of trainings would you find useful?

	Not at All	Somewhat	Very
Dashboards and other reports in Alma	☐	☐	☐
Deselection and weeding	☐	☐	☐
Electronic resource usage statistics	☐	☐	☐
Placing orders	☐	☐	☐
Sharing tips & tricks among liaisons	☐	☐	☐
Strategies and tools for selecting content for your areas	☐	☐	☐
Understanding the collection development life cycle	☐	☐	☐
Vendor-led trainings (most likely webinars) on specific databases	☐	☐	☐
Other:	☐	☐	☐

7. How useful have you found the following trainings:

	Not at All	Somewhat	Very	N/A
Fiscal Year Kickoff	☐	☐	☐	☐
Liaison Orientation with APCS and Resource Acquisitions	☐	☐	☐	☐

8. The Liaison LibGuide (https://libguides.utk.edu/liaisons) currently houses information for liaisons. How useful would you find these "ready reference" topics:

	Not at All	Somewhat	Very	N/A
E-book platforms and the types of access offered	☐	☐	☐	☐
General time frames (from order to completion) for overall item types	☐	☐	☐	☐
Procedures for ordering	☐	☐	☐	☐
Policies and guidelines for ordering	☐	☐	☐	☐
Using GOBI	☐	☐	☐	☐
Strategies and tools for selecting content for your areas	☐	☐	☐	☐
Who to contact for what	☐	☐	☐	☐
Other:	☐	☐	☐	☐

9. A goal for the approval plan review in Fall 2019 was to have fewer slips (GOBI notifications) to review. Since the approval plan has been turned back on, are you looking at fewer slips?
   - ☐ Many fewer slips
   - ☐ Somewhat fewer slips
   - ☐ No difference
   - ☐ More slips
   - ☐ N/A

10. Would you prefer that "suggest a purchase" submissions from our users go:
   ☐ Directly to the Third Floor for ordering
   ☐ To the appropriate subject librarian for vetting
   ☐ Other:

11. Do you find the Collection Updates e-mails helpful?
   ☐ Very helpful
   ☐ Somewhat helpful
   ☐ Not at all helpful
   ☐ I don't read them

12. How often would you like communication about:

	Monthly	Every other month	Quarterly	Once a semester	Never
Firm funds	☐	☐	☐	☐	☐
Continuing resource funds	☐	☐	☐	☐	☐
Gift funds	☐	☐	☐	☐	☐
Restricted funds	☐	☐	☐	☐	☐

13. When should APCS or ACR direct a vendor to a liaison?
   ☐ When advertising a new resource
   ☐ When offering training
   ☐ Never
   ☐ Other:

JENNIFER A. MEZICK
AND ELYSSA M. GOULD

APPENDIX B

Example of a Collections Updates E-Mail

This update contains collections-related information from ACR, APCS, Cataloging, Enterprise Systems, the Business Services Office, Scholarly Communications, and Collection Logistics.

Important Dates

Collection Development Listening Sessions for Liaisons (2 options):

- Dec. 11th, 2–3, rm150
- Dec. 12th, 9–10, rm150

(More sessions for everyone coming soon!)

I. New Resources!

Enslaved People in the Southeast: A Digital Exhibition is an open access resource containing images and a variety of scanned paper documents to illustrate the history of enslaved people in the southeast. This is a collaborative exhibit from ASERL and includes materials from our own Special Collections, such as an 1830s petition to the TN state legislator to abolish slavery.

International Encyclopedia of Geography is a 15-volume reference work that defines the concepts, research, and techniques in geography and interrelated fields. Created in collaboration with the American Association of Geographers.

II. Discontinued Resource

Atlanta Journal Constitution on microfilm, a subscription UT Libraries has maintained, has been canceled. When reviewing invoices for titles, APCS discovered that this title costs approx. $1,600/per use. This is a resource that is readily available via ILL.

III. Database Trials

Information gathered from vendors during the trial process, including price quotes, terms and conditions, etc., is accessible on SharePoint under "Collection Strategy Documents > Trials." If you or your teaching faculty would like to review a resource, please send the trial request to [staff member].

Current Trials:
- Entertainment Industry Magazine Archive (8/21–11/26)
- American Fur Company (9/20–12/16)
- Drama Online (10/8–11/30)

IV. Platform Updates

GALE is continuing to transition their products to their new platform. Adobe Flash will not be promoted or used on the new platform. You can find more information here: https://support.gale.com/product-enhancements.
- You can learn more about the phasing-out of Adobe Flash here: https://theblog.adobe.com/adobe-flash-update

Naxos Music Library has updated their platform. Explore the changes here: https://www.naxosmusiclibrary.com/sharedfiles/NML/en/banners/NewNML3/

V. Things to Know from outside UT Libraries

NEWS from ASERL from Nov. 11th: ASERL Statement in Support of Open Science and Scholarly Communication

"The Association of Southeastern Research Libraries (ASERL) supports principles of open science and scholarly communication, transparency in contracting, and sustainability in pricing. We believe the MIT Framework for Publisher Contract with its six core principles for library contracts with publishers, reflects a global movement of research library leadership to transform scholarly communication as a means of making scholarly content more openly available. ASERL welcomes new partnerships with the research and learning community to develop new and innovative tools in support of these goals."

Have questions and don't know who to contact? https://libguides.utk.edu/CDM_ReadyReference

HEATHER JEFFCOAT, MARLEE GIVENS,
SOFIA SLUTSKAYA, AND KAREN E. VIARS

Browse Feature in Primo

[The form below was used to record users' feedback in the course of a trial subscription to Syndetics Unbound, which integrates with Primo.]

Browse by subject and Browse by call number

Task #1

- Go to: http://search.library.gatech.edu
- Locate the BROWSE SEARCH option in the top navigation
- Try these searches . . .
    » Subject: Electrical engineering
    » Call number: TK1 .I39

Is it helpful to see library materials displayed in that order?

☐ Yes

☐ No

☐ Maybe

Why or why not?

Will you use the Browse feature?

☐ Definitely yes

☐ Probably yes

☐ Might or might not

☐ Probably not

☐ Definitely not

Why or why not?

What Is Syndetics Unbound?

Syndetics Unbound offers several virtual browsing options, including a "browse shelf" feature, "you may also like" recommendations, and tagging. It provides users with an engaging, modern, and convenient browsing experience for books and multimedia titles. Learn more about Syndetics Unbound at https://proquest .syndetics.com/Marketing/Detail/SeeIt.

Task #2

Explore the following resources and review the Syndetics Unbound features for each:

- *Harry Potter and the Chamber of Secrets*
- *Harry Potter and the Chamber of Secrets* DVD
- *Stumbling on Happiness*
- *Freakonomics*
- *Modernism Reborn: Midcentury American Houses*
- *Nanostructured Materials and Nanotechnology*
- *World Population: A Reference Handbook*

You can try your own searches via the Library Catalog (http://search.library .gatech.edu).

Which feature (of Syndetics Unbound) do you think is the most valuable? Why?

Which feature do you think is the least valuable? Why?

Did you run into any issues? Describe:

If these features went away, would you miss them?

- ☐ Definitely yes
- ☐ Probably yes
- ☐ Might or might not
- ☐ Probably not
- ☐ Definitely not

Why or why not?

eBooks & Journals

Do you expect eBooks to show up in the same list as print in both Primo Browse Search and Syndetics Unbound Browse Shelf?
☐ Yes ☐ No

Is it helpful to see the "Ebook" label in the Syndetics Full Shelf display?
☐ Yes ☐ No

Do you expect to see journals in the Browse Shelf display? Example: Search for Journal of the Institution of Electrical Engineers
☐ Yes ☐ No

KAREN E. VIARS AND SOFIA SLUTSKAYA,
CO-PRINCIPAL INVESTIGATORS

APPENDIX D

Questions for IRB Protocol "How Undergraduate Students Use the Primo Catalog"

For questions 1–5 below, all information in brackets, such as [title] will be replaced with a title, author, etc., related to the research that each class is conducting in order to make the search experience relevant to the students.

1. Find a known book, and determine if it is available.
   - Does GT Library have the book [Title]? Where is it located?
   - Does GT Library have a book by [author]?

2. Find a known e-journal and its availability
   - In Primo, look up the electronic journal called [Title]. What dates does the library have access to? List the databases in which you can find this journal.

3. Use facets to limit to a specific format
   - Find an article on [relevant topic] from a newspaper, and list the name of the newspaper and date of the article below.

4. Judging relevant books and articles.
   - Does the library have any books on [relevant topic].

5. Limit format to [relevant topic] in facets. Limit to Available in Library
   - Does GT Library have any DVD's on the topic of [relevant topic]?

Survey Questions

1. How regularly do you use GT library catalog?
   - ☐ Several times a week
   - ☐ Once a week
   - ☐ Several times a month
   - ☐ Less than once a month
   - ☐ Once a semester
   - ☐ Less than once a semester
   - ☐ Less than once a year

2. What are some of the things you have used GT library catalog for in the past?

3. What is your overall impression of the site?

4. If you could change something about the site, what would it be?

5. What do you like most about the site?

6. Does the language that we use on the site make sense to you?
   - ☐ Yes, I understand all of it
   - ☐ I understand most of it
   - ☐ I understand some of it, but some is confusing
   - ☐ Most of it is confusing or makes it hard to find what I need
   - ☐ All of it is confusing or makes it hard to find what I need

7. Have you requested an item for delivery from Library Service Center before?
   - ☐ Yes
   - ☐ No

8. Is there anything else you'd like to tell us or ask us about Primo or the library?

9. On a scale from 1 to 5, with 1 being the lowest score and 5 being the highest, rate your agreement with the following statements about the searching the GT Library Catalog:

   _____ The search function is easy to use.

   _____ The way the search results are organized on the page makes sense to me.

   _____ The search results I got are relevant and useful for my research.

   _____ I like the aesthetic appearance of the website

About the Contributors

Erin Block is the e-resources metadata specialist at the University of Colorado Boulder University Libraries. She received her MLIS from the University of Denver.

Meghan Burke is the metadata/discovery librarian at Queen's University in Kingston, Ontario. Previously, she was the metadata/electronic resources librarian at Marymount University. She has her MSLIS from the Catholic University of America.

Chris Deems joined Ohio Northern University's Heterick Memorial Library in 2018 as the systems and technology librarian. He earned his MSIS from the University of Texas at Austin.

Jenny Donley has served as the cataloging and knowledge architect librarian at Ohio Northern University's Heterick Memorial Library since 2009. She earned her MLIS and her MS from Kent State University.

Maggie Dull is the director of metadata strategies at the University of Rochester's River Campus Libraries. She holds an MLIS from the University of Washington and a Certificate in the Curation and Management of Digital Assets (CMDA) from the University of Maryland. Dull is an instructor in

Core's Fundamentals of Metadata course and is a lecturer on metadata and library systems at the University of Maryland's iSchool.

Kaylan Ellis has served as the technical services librarian at Ohio Northern University's Taggart Law Library since 2016. She earned her MSLIS from the University of Illinois at Urbana-Champaign.

Brian Falato is senior cataloger at University of South Florida Tampa Libraries. He has over twenty years of experience as a professional cataloger and has worked in all formats, both tangible and digital.

Autumn Faulkner earned her MLIS in 2011 from the University of Alabama and has been a cataloger at Michigan State University Libraries since 2012. Currently she supervises copy catalogers and helps oversee cataloging project management and workflow documentation.

Patrick Flanigan is the lead cataloging specialist at the San Diego State University Library, where he catalogs materials in both print and digital formats. He focuses on improving the discovery of library resources and collections. Flanigan received his MLIS from the University of Missouri with a focus on digital resources. He has spent the last thirty years combining his passion for music with his enjoyment of working in libraries. He currently records music for his project Punk Rock Drum Machine, and he often applies his "do-it-yourself" (DIY) approach from his musical efforts to the library challenges he encounters.

Marlee Dorn Givens is the library learning consultant for the Georgia Tech Library as well as subject librarian for modern languages, psychology, and literature, media, and communication. In this position she works with faculty to support their teaching and scholarship, supports students through classroom and online instruction, and facilitates learning for library employees. Givens first came to Georgia Tech in 2010 to lead the IMLS-funded Galileo Knowledge Repository, a statewide institutional repository. A library professional since 1994, Givens has her MLS from the University of Maryland. She has also completed two certificates in learning design from the Association for Talent Development.

Elyssa M. Gould is head of the acquisitions and continuing resource department at the University of Tennessee, Knoxville. In this role, she coordinates sixteen staff who perform acquisitions, electronic resource management, licensing, binding, and interlibrary loan activities. Gould previously served as electronic resources and serials librarian at the University of Michigan Law Library and cataloging and metadata librarian at Northern Michigan University.

Gwen Gregory is associate dean for collections management and associate professor at the Northern Illinois University Libraries. Her career has focused on management of library technical services operations, integrating technical services into the library's overall services, and working with internal and external customers to provide excellent service. She has previously held positions at several academic and special libraries. She holds an MLS degree from the University of Arizona, and a Master of Public Administration from New Mexico State University.

Hilary Hargis is the associate librarian at the Space Telescope Science Institute in Baltimore, Maryland, where she is responsible for technical services functions. Previous to this position, she worked in technical services at the Monroe County Public Library in Bloomington, Indiana and at the Othmer Library of Chemical History at the Science History Institute in Philadelphia, Pennsylvania. She obtained her MLIS at Drexel University in Philadelphia after studying history at Seattle Pacific University and religious studies at the University of Aberdeen in Scotland.

Jamie Hazlitt is the librarian for collection development and evaluation at Loyola Marymount University. Her professional areas of interest include academic library liaison programs and how they foster communication both internally within libraries and with campus faculty; textbook affordability, expanding awareness of open educational resources with faculty; intersections between collection development and outreach and communication and assessment of outreach efforts; and library leadership and representation in university governance.

Heather Jeffcoat is the web and discovery management librarian at the Georgia Tech Library. She earned her MSLIS from Florida State University. Jeffcoat has managed the library's web presence since 1998 and has been leading the technology program since 2017. As the web and discovery management librarian, she is responsible for the strategy, management, design, information architecture, and maintenance of all library websites, including the library's discovery system, Primo. As technology program manager, she works with library leadership, finance, IT, service owners, and other program and project managers to lead portfolio program execution of library technologies.

Glenn Johnson-Grau is head of acquisitions and collection development at Loyola Marymount University. His professional interests include shared print programs, library consortia and collaboration between loosely affiliated higher education institutions, and the impact of campus governance and politics on library operations and decision making.

Kimberly Lawler is the e-resources and serials specialist in the University Libraries at the University of Colorado Boulder. She received her MLIS from the University of Denver.

Jennifer A. Mezick is the collections strategist at the University of Tennessee, Knoxville. In this role, she provides guidance on collection decisions with a holistic approach by utilizing quantitative and qualitative data. Mezick previously served as interim director of library services at Pellissippi State Community College and as acquisitions and collection development librarian at Pellissippi State Community College.

Xiying Mi is a metadata librarian at University of South Florida Tampa Library. She is focused on digital collections metadata creation and curation. Her research interests lie primarily in linked open data, metadata, and data management. She received her MLIS from University of Illinois at Urbana-Champaign.

Melissa Moll is the music cataloging librarian at the University of Iowa Libraries. During 2016–18, she temporarily shifted to project work related to Cataloging-Metadata Department efforts towards UI Libraries systems and collections moves. Melissa holds a Master of Arts in library and information studies from the University of Wisconsin—Madison and a Doctor of Musical Arts in organ performance and pedagogy from the University of Iowa.

Jenny Novacescu is the current chief librarian at the Space Telescope Science Institute (STScI). At STScI, she focuses on facilitating access to astronomical and astrophysical research materials, mission and staff bibliographies, data citation standards, and scholarly publishing. Prior to joining the physics and astronomy library community, she worked in Maryland public libraries and the U.S. Army Medical Research Institute for Infectious Diseases (USAMRIID) Medical Library.

Bonita M. Pollock is currently the coordinator of metadata/cataloging at USF Libraries Tampa. Her research agenda entails developing semantic web and linked data technologies for libraries. She holds an MLIS from Kent State University and has published and presented on various subjects related to metadata and cataloging.

Emily Sanford has been the serials catalog librarian at Michigan State University Libraries since 2011. She has a quarter-time appointment with the libraries' User Experience Unit, where she contributes to usability and assessment projects. She earned her MSI from the University of Michigan in library and information services and archives and records management in 2010.

Anna Seiffert is the electronic resources and collection assessment librarian as well as the head of collection management services at Arthur Lakes Library. Since she joined the Mines faculty in 2016, she has worked on assessment, collection development and management, and the eResource lifecycle. Seiffert earned her MLS at Indiana University and her BA from Purdue University. She currently serves on various regional and local committees including the Colorado Alliance of Research Libraries' Shared Collection Development Committee, Faculty Senate Library Committee, Arthur Lakes Library Assessment Committee, and Technology Initiatives Committee. Prior to this position, Seiffert was the electronic resources manager for Purdue University Libraries.

Sofia Slutskaya is the head of resource description at Emory University Woodruff Library. She holds an MLIS from University of Tennessee, Knoxville, and a PhD in Library Science from Moscow State Art and Cultural University. Over the years, she has held a variety of positions in both public and technical services. Her professional interests include cataloging print and electronic materials, e-resource management, and e-book acquisitions. Currently, Slutskaya provides strategic and technical guidance on cataloging practices for the Emory University Robert W. Woodruff Library's physical and digital collections.

Shelby Strommer is the collections care coordinator in the Preservation Services Department of the University Library at the University of Illinois at Urbana-Champaign. She previously worked as the preservation processing coordinator librarian at the University of Iowa Libraries. Strommer holds an MSI, with a specialization in preservation of information, from the University of Michigan.

Karen E. Viars is the instructional technology librarian at Oglethorpe University. She earned an MS in Information Sciences from the University of Tennessee, Knoxville, an MS in Instructional Technology from Georgia State University, and a BA with honors in English Literature from the University of Georgia. She has held a variety of instruction-focused library positions in large and small academic libraries, including the humanities and science fiction librarian at the Georgia Tech Library. Viars offers training and support to faculty at Oglethorpe University in designing and developing hybrid and online learning.

Index